The Complete Guide to
REQUIREMENTS MANAGEMENT
Using the REPAC®
FRAMEWORK™

PERRY J. MCLEOD
PMP, PMI-PBA, CBAP

J.ROSS
PUBLISHING

ISBN-13: 978-160427-135-5

Printed and bound in the U.S.A. Printed on acid-free paper.

10 9 8 7 6 5 4 3 2 1

Library of Congress Cataloging-in-Publication Data

Names: McLeod, Perry J., 1969– author.
Title: The complete guide to requirements management using the REPAC
  framework / Perry J. McLeod.
Description: Plantation, FL : J. Ross Publishing, 2019. | Includes
  bibliographical references and index.
Identifiers: LCCN 2018055562 (print) | LCCN 2018061777 (ebook) | ISBN
  9781604278064 (e-book) | ISBN 9781604271355 (pbk. : alk. paper)
Subjects: LCSH: Project management. | Organization.
Classification: LCC HD69.P75 (ebook) | LCC HD69.P75 M337 2019 (print) | DDC
  658.4/04--dc23
LC record available at https://lccn.loc.gov/2018055562

Direct all inquiries to J. Ross Publishing, Inc., 300 S. Pine Island Rd., Suite 305, Plantation, FL 33324.

Phone: (954) 727-9333
Fax: (561) 892-0700
Web: www.jrosspub.com

Dedication

For my family.

*My beautiful wife, Janice, my two sons, Aidan and Tristan,
my sister Dawn, and my parents, Michael and Susan.*

Thank you for all your love and support.

CONTENTS

FOREWORD

I have been a business analysis practitioner for more than 22 years—the past 16 as a business analyst (BA) contractor. By the time I met Perry through a mutual colleague, I had been a BA almost 12 years and had had my fair share of project failures. If he had told me that he would one day write this book, I would have insisted he write it then. It would have saved many years of missteps, obstacles, frustrations, and the hardships which come with challenging personalities.

The Requirements, Elicitation, Planning, Analysis, and Collaboration Framework™ (REPAC®) is a unique set of words and ideas packaged together under four simple concepts: context, focus, perspective, and depth. Whether we are working within an agile, waterfall, or a hybrid environment, REPAC helps us decide which conversations are worth having and which are not.

I think the most profound statement Perry reinforces throughout his book is that we must stop asking for requirements and ask for simple stakeholder needs, which, with the help of the whole team, determines what we require to fulfill those needs. It's a small thing but it's a big thing!

Social styles and emotional intelligence play a crucial role in our profession. Perry spends a lot of time teaching us that we must first understand our stakeholders before we attempt to understand their needs, wants, and expectations.

As you read through this book you can tell that Perry seeks to understand business analysis using a scientific approach. His REPAC Framework is an entirely new communication and collaboration model for business analysis and adaptive/predictive project management. At many levels of applicability, Perry takes us through dozens of knowledge sets, which contain hundreds of words and concepts organizing everything from what is customer value and corporate purpose to how understanding data tuples and machine logic make for better data analysis requirements. I think what surprised me the most was how I can use his framework to vertically slice my user stories into small enough bits which any team member can complete in just a day or two. He literally built a lexicon of business and systems analysis and design. No small feat, simply elegant and amazing!

Both predictive and adaptive project methods need communication frameworks so stakeholders' needs and *what we require to fulfill them* (my new mantra, thanks Perry) are accurate and unambiguous. Finally, we have a book that uses every page to teach us how to truly elicit, slice, and analyze stakeholders' needs through organizational awareness and social understanding, collaboration, context, focus, perspective, and depth.

Thanks to Perry's diligent efforts, tenacity, quest for knowledge expansion, and betterment of all project success, we now have this amazing addition to the business analysis literature. Perry has done all the heavy lifting on our behalf. It doesn't matter whether you are a PMP®, CBAP®, PMI-ACP®, or PMI-PBA®, you need to read this book.

Jacqueline J.D. Young
Senior Business Analysis Consultant
Ontario, Canada

INTRODUCTION

"No matter how one may think himself accomplished, when he sets out to learn a new language, science, or the bicycle, he has entered a new realm as truly as if he were a child newly born into the world."
—Frances Willard, *How I Learned to Ride the Bicycle*

There are many ways of talking about business opportunities, problems, and solutions—each of which captures different characteristics of the whole. As an analogy to business analysis, poetic naturalism offers us a way to describe our organizational environments appropriately with the right audience. This book uses the philosophical approach poetic naturalism to give business teams a variety of ways of talking about their projects. The pillars of poetic naturalism can be summarized in three points: (1) there are many ways of talking about the world, (2) all good ways of talking must be consistent with one another and with the world, and (3) our purposes in the moment determine the best way of talking.[1] It is this philosophy that forms the fabric of this book.

Solutions and all of their components look and behave differently from the largest to the smallest of scales. Business solutions move from one moment to the next—dependent only on their current state. Because we are as much a part of a business system as the machines with which we interact, we must always remember to move the system toward its future purpose and value with efficiency and effectiveness while relying on the business system's previous state as our guide.

Through elicitation, discovery, observation, and analysis, we define needs and what is required to fulfill them using tables, equations, statements, models, theories, vocabularies, and stories as our communication tools. It is not enough that the stories and their relations make sense in and of themselves, they must fit together. As we dig deeper into that which is required to satisfy needs, their stories become harder to perceive. Because of this, we need a framework in which to place our tables, equations, statements, models, theories, vocabularies, and stories. This framework must allow for a variety of ways to talk about our problems, opportunities, and solutions by using language that is dependent upon the focus, perspective, and depth of the resolution at which we are looking. Our business solutions are the products of those aspects.

As an analyst, in addition to the six basic interrogatives,[2] our keyword is *emergence*; that which is required to satisfy a need emerges from the need itself.[3] A component of a business solution is emergent if it is not part of a detailed fundamental description of the business system itself, but becomes useful or even inevitable when we look at the system as a whole. Forming a necessary base or core of central importance to value and purpose is obvious in business analysis and project management. A business analyst (BA) knows that all business systems emerge from the complex interplay between people, processes, technology, information, and all of the individual components comprised therein.

Emergence is ubiquitous in business systems. When we discuss the needs of our high-level stakeholders we should not speak to the functions and the arrangements of particular specifications. We should invoke values based on the Bain and Company Elements of Value model[4] and then build purposeful sets of components that will emerge as the required arrangements of functions and specifications. The closer your stakeholder is to the fundamental components of the solution, the less extensive and emergent the conversation.

The Requirements, Elicitation, Planning, Analysis, and Collaboration Framework™ (REPAC®) is an ontology for projects and project professionals built using poetic naturalism, communication theory, mathematics, set theory and propositional logic, and organizational and behavioral psychology. How a solution makes you feel when you use its purpose or receive its value is an emergent property. It is larger than the sum of the parts of the solution and difficult to quantify, but no less critical. This notion is where the BA must first focus conversations.

Emergence depends on your perspective. What is microscopic to one stakeholder may be macroscopic to another. Think of *purpose* as the sum of all emerging properties, the arrangements of functions, and the positions of all specifications. Think of *value* as emerging properties of use. We receive benefit through intention. The more purposeful a solution becomes, the more value we deliver, and the more applicable we find the business solution.

A cell in your body is another example of emergence. All of the components in any one of your cells are inert; they are not alive. Put all of those proteins together in the right arrangement, and we get the emergence of life. In this example, the cell represents a stakeholder's need. We cannot call it alive until all that is required, the components of the cell, are arranged in just the right way.

Organizations that can foster a culture of learning will remain sustainable indeterminately. We must reexamine our requirements, seeing them through new eyes, and build a new glossary of terms. According to Gartner.com, the term *business glossary* is an umbrella term that includes the applications, infrastructure, tools, and best practices that enable access to and analysis of information to improve and optimize decisions and performance.

This would seem to support my vision of the myriad interactions and interdependencies that happen every moment of every day, in every organization, everywhere. These domains of applicability require different language sets. Indeed, this is ground zero for a business analysis professional. It would seem, therefore, that we must always be learning about the people, the processes, and the tools on which our organizations depend—to say nothing of learning about the nuances of business analysis itself. I have contracted to and consulted for dozens of organizations over the years. We all agree that their employees need training on practical subjects, including business analysis and project management. Sadly, though, when it comes to planning an educational program that extends beyond the hard skills, I tend to hear "we just don't have the time" or "it is not in the budget—perhaps next year." When it comes to plans for follow-up and learning reinforcement, well let's just say it feels like my message falls on deaf ears.

I used to believe these things were said to me sarcastically. Over the years, I have begun to recognize their sincerity, but that does not change the reality that many organizations need to provide educational programs that move past simple training to empower, offer personal growth or self-improvement, and perhaps most important, build teams of learners. "[The purpose of education] has changed from that of producing a literate society to that of producing a learning society" (Ammons 1964). This is where

REPAC enters the playing field as a learning aid for organizational intelligence and business analysis alike. Its purpose exceeds planning by helping to organize all of the information we need to elicit, learn, and analyze organizational issues so we can build lasting solutions.

I am always reminding my sons that learning requires making mistakes. When we experience, reflect, and apply new ideas we are bound to make errors. Unfortunately, some organizations do not celebrate those of us who are brave enough to ask questions. We are just expected to know the answers. One of my goals for the acceptance of REPAC is as a learning tool—a requirements learning tool for project teams; a way to learn what and why stakeholders need the things they need. Inspired by meaningful and ongoing communication, REPAC is not just a planning tool, it is a device that helps us determine which conversations are worth having and which are not.

REFERENCES

Ammons, M. 1964. Purpose and Program. Educational Leadership, 22(1), 15. Retrieved from http://ascd. com/ASCD/pdf/journals/ed_lead/el_196410_ammons.pdf.

Carroll, Sean. 2017. *The Big Picture: On the Origins of Life, Meaning, and the Universe Itself.* Dutton.

ENDNOTES

1. Sean Carroll. 2017. *The Big Picture: On the Origins of Life, Meaning, and the Universe Itself.* Dutton.
2. The six interrogatives: who, what, when, where, why, and how. Also known as the 5Ws.
3. Needs emerge from goals and objectives, which are either strategic or tactical.
4. I write about this model in more detail later. For more information visit: bain.com.

CASE STUDY

Today, content management systems (CMSs) are critical to an organization's overall enterprise communication strategy. Your company has decided to invest in the development of a web-based CMS. In general, a CMS is capable of creating, distributing, editing, and managing information through web portals within a collaborative environment. Your company has been expanding very quickly over the past few years and has outgrown its structured, homegrown document management system.

You work for The New Business Analyst (TNBA) International Learning, LLC. Founded in 1969, TNBA has become a global organization with offices in the Americas, Europe, India, the Middle East, and Asia. As a leading service provider of business analysis, project management, and leadership training, TNBA differentiates itself from competitors by only employing educators with business training and formal education in adult learning. As with many companies, TNBA grew over the decades and continued to expand and patch its current systems without regard to the possible consequences. It is no longer possible to continue with this strategy.

With the acquisition of some major clients, your organization has decided to take advantage of this system threat and redesign the way it creates, distributes, and manages all of its content—including its proprietary learning material. Also, TNBA has decided to make a substantial investment in online education and is intending for the CMS purchase to accommodate this initiative. You have been selected to be the lead business analyst (BA) for this massive undertaking. You have been given a team of four other BAs to help you with your research, elicitation, and analysis. You are directed to provide the following deliverables:

- Root-cause analysis
- Strategic and tactical goals and objectives
- Detailed stakeholder analysis
- Business case
- Requirements management plan
- Requirements team charter
- Stakeholder needs analysis
- Solution requirements
- Logical design
- Requirements package
- Test and acceptance strategy

Before you begin your elicitation, planning, analysis, collaboration, and documentation efforts, you decide to educate yourself on the CMS and the Requirements, Elicitation, Planning, Analysis, and Collaboration Framework™ (REPAC®), which you have been asked to follow on this initiative. As you inform yourself, you begin to identify features that you include in the business case for possible scope inclusion. Your REPAC research provides you with interesting results.

First, you realize that the REPAC Framework is very needs driven and does not discern between various types of requirements such as business, stakeholder, functional, nonfunctional, traditional, system, or technical. Using concepts like focus, perspective, and depth, you build collaboration sets containing members who help you elicit, plan, analyze, and assemble requirements that are quantized.

Thinking about building blocks, you realize that REPAC finds a requirement as made of smaller bits known as *enablers*. Together this creates a closed-looped superstructure consisting of interrelated and interdependent entities. This reminds you of Legos. Each whole piece is a requirement, while each stud represents a separate enabler. Lego bricks *stick* together because each stud or enabler has a corresponding slot waiting for it on a different block. You image this choreography as one of the elemental principles driving the REPAC Framework.

These encapsulated requirements start with a source, which is a cause of some sort. It may be an opportunity or a threat. In any case, each source must pair with one or more stakeholders. Thus, a stakeholder analysis becomes part of source identification. As you continue to learn more about REPAC you notice that the framework *listens* for stakeholder issues, complaints, problems, threats, and the like, and then identifies those as sources.

Next, it examines the source at a focal point with a particular perspective and depth of analysis to create a legitimate need that can be traced back to an organizational objective. You notice that, from the source, REPAC asks, "What is *needed* to resolve the issue?" Further, it continues to ask, "What is *required* to satisfy the need?" Last, REPAC queries, "*How* do we *specify* what is required to fulfill the need?" This slight change in semantics alters the REPAC Framework's point of view from being a requirements management structure to a needs management structure.

Bubbling with complexity and plurality, you are anxious to see how this process can help you create better solution packages for all of your stakeholders. Considering the deliverables ahead, chief among them are the causal events leading to this new organizational direction; you realize that the natural order of things is change. These changes happen according to patterns that we can observe, analyze, and predict—relative to the data collected about the phenomena. With all of the various events in mind, you are concerned that your stakeholders will be *all gung ho* to repair the new system without fully understanding the causal issues.

It is common for organizations to over-purchase in these cases, leaving a large number of capabilities seldom or never used. You realize that often there are actual causes to business situations, but that does not preclude random events which have no cause—a random convergence of happenstance if you will. You will have to be careful to conduct a thorough current state analysis to determine the gaps that must be filled by the new solution. This is your chance to shine as a trained professional.

In the chapters that follow, we will use this case study as input for the REPAC Framework. Beginning with source identification, we will conduct a causal analysis and build a stakeholder list for our requirements team.

ACKNOWLEDGMENTS

This book is my first solo publication. For me, it is the result of a five-year journey. I wanted to genuinely understand why we needlessly challenge ourselves when it comes to practical and efficient project delivery. After countless interviews, observations, surveys, and workshops, I arrived at three central themes: communication, coordination, and collaboration. This discovery led me to create the Requirements Elicitation, Planning, Analysis, and Collaboration Framework™ (REPAC®). REPAC is a methodology; a study of projects and project professionals, as seen through the lenses of communication theory, mathematics (in particular), set theory and propositional logic, and organizational and behavioral psychology.

This project has, indeed, been a long journey but I cannot take full credit. Over my many years of managing requirements and plans, coaching and training, and mentoring and consulting, I have met with and learned from hundreds of professionals; all of whom have enhanced my life, refined my thinking, improved my methods, and in some way, contributed to this book. For example, Amy Paquette, a former student, taught me a team building activity called the Ball of Yarn Game, which inspired me to use mesh theory for my communication model.

My first *real* job in information technology was with a start-up called Requisite Technology. They no longer exist but, for me, their memory lives on—it was like a university dorm, full of fun and fellowship. We were all very young and excited to make our mark in the early days of business-to-business internet e-commerce. I want to call out Liz Litkowski, Requisite's former VP of operations and marketing. I doubt she would even remember me, but Liz was kind enough to help me understand the importance of communication—particularly the type of information that is critical to leaders and in which ways I should present that information. In my role as Unix Administrator and Jr. Oracle DBA, I worked with an applications specialist whose name escapes me. He and I had our unique roles, but we were also supposed to back each other up, as needed. Soon after the millennium came, I decided to plan a long trip to Africa. I distinctly remember Liz telling us, "I want to be able to chop one of your heads off and have the other pop up in its place." Not only did she appeal to my dark sense of humor, but again, she helped me understand the importance of natural language and building lasting relationships. Liz, if you are reading this, thank you.

Soon after September 11th, 2001, Requisite substantially reduced its staff. It was not long before I found myself at the Canadian Standards Association (CSA). My manager, Sandra Quinn, currently the eHealth program manager at Central West Local Health Integration Network, gave me the freedom to explore business analysis. She did not prescribe any one method. I was free to determine the best approach, be it adaptive or prescriptive. Thank you, Sandra, for giving me space to learn and grow.

After my time with the CSA, I decided to become a contract project manager and business analyst on the advice of Thomas Palantzas, client solutions specialist: business process improvement, Global Knowledge Training. I had stopped growing as a professional and was spending too much of my time in operations, fixing month-end data processing errors. Thomas encouraged me to break free of the mold and excel as a contract professional. The next time I met Thomas, my life took off in ways I could not have imagined.

My first contract served to be a watershed opportunity. I joined the International Institute of Business Analysis (IIBA) (a brand new organization at the time) where I met Jacqueline Young, possibly the most exceptional business analyst working today and the author of the foreword for this book. Her insights and advice have kept me grounded over the years. Interestingly, Jacquline introduced me to the original IIBA leadership. That single event set off a path of dominoes that has led me to these very words.

After meeting Jacqueline, I met Jason Questor, co-founder of ACHIEVEBLUE™ and founder of the IIBA Toronto Chapter (who was kind enough to mentor me for a time), with whom I served as vice president of education. I also met Amy Ruddell, senior portfolio director at Diversified Communications Canada and editor-in-chief of PMTimes and BusinessAnalystTimes, and David Barrett, program director at Schulich Executive Education Centre, Schulich School of Business. With David and Amy, I served on Diversified's Project World Business Analyst World advisory board. Through Jason and the IIBA, I was reintroduced to Thomas, the gentleman who has been the single most influential professional in my life. I had expressed an interest in teaching and Thomas, who at the time also served on the IIBA Toronto Chapter board, suggested I come to Global Knowledge for an interview and audition. Since then, Thomas and I have become close colleagues and a great team. Thank you, Thomas, and all my students, for my career and the best years of my professional life.

Finally, I would like to say thanks to Cheryl Lee, fellow instructor, BA supreme, and core team contributor to the *PMI Guide to Business Analysis*, whom I replaced as chair for the PMI Toronto Chapter's Business Analysis Community. Thanks, Cheryl, for your faith in me. I hope I live up to your expectations.

I would be remiss (and possibly in much trouble) if I did not end these acknowledgments with the most important people in my life—my family. To my parents, Michael and Susan, and sister, Dawn, I say thanks for not killing me during those troublesome teen years. Last, to my fantastic wife, Janice, and sons, Aidan and Tristan, it is a foregone conclusion that without their unflinching support this book would not have been possible. Janice has more than fifteen years of experience building lasting customer relations. Her personal toolkit was of great inspiration. At eleven and six respectively, my sons have been surprisingly insightful in helping me simplify some of my more complex ideas. Thanks, boys!

ABOUT THE AUTHOR

Perry McLeod is a senior management consultant, facilitator, and educator with over 25 years of experience in business analysis, workshops and facilitation, agile adoption, process re-engineering, project management, business and systems modeling, strategic alignment, mentoring, and training. Perry's professional experience includes delivering industry-recognized best practices and standards for some of North America's most successful companies across many sectors, including banking and finance, agriculture, supply chain, consumer products, software design, insurance, and payment processing. He holds the following certifications: CBAP®, PMP®, PMI-PBA®, PMI-ACP®, SMC®, and is currently working toward his masters in education.

McLeod is deeply involved in the development of business analysis and project management methodologies. He has served as past vice president of education for the International Institute of Business Analysis, Toronto Chapter and as an advisory board member for Project World Business Analyst World. Perry is currently the chair for the Business Analysis Community, Project Management Institute, Toronto Chapter. He was also a contributor to the development of *A Guide to the Business Analysis Body of Knowledge (BABOK® Guide) v2.0.*

McLeod has developed requirements elicitation and analysis models and written courses for and taught at most of the major universities across Canada including the University of Toronto, York University's Schulich School of Business, Sheridan College, and Seneca College. He has also written dedicated courses for clients including TELUS; CIBC; Deloitte; John Hancock; the governments of British Colombia, Ontario, and Canada; Rogers Communications; Manulife Insurance; Shoppers Drug Mart; and the Toronto Dominion Bank.

McLeod's disciplined approach to teaching starts with the premise that his participants are equal partners in the learning experience. As a servant leader, Perry begins by developing a custom running case that is specific to the learner's background. Using positive language, real-world examples, humor, and passion, he creates an environment of trust and credibility. His enthusiasm is unmatched and he firmly believes that learning is a biological imperative that allows participants to take advantage of their propensity to tell stories, find meaning, and be social. McLeod has a unique passion for business and is an active believer that effective communication along with a deep understanding of behavioral and organizational psychology is the foundation for all endeavors—both professional and personal.

Web Added Value™

This book has free material available for download from the
Web Added Value™ resource center at *www.jrosspub.com*

At J. Ross Publishing we are committed to providing today's professional with practical, hands-on tools that enhance the learning experience and give readers an opportunity to apply what they have learned. That is why we offer free ancillary materials available for download on this book and all participating Web Added Value™ publications. These online resources may include interactive versions of the material that appears in the book or supplemental templates, worksheets, models, plans, case studies, proposals, spreadsheets and assessment tools, among other things. Whenever you see the WAV™ symbol in any of our publications, it means bonus materials accompany the book and are available from the Web Added Value Download Resource Center at www.jrosspub.com.

Downloads for *The Complete Guide to Requirements Management Using the REPAC® Framework* consist of the following:

- An advanced pre-project survey that identifies initial requirements management risks and identifies initial probabilities for success
- A requirements activities management table that accounts for effort, duration, productivity, and efficiency to determine probabilities of task completion
- A use case points analysis sheet

1

THE REPAC® FRAMEWORK¹

Words are important. Let's begin the project with the right ones. Ask not, "What is the requirement?" Ask, "What is required—strategically and tactically—to solve the problem, take advantage of the opportunity, envision the goals, meet the objectives, serve an organizational purpose, fulfill customers' needs to bring them value, or design the solution."

The Requirement Elicitation, Planning, Analysis, and Collaboration Framework™ (REPAC®) is an ontology; meaning it describes the properties it possesses. It starts with an input source such as a vendor, regulatory, or legal issue; an interruption in services; an opportunity (i.e., a new partnership or innovation); or even a simple change request. It provides a means to organize ourselves. Sources filter through points of focus, perspective, and depth to identify a set of quantifiable needs. It ends with an assembly of elements that transforms the need into *REPAC-aged* capsules of information. The framework redefines requirements management at a quantum level. We build *what we require—no more, no less.*

Atoms make up the observable universe. Similarly, everything in business solutions is, in a sense, made up of requirements, which like atoms, serve as building blocks for all that *matters* to an organization. What if we could see our requirements as atoms, how would they appear? If we could split one open, what would be inside? Einstein taught us through the special theory of relativity that time and space are two parts of the same whole. I see requirements in this way. I observe essential elements of a requirement, which upon closer examination, link to each other to the point where they are inseparable.

> *A requirement is a usable representation of a need. It focuses on understanding what kind of value could be delivered if fulfilled. The nature of the representation may be a document or set of documents, but can vary widely depending on the circumstances.*—BABOK® Guide, IIBA, 2015

> *A requirement is a condition or capability that must be met or possessed by a system, product, service, result, or component to satisfy a contract, standard, specification, or other formally imposed documents. Requirements include the quantified and documented needs, wants, and expectations of sponsor, customer, and other stakeholders.*—PMBOK® Guide, PMI, 2013

Stakeholders do not have requirements—they have needs. Solution providers and agents of change assemble requirements that are designed to satisfy those needs. The International Institute of Business Analysis

(IIBA) and the Project Management Institute (PMI) have done an exceptional job of helping practitioners understand the extrinsic value of a requirement, and the idea to use them to solve problems and build solutions. Requirements have purpose because they begin a causal chain of events that eventually bring us to realized value for stakeholders—but there is more to them than meets the eye.

What are the elements that give rise to the fundamental purpose of requirements? Understanding the very nature of how requirements are constructed is essential to eliciting, planning, analyzing, communicating, and managing them. Without this recognition, requirements tend to appear as random arrangements of text, tables, and diagrams, which may or may not reside within a single document. Often conceived with minimal traceability, interdependent and interrelated requirements exist as seeds spread across many packages or many pages of the same material. What if there was a way to solve this problem? It would mean we would have to abandon decades of thinking—redefining the very nature of the word *requirement*. When we understand requirements extrinsically, we are doing so in a classical sense. When we add an intrinsic aspect, we experience requirements at a quantum level. This approach is central to the REPAC Framework.

There are two ways to think of requirements—classical and quantized. Requirements conveyed to stakeholders as textual specifications or graphic images are classical when they are elicited and recorded as declarative statements or images across a single document or a collection of artifacts packaged together in separate smaller reports. Some of these demands may be poorly stated and disorganized. This obstacle is representative of many of the requirements that I have come across over my twenty-plus years as a business analyst. Many of these elements relate to each other in some way. Without adequate traceability, it becomes nearly impossible to understand the nuances of those interdependencies and relationships.

The REPAC Framework encapsulates requirements and all of the elements that went into building them into sets. REPAC considers requirements as both behaviors and enablers of behavior at the same time—there is no difference. Think of a requirement as an object made up of elements, like an atom or a cell in your body, built exclusively from a stakeholder's point of view. Requirements separated within the document, perhaps by many pages, create a potential for design, development, and testing errors. Slicing stories in an agile environment remains a challenging task for many adaptive teams. The REPAC Framework helps agile partners by understanding the vertical nature of a stakeholder's needs, from organizational purpose and customer value down to data tuples and machine logic. REPAC brings a new understanding to user stories.

REPAC identifies where our needs come from, why they are important, and what to do with them. It is based heavily on *set theory*, a branch of mathematics where things are grouped into collections. Sets usually represent numbers, but a set can be an assemblage of anything we want it to be. A simple example of a finite set would be the alphabet: a, b, c . . . x, y, z. Another example is your entire wardrobe. Consider all the different ways you can group all of your clothes. The combinations of unique outfits might number in the hundreds. When we reorganize or combine and apply sets in different ways for unique situations, they become very useful building blocks for understanding complex problems. This is the power of REPAC.

The framework provides hundreds of ways to combine and reorganize different elements that are pertinent to organizational issues. Using set theory, the REPAC Framework asks a business analyst (BA) to assemble a set of information that can be used to plan business analysis activities and deliverables, elicit needs or user stories from stakeholders, analyze those needs, and determine what is required to slice the stories and realize the needs. We do not ask our stakeholders what their requirements are. We construct a

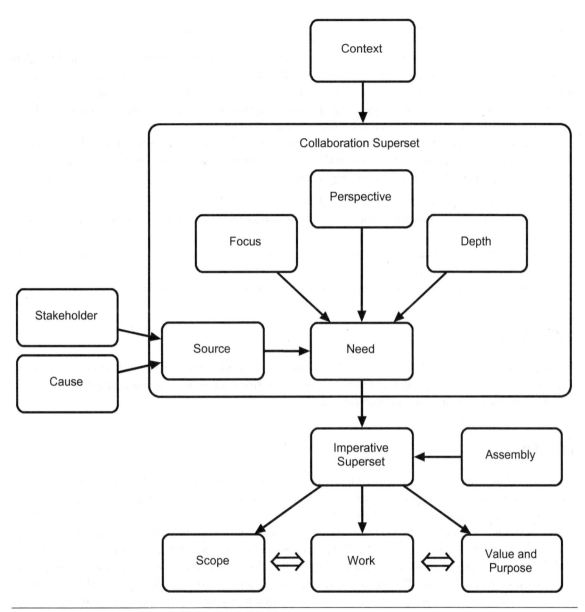

Figure 1.1   REPAC Framework (© The New BA, Ltd.)

requirement, element by element, based on the information learned from a REPAC *set*. Using the REPAC *assembler*, contained within the framework seen in Figure 1.1, we identify a topic source, a perspective to be examined, and depth to explore. With an instance of the REPAC set we can elicit, plan, analyze, collaborate, slice, and assemble imperatives of any level or type, across any domain. Each element of the framework is outlined in this chapter.

SOURCE

REPAC uses the word *source* to refer to the initial someone or something that presents the initial problem to be resolved or an opportunity to be exploited, as well as the problem, issue, or opportunity itself. It is the fuel for the REPAC set builder. Identifying a source infers raw data such as documents and diagrams, stakeholders, or the results of a causal analysis. This inference implies the source as a generative force, capable of producing organizational purpose and value-based stakeholder needs.

We must never attempt to resolve an issue until we fully understand it and the stakeholders for whom the problem persists. We engage our stakeholders to identify the root cause, understand various issues, or exploit some opportunity. REPAC source requires us to:

- Determine the reason we are engaging the stakeholder
- Understand the problem or opportunity space enough to proceed with planning (this is a matter of perspective)
- Conduct a stakeholder analysis for establishing/managing expectations and alignment to project and business objectives
- Create a requirements team charter with which to manage our engagement

CONTEXT

Without context, there is no meaning to the circumstances, conditions, factors, and states that form the setting for the events, ideas, and terms that we experience from our reality. We use context to assess fully, understand, and bring meaning to everything we experience.

FOCUS

There are many conversations that must take place, even for the smallest plan. Projects of all shapes and sizes rely on mindful and immersive communication. REPAC *focus* acts as an anchor to concentrate attention and a point of emphasis for a REPAC set.

When you have a meeting, do you know what discussions must take place? When you have a workshop, what is the agenda? How will you decide? REPAC focus is a means to identify what is important to address and the primary purpose of a meeting or workshop. It is the anchor to a REPAC superset, a grouping of elements used to elicit, plan, slice stories, and assemble requirements. The point at which images form within our mind is the REPAC point of focus. We carry that focus into a collaboration event and examine it from different perspectives and layers of analysis.

PERSPECTIVE

REPAC *perspective* is a state or condition permitting clear perception or understanding of focus. It is the interrelation in which the subject or its parts, *cognitively examined*, allow us to realize points of view on the selected focus and is a reference for considerations, expatiations, opinions, beliefs, experiences, and such.

Perspective is our ability to see things as they truly are—a matter's importance and meaning as it relates to the needs of stakeholders and the organization.

But herein lies the rub. At the opening of this chapter, I cited English Biologist Thomas Huxley. Huxley's arguments with English bishop and then great orator Samuel Wilberforce were instrumental in the acceptance of evolutionary biology across a wider audience. The quote is apt, in that, no matter how powerful, loud, or passionate an emotional appeal is, it is just that, an emotional appeal—something that we can neither defend nor compete. As business analysis professionals, we must facilitate unbiased debates about what is best for the stakeholders and organization, regardless. "But what is right?" Indeed—oh to live in a world of reason!

When you discuss something with a stakeholder, what points of view are considered? The perspective of focus is the interrelation in which the focus and elements of discussion are explored and analyzed in depth. Perspective has a tendency to become a personal assessment of attention and, as BAs, it is our duty to keep the impressions as unbiased as possible.

DEPTH

REPAC uses several strata to organize information into sets. Depth—more accurately identified as the depth of analysis—is the level of thoroughness or completeness with which we wish to explore our focus and the perspective. This method of analysis allows us to examine a stakeholder's needs through distinctive layers of abstraction.

In advance of any discussion about a stakeholder's needs, it is to our benefit, and theirs, that we identify how detailed the conversation will be. Without this pre-identification, we risk analysis paralysis or digging too deeply into a subject prematurely. Despite the behest of our stakeholder's demand for stating the *solution* at the onset, we must layer our analysis. REPAC depth helps us pull back layers of abstraction through a classification scheme that starts with contextual patterns and ends with executable logical or physical models that are quickly realizable and refillable. We analyze perspective and focus at an appropriate depth or level of applicability. It is a way to examine a point of focus and perspective (an anchor of conversation, planning, elicitation analysis, and collaboration). In the chapters that follow, I will continue to introduce and detail what REPAC is, the extensibility it offers, and the concepts it employs.

The REPAC set builder, the framework's main interface, acts much like a recipe. We build a REPAC set using the elements and policies outlined in the set equation, which I will detail in the next chapter. After conducting an in-depth stakeholder analysis, the BA selects one or more parties of interest and asks them to present an issue, problem, threat, or some other topic that must transform into a need or set of needs; this begins the REPAC process.

THE REPAC PROCESS

The following text explains how the recipe comes together as a tool for exploration, conversation, collaboration, and story analysis.

DISCOVER NEEDS, ALIGN OUR PURPOSE, AND VALIDATE VALUE

Everything we do is from the stakeholder's point of view. The stakeholder may represent operational, technical, nontechnical, or testing processes, or any other aspect of a problem space. Notwithstanding classical approaches to analysis, we will always understand the problem and subsequent needs from the stakeholder's point of view. When conducting a needs assessment, our attention should be on what is missing from the stakeholder's viewpoint so we can identify what is *needed* to fill in the gaps. We never elicit requirements directly. We elicit problems, issues, and the like, which we transform into specific needs that will later be assembled into requirements.

Assembly

Through a technique known as REPAC *requirement assembly,* we identify what behaviors and enablers are *required* to fulfill the needs and fill in the gaps. This technique results in quantized imperatives.

THE REPAC SET BUILDER

Recall that I do not believe that BAs should elicit requirements directly from their stakeholders. Requirements, constructed into executable and testable statements from stakeholders' opportunities, wants, desires, issues, problems, and the like, should be done using the REPAC Framework. Using the REPAC tool allows you to identify which conversations, plans, sessions, and so on *need* to take place using the three aforementioned simple concepts: focus, perspective, and depth. Within REPAC, we re-identify requirements as abstract ideas containing elements necessary to satisfy the needs of the stakeholder and provide purpose for the organization. By abstracting the requirement and encapsulating it within a structure of terms vital to its nature, we create a closed-looped system of interdependent and interrelated components. The encapsulated imperative is a system unto itself, interacting with other systems creating a harmonious whole. The REPAC set builder is the framework's primary interface (see Figure 1.2). The REPAC set builder employs four simple parameters:

- *S*: refers to the source of our need
- *N*: refers to the need, as defined by the elements of the REPAC set builder
- *A*: relates to the assembly of an imperative
- *I*: refers to the imperative of what is required to satisfy the need

With user stories or other traditional methods, once we identify and analyze the stakeholder and source, we examine their needs concerning a focal point of interest, a perspective of that focus, and a depth of discussion. From this, we identify a stated need that we assemble into an imperative, which distributes across the team as scope and work realized as customer value and organizational purpose.

The REPAC Framework is designed to support all business systems, which includes elements of information, software, and process engineering as well as organizational physiology—all determinants of the people, process, and tools/technology triad. Business systems characterized by both organic and mechanical elements and manual and automated processes are incredibly complex because they encompass these devices—all of which embody aspects of an organization's culture.

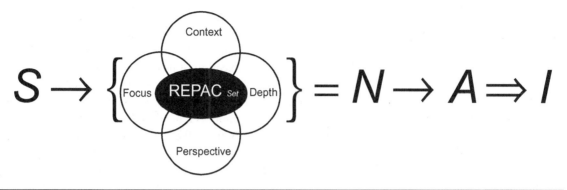

Figure 1.2   REPAC set builder (© The New BA, Ltd.)

Information engineering is not a new term. It is the method of developing software where we place a high level of importance on the data. Data is analogous to raw material or pieces of wood. Organized or processed data with context is information. Hence, information is comparable to a chair made of wooden pieces. The generation, distribution, analysis, and use of data in information technology systems is known as information engineering. We must keep our focus on data and its movement as we identify needs and provide solution options.

Software engineering, an equally familiar term, is a systematic and disciplined approach to developing computer programs that interface between user (often a person) applications, operating systems, and hardware. Developers create solutions in either a structured, imperative mode or an object-oriented environment using protocols or objects and classes, respectively. It applies techniques from both computer science and engineering principles and practices to the creation, operation, and maintenance of software systems. We must also keep our attention on the protocols or behaviors and enablers of the solution, and its components.[2]

Stakeholders use processes and machines to reach objectives and accomplish tasks. Process engineering, a relatively new term, involves observing operational duties and interpreting the results for translating the needs of stakeholders into processes and facilities that convert *raw materials* into value-added segments. Through process engineering, analysts oversee process improvements across domain lines.[3]

Organizational psychology, a practice still not widely applied in business analysis, is the people side of the equation—more specifically, how people interact with data, processes, technology, and each other.

BAs should always elicit and analyze the right blend of people and culture, processes, and machines into a seamless integration of solution behaviors and enablers. The REPAC Framework provides us with the tools we *need* to establish that integration.

The presence of a *need* implies the assembly of what is required to satisfy the need. We find needs at the intersections of focus, perspective, and depth. Needs, however, come with many different points of view and are separate from wants. Needs are what the solution requires from a stakeholder's point of view in terms of behaviors and characteristics. Needs solve problems or take advantage of opportunities, which trace to customer value and organizational purpose. Wants are rational (or irrational) subjective desires expressed by stakeholders and may not connect to customer value or purpose.

Stakeholders' areas of interest are pluralistic, stretch across different levels of applicability, and are interdependent and interrelated. There are many perspectives on a dizzying array of topics and terms. REPAC uses a set of concepts and categories in a subject area or domain to organize different areas of focus with points of view at various depths. The system allows for the selection of more than one element from the perspective set, for instance. The selection is a combined order. This allows the user to remain focused on a discrete set of topics while still allowing for a broad range of discussions. The REPAC Framework creates manageable sets of terms. It can be as complex or as simple as it needs to be. It can focus on the big questions or the little ones. It can have profound points of view, using the perspective policy, or it can keep things engaging and straightforward.

To mortgage the future of a project without a clear picture of what to focus on sets it up for failure like so many projects that have come before. As we delve deeper into this framework, each step emerges in full detail. Let us begin our journey by getting to know our stakeholders.

REFERENCES

A Guide to the Business Analysis Body of Knowledge (BABOK® Guide). 2015. International Institute of Business Analysis (IIBA), p. 48.

A Guide to the Project Management Body of Knowledge (PMBOK® Guide). 2013. Project Management Institute (PMI), p. 371.

Murphy, Kevin R. and Frank E. Saal. 1990. *Psychology in Organizations: Integrating Science and Practice (Applied Psychology Series)*. Psychology Press.

ENDNOTES

1. This chapter adopted from: white paper written by Perry McLeod for Global Knowledge: Stop Gathering Requirements and Start Building Them. http://www.bitpipe.com/detail/RES/1435007237114 .html (accessed March 25, 2016).
2. Adopted from: Home | Software Engineering, https://uwaterloo.ca/software-engineering/ (accessed April 17, 2016).
3. Adopted from: Process engineering—Wikipedia, the free encyclopedia, https://en.wikipedia.org/ wiki/Processengineering (accessed April 17, 2016).

SECTION 1:
Building Relationships

2

THE PERFECT INTERVIEW

"An interview is a formal or informal approach to elicit information from stakeholders."
—Project Management Institute, *Business Analysis for Practitioners: A Practice Guide*

BUSINESS ANALYSIS INTERVIEWS

Successful business analysis interviews hinge on preparatory work. A structured business analysis interview is not a spontaneous ad hoc means to gather requirements. Formal interviews require meaning, a well-understood objective, knowledge about the interviewee, and careful research, planning, execution, and follow-up. In ordinary usage, the word *meaning* implies intention, intention implies design, and design implies a designer. The design is the interview and the designer is the business analyst (BA). The intent is to design the interview rather than just plan it. BAs depend on interviews as a technique for conducting research, asking and answering questions, building rapport, and acquiring issues, problems, needs, and the like.

Too often, however, a formal interview focuses directly on requirements rather than the information or raw data needed to build the requirements during requirement analysis and design definition. In extreme cases, the BA may only rely on interviews. Because of misuse, poor preparation, and execution, interviews are one of the least successful ways to build requirements. In the pages that follow, we will examine some design practices that will elevate the common business analysis interview into a well-designed, carefully constructed, and seamlessly executed event.

Ask not what the requirement is, ask what do we require to meet expectations and fulfill the stakeholders' needs. In *A Guide to the Business Analysis Body of Knowledge* (*BABOK® Guide*), the International

Institute of Business Analysis (IIBA) (2015) suggests that the intended use of an interview is to "elicit business analysis information from a person or group of people. The interview can also be used for establishing relationships and building trust between BAs and stakeholders."

A business analysis interview falls under two basic types: structured or unstructured.

Structured Interview

In a structured interview, the interviewer has a predefined set of questions. The discussion, which is sensible, planned, and intended to provide the analyst with specific answers, is often a means to gather information that is not suited for other business analysis techniques.

Unstructured Interview

An unstructured interview lacks predefined questions. The interviewer and interviewee discuss topics of interest in an open-ended way. This technique is best suited for building a social connection to the stakeholder. When considering a structured business analysis interview as the means to gather the raw data needed to build requirements, follow the *BABOK® Guide* (2015):

- Elicit information (raw data)
- Establish rapport, expand relationships, build trust
- Increase stakeholder involvement
- Observe nonverbal responses
- Seek support
- Require full discussions with stakeholders
- Explore topics in detail
- Allow for privacy

The IIBA also suggests limitations or drawbacks to the interview process such as the time required of all parties concerned, unintentionally leading the interviewee to a biased conclusion, and the amount of training needed to conduct effective interviews.

GOALS AND OBJECTIVES

Why must this interview take place? What must and should we accomplish? Goals are qualitative; they describe an end state. Imagine that I have come to your office to train you and some of your colleagues. The class finishes, but my flight is not until the next day. You suggest I spend some time taking in the local sights. I agree and tell you my goal is to learn about the history of your city. My target does not describe what I must see or where I must go. We have to objectify the goal. A structured business analysis interview is more than a conversation; it is a social event requiring careful planning. According to the *BABOK® Guide* (2015), a successful meeting depends on factors such as:

- A level of understanding of the domain by the interviewer
- Experience of the interviewer in conducting interviews
- Skill of the interviewer in documenting discussions

- Readiness of the interviewee to provide the relevant information
- Ability of the interviewer to conduct the interview
- Degree of clarity in the interviewer's mind about the goal of the interview
- Rapport between the interviewer(s) and the interviewee

We have already explored some reasons for conducting a structured business analysis interview; however, we have not discussed the intent of any particular interview. Stating the specific objectives of the interview is challenging, they must be SMART (specific, measurable, actionable, realistic, and time-bound). It is helpful to frame a goal with this simple statement, "For this interview to be successful, I must have:"

- A short declarative statement describing why time has been taken from the interviewee
- A fit criterion or simple test to verify the objective
- A set of items on which to follow up
- A sense that the information obtained is useful
- A timeline for each question including how much time is allotted for follow-up

A successful, structured business analysis interview depends on many factors. Oftentimes, the BA does not have the required experience or has developed poor habits. Understanding the difference between your wants and needs as well as those of the stakeholders is the first step to creating an acceptable goal that is agreeable to both the interviewer and interviewee. Common mistakes include:

- Not following a key thread from a given answer
- Not exploring why some answers are given
- Not understanding interview notes after the interview
- Poor active listening
- Making assumptions about what was said
- Asking too many closed questions
- Allowing for monosyllabic answers
- Not drawing the interviewee out enough

Planned, well-executed business analysis interviews tend to be the best technique to elicit important information from managers and executives. Their time is precious, their perspectives are unique, and they often have a very clear message. The structure of the interview will depend on many aspects, such as the overall goal, the location, the parties involved, the BA's experience, time, the questions themselves, various personalities, and the organizational culture. We will explore these topics in more depth in a later section. A paradigm approach to the initial structure of the interview known as a situation, target, and proposal (STP) can be a fast way to begin the planning process. Table 2.1 provides an example of how an STP is used:

- Situation: topics of discussion
- Target: for each topic of discussion or for each line of questioning, what is the desired outcome?
- Proposal: an idea that could resolve the issue or, in this case, a line of questioning

Table 2.1   Situation target proposal example

Situation	Target	Proposal
Poor sponsor support. When a problem arises, the sponsor may not have the authority, or perspective, to support the project adequately.	Obtain a greater understanding of the sponsor's level of interest and authority over the project.	Begin with a rapport building exercise. Casually address issues of authority and interest. Slowly begin to increase the importance of the questions.

THE INTERVIEWEE

Understanding your stakeholder will help lay a foundation of trust and credibility while easing the difficulty with delayed reciprocity. As BAs, we expect a lot from our stakeholders. What we promise them, when not seen for months or even years, could greatly affect the trust and credibility we have worked so hard to achieve. Unlike a direct barter system, our half of the exchange may take weeks or months to reciprocate—common where information or specific actions are required—and therefore puts relationships in jeopardy before they even begin—another reason to use an adaptive approach. A structured business analysis interview is often a *first contact* situation for the BA and stakeholder. First impressions, forged in seconds, make or break a reciprocal exchange, which could go on for a very long time.

We would be remiss if we did not understand the stakeholder both personally and professionally. We research stakeholders in two ways. First, we determine their importance within the organization and our requirements. Second, we explore who they are as people—what motivates and demotivates them, are there any special needs we should be aware of, do they have precise awareness of the upcoming change, do they have a desire to help us, and do they possess any special abilities that could be of value toward our goals?

Our ultimate goal in an interview, or any engagement, is to merge the source data we obtain from our stakeholders with the contextual patterns that make up every day organizational life. From this a conceptual framework begins to take shape, and we can begin to understand which needs to address. We understand this conceptual framework in a logical, non-solution-specific and physical, solution-specific approach. The result is knowledge, which we can use to make strategic and tactical decisions. Over time, this knowledge becomes wisdom, which we share with others. Finally, when faced with new data, we reinforce our understanding of contextual patterns with the wisdom we have obtained.

The golden rule teaches us that we should do unto others as we would have them do unto us. Travis Bradberry and Jean Greaves at The Good Men Project suggest that there is a better approach to take when we want to understand our stakeholders:

> *"The Golden Rule—treat others as you want to be treated—has a fatal flaw: it assumes that all people want to be treated the same way. It ignores that vastly different things motivate people. The Platinum Rule—treat others as they want to be treated—corrects that flaw."*

Although this may seem slightly pandering, it is an acknowledgment of who we are as a people. As Bradberry and Greaves suggest, if someone needs public recognition, give it to him or her. If they do not like to be the focus of attention, however, keep them from feeling uncomfortable. This idea maintains the importance of understanding the four basic personality styles and the structure of emotional intelligence. In addition, it also agrees with Belbin's Team Roles. We explore both of these soon.

So far in this chapter, we have discussed some business analysis interview preparation techniques, including identification and analysis of objectives, structures, and stakeholders for a seamless interview. I have shown the importance of laying the interview groundwork as a necessary first step. Conducting the actual interview presents its own obstacles; thereby it requires its own set of procedures. I prefer the word *design* over the word *plan*, let's examine why.

GETTING READY

Often stakeholders use an interview as a means to defuse or *get things off of their chest*, which is acceptable as long as the grievances and grumbles are controlled and contained. If they become inappropriate or too far out of the interview's scope, the BA must work to bring the interviewee back to the goals of the interview.

Design the Event

When designing a structured BA interview, it's crucial to have a goal in mind, a clear set of questions planned, and an understanding of how those questions may deviate from the intended goal. An interview has an intended line of questioning; it may also have alternate lines of questioning and unanticipated paths where the interviewee has raised issues or answered questions in a way in which the BA had not considered or planned. In short, an interview is a social process.

Referring to the example in Figure 2.1, we can see the interview has an intended line of questioning but also has an intended follow-up. Along the way, unintended responses were either resolved or set aside. All concerns raised by the interviewee, addressed during the interview, or documented for follow-up after the interview or in a subsequent interview, must leave the interviewee with a sense of closure. Use follow-ups with caution; stakeholders, such as managers, are busy and may be upset if more of their time is required. Table 2.2 presents a possible scenario to the business analysis interview design structure seen in Figure 2.1.

Structure the Flow

As seen in Figure 2.1, the flow of an interview may become quite complex. The BA must keep excellent notes and in those notes trace the line of questioning for further analysis. This requires something more than a plan; it requires a design. Traditionally, the terms *plan, planning,* or *making a plan* are seen as overhead activities, unavoidable, or non-value-adding work which force managers and team members to skip important project steps and compromise quality. "We don't have time to plan. Just do it!"—is the refrain we hear most often. The term *design*, however, conjures up specific things needing fulfillment. A design is:

- A specification of an object
- Manifested by an agent
- Intended to accomplish goals
- In a particular environment
- Using a set of primitive components
- Satisfying a set of requirements that are subject to constraints
- In this context, the interview is the object under design

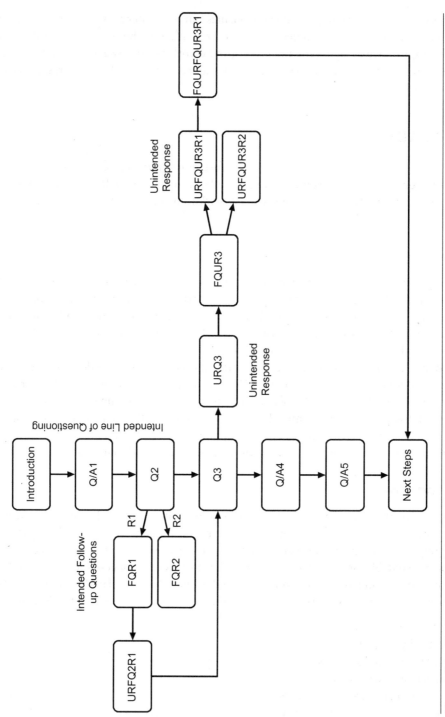

Figure 2.1 Business analysis interview structure example (© The New BA, Ltd.)

Table 2.2 Business analysis interview structure example path description

ID	Scenario	Description
Introduction	Establish rapport	The BA and the interviewee spend a few minutes setting the tone of the interview by engaging in a social tête-à-tête and establishing some guidelines.
Q1/A1	Question one and answer one	The first open-ended question formally sets the tone of the interview and inexorably leads to questions that are more important. The BA is satisfied with the answer and the interview proceeds according to plan.
Q2&R1	Question two and response one	The BA anticipates that there may be two different responses to question two and has planned for this by writing follow-up questions. In this scenario, response one is given.
FQ2R1	Follow-up question to response one	As expected, the interviewee has responded with an anticipated answer to question two. Prepared for this, the BA asks a follow-up question for the response given to question two.
URFQ2R1	Unintended response to follow-up of question two's response one	The BA did not anticipate this response. He decides to continue with his planned line of questioning and suggests that they follow up on that response at another time.
Q3	Question three	Question three is starting to get at the significant part of the issue at hand. This question might be sensitive and politically based.
URQ3	Unintended response to question three	The BA receives another unintended response and decides to leave the normal line of questioning and explore this new path further.
FQUR3	Follow-up question to the unintended response from question three	The new line of questioning continues to bring up surprises for the BA.
URFQUR3R1	Unintended response from follow-up question of unintended response to question three's response one	Responses continue to be unintended. The BA begins to suspect that he may need to book more interviews with different stakeholders to determine if this new information is consistent across the project team.
FQURFQUR3R1	Follow-up question to unintended response from follow-up question of unintended response to question three's response one	Realizing that time has run out, the BA asks his last question and continues to the next steps, and is likely planning how to proceed with this stakeholder.

Design the Questions

A major component of the interview design is its questions. Each question has its own objective, which contributes to the overall goal of the interview. Stakeholders, eased into an interview using a technique that slowly builds the importance of the questions over time, feel more comfortable and more willing to divulge information. We use four basic types of questions to build this trust and credibility. Figure 2.2 and Table 2.3 demonstrate the four question types and their basic application.

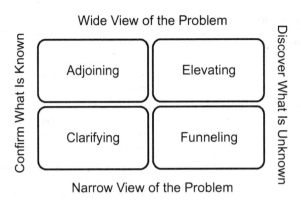

Figure 2.2   Four basic question types model (© Pohlmann and Thomas 2015)

Table 2.3   Four basic question types descriptions (© Pohlmann and Thomas 2015)

Clarifying	Clarifying questions help us understand what transpired so we can avoid making assumptions. Two monologues do not make a dialogue. It is important to remember not to speak over, past, or through each other; waiting for the other to finish so you can say your piece. Ask clarifying questions such as, "I believe you mean this" or "Let me see if I understand" to remain focused on the message your sender is trying to get across. A clarifying question will naturally lead to another follow-up question such as, "Please tell me more" or "Describe what that felt like."
Adjoining	These questions explore related and ignored aspects of the problem related to the dialogue. There are many types of contexts; here we can use modal verbs to ask questions which explore different contexts. In linguistics, we use modal verbs or auxiliaries, which provide additional help and support to the messages we are trying to convey. Words like "can," "could," "shall," "should," "will," "would," "may," "might," and "must" indicate likelihood, permission, obligation, and ability. Sentences that use these terms can help us obtain more information and gain a better understanding of our sender's intent.
Funneling	Funneling questions dive deeper into responses. Why was that answer given and not another? What assumptions do we challenge? What are the root causes? Exploring and sometimes challenging our senders with questions such as, "why did you do it this way," or "what was the method you followed," compel our sender to reason conically and funnel their thoughts into the details of their message. This line of questioning can take us from a contextual or conceptual analysis to a physical one, which is helpful in process re-engineering.
Elevating	These questions raise broader issues and highlight the bigger picture. Elevating questions help us zoom out because it is harder to see the overall context and patterns driving it when you completely immerse yourself in the problem space. Example questions include "Taking a step back, what are the larger issues?" or "Are we even addressing the right question?" Think of this as a reverse conical analysis. Here we want to focus on context and identify patterns which we can use to relate to our own problem space.

Organizational culture rewards those who answer questions, not those who ask them. Questioning conventional wisdom can lead to sidelining, isolation, or even threats (Pohlmann and Thomas 2015). The BA must be courageous and be willing to take a line of questioning wherever it needs to go. Do not plan—design! Design your requirements, design your workshops, and design your interviews.

What to Talk About

There are three concepts to understand when considering what questions to ask and how to ask them. The BA must first identify the source of the interview—what is driving this conversation? Next, we must decide what to focus our attention on, followed by what perspective they want to take, and how deep to take the conversation. The Requirement Elicitation, Planning, Analysis, and Collaboration Framework™ (REPAC®) will help us create these questions. REPAC provides thousands of possible subjects, perspectives, and depth combinations, which takes the guesswork out of determining what conversations should take place and when. With this framework, we can apply a linear approach to our questions.

A Linear, Logical Approach

This technique helps to plot interview questions across a normal distribution curve. The statistical terms *mu* and *sigma* symbolize the mean and the standard deviation, respectively, of a probability distribution, which is how the line of questioning technique is applied. In probabilistic terms, the interviewee is more likely to answer the questions you need answered on the upswing of a normal curve than they are on the downswing. Interviews can be emotional, intense, or politically charged events. Allowing for a natural decrease in importance and intensity creates a stronger sense of closure. In this model, the level of importance of the questions increases at a steady rate until the critical questions, once asked and answered, bring the interview down to a natural conclusion and sense of closure. Figure 2.3 demonstrates this process.

Following Figure 2.3, we see the introduction and the first question open up the lines of communication. As the interview proceeds, the importance of the questions increases at a steady pace. This approach allows the interviewer and the interviewee to ease into the subject matter at a natural pace. Review Figure 2.1 and compare it to Figure 2.3. Here we can see that the interviewee has escalated the line of questioning, creating a disjointed curve, representing an unexpected direction for the BA. Best practice tells us the BA must do their best to prepare for this by researching the topics at hand as well as the stakeholder's personality and bring the interview home safely.

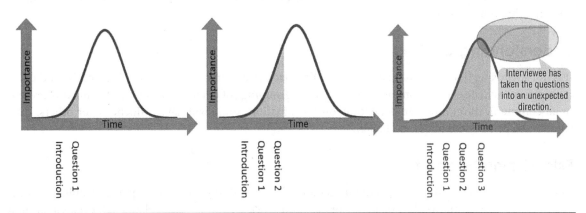

Figure 2.3   Normal distribution curve of a structured interview (© The New BA, Ltd.)

The Pre-Interview

An important step to a successful interview is setting up a safe, trustworthy, and credible environment. Setting up a pre-interview with the stakeholder, either by phone, text, in person, or by whatever mode seems appropriate, often helps to clarify issues, refine the interviewer's objectives, and begin the process of building trust. A good interview is about:

- Establishing rapport
- Situational awareness
- Helping the stakeholder understand delayed reciprocity
- Encouraging honesty
- Asking the right questions and encouraging dialogue
- Active listening
- Summarizing and consolidating what you have heard
- Managing bias
- Troubleshooting difficult situations

The pre-interview is a simple but important step. Take the time to understand your stakeholder on a personal and professional level. If possible, meet face-to-face to introduce yourself, briefly discuss the interview, and ensure that the interviewee fully understands their purpose. If a face-to-face interview is not possible, arrange some other mode such as text messaging or a telephone call. Do not give the interviewee a list of your questions; just introduce them to the ideas you wish to cover. If the stakeholder is not willing to discuss a certain topic, it is best to remove it from the interview and discuss the matter with the project manager and sponsor.

THE INTERVIEW

The most important influence on how we interpret messages is context and the patterns within. The interview itself is an exchange of raw data in the form of verbal and nonverbal packets. This raw data is given meaning through context.

Understanding Context

It is not surprising that some aspects of context link back to emotional intelligence. We understand communication exchanges by becoming aware of the six groupings of context. Each type of context is present in all communication; however, depending on the situation, some will have influence over others. This subject will be revisited in a later chapter.

Establishing Rapport

The first task in successful interpersonal relationships is building rapport. Rapport establishes common values, beliefs, knowledge, or behaviors around work and non-work-related subjects. Creating a common ground puts the interviewer and interviewee at ease and helps to couch the pain of delayed reciprocity. Some examples of ways to build rapport include:

- Identify common ideas and interests to open the interview
- Use nonthreatening project related topics for initial small talk
- Listen to what the other person is saying and look for shared experiences or circumstances
- Inject a small amount of humor about the project, but be careful not to offend
- Be aware and respond to nonverbal cues from yourself and the interviewee

Make sure the interviewee feels included but not interrogated during the interview. Put the stakeholder at ease. This will enable you to relax and allow the conversation to progress comfortably.

Situational Awareness

Situational awareness takes critical thinking and the ability to be aware of what is happening in the vicinity in order to understand how information, events, and one's own actions affect goals and objectives, both immediately and in the near future. As the BA works through the interview, myriad things are happening around them. Communication and understanding are complicated human endeavors. Many of us explain issues by telling stories filled with metaphors and hidden meaning. Be mindful of all the nonverbal nuances happening while the interviewee tells his or her story.

Reciprocity and Fair Exchange

Reciprocity is simply responding to a positive action with another positive action based on an agreed-upon exchange which is/should be fair to both parties. Delayed reciprocity is a little more complicated in that it asks for something now in exchange for something later (or in some cases, much, much later!). As business analysis professionals, many of the things we ask for in terms of a solution are not returned for many weeks, months, or even years. Not using an adaptive approach can create a cloud of distrust.

Encourage an Honest Dialogue

About two-thirds of all human dialogue is gossip (Dunbar 2004). It is in our nature to talk about other people. Anthropologically, this behavior serves as *verbal grooming*—equivalent to the social grooming seen in other primates. When not of a malicious nature, verbal grooming serves to reinforce social relationships (Fox 2002). It is important, however, to verify gossip within the interview setting.

Listen Actively

Often used in counseling and conflict resolution, active listening is the most important skill for a BA to possess. How well we listen has a major impact on our effectiveness and on the quality of our relationships with others. Good communication skills require a high level of self-awareness. By understanding our personal style of communicating, we create lasting impressions and become better communicators and collaborators.

Manage Bias

BAs must ensure that the information obtained through an interview is indicative of the actual situation rather than an artifact of the interview or the individual interviewee's perceptions. Interviewee responses, biased by the actual interview situation itself, lead BAs in the wrong direction and potentially cause weeks of delay. Specifically, interviews are conducive to people receiving attention and feeling heard and validated.

Stakeholders may also alter their own perceptions of their current situation and prime themselves to give biased responses that are disproportionately positive or negative. Referred to as the Hawthorne Effect, this temporary phenomenon—first discovered from data collected during a factory study to determine if workers would become more or less productive with an adjustment in light levels—had some unexpected results. As a side effect, the workers taking part in the study did increase their productivity but not through any change in factory luminosity. As a result of the attention they were receiving from the study itself, their productivity noticeably increased (Noland 1959).

Manage Conflict

Oddly, when we consider conflict, images of people screaming at each other or emotionally hijacked words of discomfort, tension, and crisis tend to come to mind. These concepts refer to how we deal with conflict, which tends to be fallacious and illogical. Conflict is just a difference of opinion. Our inability to manage conflict using rational arguments, emotional intelligence, contextual thinking, and other concepts reduces the conflict to fights, which forces our brains into a fight-or-flight mode and severely limits rational thought.

Fights and arguments are two words used synonymously but could not be further apart. We all know that a fight is a disagreement based not on rational thought but rather on an emotional position. Emotions and feelings are not the same. Emotions are biological responses to stimuli and more or less out of our control. Research classifies six distinct emotions: disgust, sadness, happiness, fear, anger, and surprise. How we "feel" about our anger or disgust is interpretive, subjective, and under our control. Fights, filled with fallacious thinking and emotional hijacking, seldom do anyone any good. Argumentation, on the other hand, is reason giving. Argumentation, the gateway to effective reasoning, is an essential skill for any BA.

According to Merriam Webster, argumentation is the "act or process of forming reasons (based on inference and logic) and of drawing conclusions and applying them to a case in discussion." Consider argumentation as a means to justify claims where absolute proof is unavailable. Reasons are the justifications we give for our claims. Without reasonable discourse, we will give in to sentiments in a *knee-jerk fashion*, on a whim, or at the command of an authority figure. We keep arguments clean and reasonable by fully understanding our claims, assumptions, or premises and by determining the method we will use for our line of reasoning—building an argument on a set of successive truths which inexorably lead to one (and only one) conclusion or point.

It would seem, therefore, that our first step to manage conflict is to remove the emotional ingredient. A difficult task indeed, considering most of us do not have training in rational thought and we tend to give in to emotional hijacking.

FOLLOW-UP

It is important to organize the information and confirm the results with the interviewees as soon as possible after the interview. Sharing the information that was learned allows the interviewees to point out any missed or incorrectly recorded items (*BABOK® Guide* 2015). If all has gone well, the interview follow-up is a straightforward matter. Interviewing is a very effective way to capture information from stakeholders who have specialized information or a unique perspective. It takes a great deal of time to prepare and conduct the perfect interview. Thus, the follow-up is the step where we ensure that we got what we needed; satisfied any needs that the stakeholder had; built some trust, credibility, and rapport; and have a clear direction. At the end of an interview, be sure to:

- Thank the interviewee for their time
- Discuss plans to address anything that might not have been covered in the interview
- Let the interviewee know that he or she will receive a rough transcript of the interview for approval
- Advise them if you anticipate needing their time again in the future
- Formally end the interview with a positive comment—something related to the matters at hand

As the interview begins to wind down, give the interviewee a chance to volunteer additional data to ensure that they have *said their piece*. End the interview by summarizing the main points. This gives you a chance to review your notes and ensure that there are no misunderstandings. Once again, thank the interviewee for their time and remember not to pander. Let the interviewee know when you plan to summarize the interview notes and submit them for approval. Doing so just after the interview while it is fresh in everyone's mind will make for accurate results. The review and feedback process will improve the quality of the notes and may provide important clarifications.

Always prepare to interview stakeholders by reading background documentation. This technique, known as document analysis, is the basis for all interview-planning efforts. Every interview is unique; however, there are some key items to remember when planning the perfect interview is the goal:

- Is the pre-interview research complete?
- Do they or we need context? What type?
- Will the interview be formal or informal?
- What are the goals and objectives?
- What do we know about our stakeholder, professionally and personally
- What is their importance within the organization and the project?
- Will we plot a normal curve, allowing for a natural progression?
- What will our questions focus on; what perspective and depth will they take?
- How will we respond to unexpected questions?
- Are we using a linear and logical approach?
- Have we taken time to establish rapport?
- Are we sure that the interviewee is fully aware of the situation?
- Do we have an honest dialogue?
- Are we listening actively?
- Are we managing bias—theirs and ours?
- Do we understand how to manage conflict, should it arise?

- Have we agreed on next steps?
- Have we closed the interview with professionalism?

An interview is about doing the right research, asking the right questions of the right person within the correct context, and listening for the right response. It takes a lot of concentration and determination to be an active listener. Not all of the interviews will require this much diligence, but when they do, a careful, methodical, and persistent approach will go a long way toward building credibility and trust. As you progress through this book, my hope is that you learn about many ways to build trust and foster lasting relationships.

REFERENCES

A Guide to the Business Analysis Body of Knowledge (BABOK® Guide). 2015. International Institute of Business Analysis (IIBA), p. 48.

Dunbar, R.I.M. 2004. Gossip in Evolutionary Perspective, Research Article, https://doi.org/10.1037/1089-2680.8.2.100.

Fox, Kate. *Evolution, Alienation and Gossip*. Outlook, May 15, 2002.

Noland, E.W. 1959. *Hawthorne Revisited*. By Henry A. Landsberger. Ithaca, NY: The New York State.

Pohlmann, Tom and Neethi Mary Thomas. *Relearning the Art of Asking Questions*. https://hbr.org/2015/03/relearning-the-art-of-asking-questions (accessed December 14, 2016).

3

UNDERSTANDING OUR STAKEHOLDERS

Star Trek's Admiral Christopher Pike to First Officer Spock during a dressing-down for violations of the Prime Directive. "That's a technicality." Spock: "I am Vulcan, sir, we embrace technicality." Pike: "Are you giving me attitude, Spock?" Spock: "I am expressing multiple attitudes simultaneously. To which are you referring?"
—Star Trek Into Darkness, Dir. J. J. Abrams, Bad Robot Productions

The first step to identifying the Requirements, Elicitation, Planning, Analysis, and Collaboration Framework™ (REPAC®) source is building an effective requirements management team. In my experience, project managers only perform one of its steps—the stakeholder analysis. This project activity is an essential step for any project, however, there is much more to building an effective stakeholder engagement strategy. Everything, literally everything the project produces—communication plans, requirements documents, process diagrams, and acceptance tests—can be linked back to our engagement strategy. A project does not "have" stakeholders, a project "is" stakeholders. They hold the needs, objectives, problems, opportunities, risks, everything. Without its stakeholders, the project cannot exist. Remember, the team itself is part of the stakeholder list. Over the next few chapters, I will discuss some of the theories and practices behind building an effective requirements management team.

Partially ironic since Spock is only half human, the quote at the beginning of this chapter from *Star Trek Into Darkness* speaks to our tendency to misunderstand the attitudes of our coworkers and stakeholders. This form of miscommunication causes an incongruence, a deviation between what we intended and how something was perceived. In this chapter, we will take a look at attitudes, along with how they form and are manifested, in the hopes that we may have better conversations with our teams.

As your career in business analysis progresses, you will affect many people in profound ways. Some of them may try to undermine your efforts, while others may be great supporters. Building a requirements team elevates our methods and recognizes the importance and necessity of a group of people dedicated to providing purpose and value through requirements. With every class I teach, I ask, "Do your projects always have a development team?" The answer is always, "Yes." "Do your plans have solution design or testing teams?" Again, the answer is always, "Yes." "What about a requirements team?" To this, my students often look confused. I am bewildered when I ask myself why one of the most (if not *the* most) important part of a project does not get a dedicated team. I am sure you have read or heard this many times before, but it is worth repeating.

A stakeholder is any person, group, organization, or system that expresses interest in or can affect or is affected, either directly, indirectly, upstream, or downstream, by the project or any of its deliverables or resources, in either a positive or negative way—this means you!

Did I leave anyone out? Thankfully, we do not need to meet the expectations of this entire list. We focus our efforts on the stakeholders that score highly on whichever classification scheme we are using. There are a few scoring methods, some of which we will review later. Regardless, they all center on salience, the degree and quality of importance or prominence that any stakeholder or stakeholder group has over the project or its scope.

ATTITUDES

We all express many attitudes about many things every day. Understanding how your stakeholders form their opinions and their evaluations of ideas, events, objects, and people will help gain support for your efforts and influence your decisions and your ability to persuade, as the need arises. Our attitudes often define our actions—and our actions are directly attributable to project success or failure. In varying degrees, attitudes are made up of three components, which are known to behavioral psychologists as the ABC Model of Attitudes (McLeod 2014).

- *A*: affectively-based attitudes are the emotional reactions we have to an attitude object. Using a simple project related scenario, one of the stakeholders in our case study (we will call him Bob Palindrome) has an aversion to using the use case method for analyzing stakeholder needs and project scope; he feels the technique is too technical. In this example, the attitude object is the use case method. We can manage stakeholder Bob's anxiety by offering one-on-one coaching in the hopes that he will see the method is simple and easy to learn. Affective-based attitudes are value-based and often stem from the moral patterns we create in our minds.
- *B*: behavioral attitudes express themselves when we react to an attitude object. When we asked Bob if we could apply the use case technique to flush out his needs, he may have had a strong visceral reaction because of negative memories or he may react more casually, suggesting the possibility that we might persuade him to *change his attitude*. Behavioral-based attitudes are rooted in the response patterns we create for various situations. Our emotions are hardwired. Our feelings are reactions to our emotive responses—these we can change.
- *C*: cognitive attitudes root into the beliefs we have about the attitude object itself. Once again, we know that Bob expresses anxiety about use case techniques. If he does indeed feel that use cases are too technical, then he has expressed his cognitive attitude on the matter. Cognitive views, based on actual experiences, create our response patterns, which form our affective values—do you see a pattern emerging? If stakeholder Bob has attended too many workshops where use cases did not provide useful results, this may explain his aversion.

All three components come together to define an attitude. If we are to influence or persuade our stakeholders to support our requirements efforts, tell us their user stories, join the requirements team, and give us their time and commitment to the project, then we must uncover their attitudes. Many of the challenges we face are the result of our stakeholder's unique combinations of opinions and attitudes about the project and the proposed solution. Views seem to change every day. How can we keep up? If we take the time to understand our stakeholders as people, what makes them tick if you will, then we can predict, to some degree, changes in attitude before the project's circumstances change. We may perceive changes in attitudes but the underlining patterns that drive them seldom change. Once an attitude forms, how does it manifest? If a stakeholder does not share his or her opinions with us, how are we to help?

Attitudes express themselves explicitly or implicitly. Explicit attitudes are at the conscious level, while implicit attitudes are deep within our unconscious selves. Explicit attitudes form deliberately and are easier to self-manage and communicate. Conversely, we believe unconscious attitudes emerge involuntarily. We commonly use our explicit attitudes to make decisions about the people we will spend time with, things to do or not to do, and whether we believe certain things are right or wrong. In our earlier example, Bob was able to express his dislike for use cases because he consciously formed his conclusion based on past experiences. His attitude, not fixed due to his awareness, can be modified. However, if Bob is not aware of his reasons, he may have formed them implicitly through bias or prejudice and this would be much harder to resolve.

It is possible and quite probable for explicit and implicit attitudes to contradict each other. Prejudice is a frequently used example. Stakeholders may hold resentment about things or people of which they are not aware. Outwardly, they encourage fellow teammates and the project's objectives but inwardly and unknown to them, they harbor negative feelings, exhibiting unsupportive patterns. This mode affects their behavior and will cause confusion and bias. Identifying explicit attitudes is natural, with the right level of emotional sensitivity, but implicit attitudes are a challenge to uncover. Psychologists typically use the Implicit Association Test (IAT), in which subjects promptly categorize words or pictures. Psychologists use test outcomes to determine non-self-regulating associations between concepts and attributes. Marketers often use IAT to study brand awareness and affiliation.

Stakeholders base their perceptions of purpose, value, importance, and influence on their beliefs, which are a product of the patterns they create in their minds. In a project environment, these ideas translate into rights. Rights reinforce the beliefs a stakeholder has to his or her claim to project value.

Understanding the cause of the attitudes tabled by a belief system is critical to gaining support and cooperation. Patterns become stakes, and models and agents are important to understand because they form the basis of the stakeholder's position. It is through our beliefs that we lay claim to a stake in something.

Incidentally, it is worth mentioning stake as it relates to cooperation and competition between stakeholders—the higher the stake, the lower the probability of a stakeholder forming cooperative bonds with others. Stakeholders tend to cooperate or compete on what is required based on rights, which stem from patterns, which form beliefs, and express as attitudes. The more urgent a right or belief is, the higher the tendency to compete rather than cooperate.

Using a psychological approach to discover and analyze stakeholders and their needs encourages us to understand the underlying motivations that drive their support, resistance, and decisions. This proposition builds an effective stakeholder engagement strategy, which translates into lasting and productive relationships. We are all pattern-seeking, story-telling, social primates that want to believe—and as such, we have predictable behavior that can be identified and addressed as a matter of cooperation and compliance—our patterns of belief.

Stakeholders play a role within the project context and have responsibilities, just as we do. They have expectations of us, and we should have expectations of them. As we continue to explore these relationships, ultimately creating a requirements team charter, I will explain how these mutual agreements manifest and manage.

SOCIAL STYLES

All projects change something. George Bernard Shaw once said, "The single biggest problem in communication is the illusion that it has taken place." We are, in fact, agents of change. Transformation requires communication; thus George's quote is suitable. I will never understand the irony of poor project communication. It is so fundamental to success, and we all know this, yet many times we perform it so poorly.

The ability to identify patterns and their characteristics is central to the profession of business analysis. This capability applies to stakeholders as much as it does to anything under the magnifying glass of the business analyst (BA). In his book *Personal Styles and Effective Performance*, David Merrill and his team identified four basic personality styles that are used today by educators, consultants, and analysts to help understand human relationships within a business context. David and his team based their work on Carl Jung and his work on psychological types.

The Merrill & Reid model (1981) balances the *specificity needed for explanatory usefulness and the generality need for broad applicability*. The model uses four distinct social styles: controllers, analyzers, promoters, and supporters. Robert Bolton and Dorothy Grover Bolton, in their book *People Styles at Work*, reference the same social styles as driver, expresser, amiable, and analytical. As individuals, we have a primary and a secondary form that we exhibit while in and out of our comfort zone. Proportionally, however, we express all four styles. Figure 3.1 reflects the Merrill & Reid model and illustrates a comparative view of how the model reflects an individual.

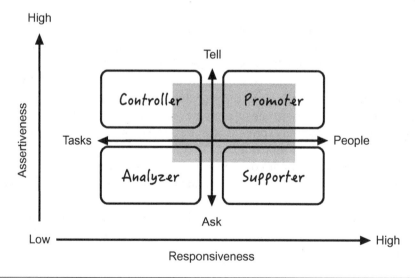

Figure 3.1   Social styles (©Merrill & Reid, 1981)

Thinking back to our case study, imagine that you recently completed a stakeholder engagement plan and requirements team charter and that you are very excited to present your work to the project manager. You take the time to fill her in on all the details, processes, and people with whom you have spoken. Rather than appreciating your thoroughness, she flicks her pen angrily, presents a defensive posture, and speaks to you curtly. She tells you that she does not care about the details and next time to spare her the pain of your obsessive need to belabor every little detail. What just happened? You missed an important step—understanding your stakeholder's behavior patterns.

Attitudes, social styles, personal and professional habits—navigating it all can seem overwhelming at times. Some of us feel very comfortable in and look forward to working in social settings, while others cringe at the idea of in-person collaboration. When we meet or work with someone who *just gets us*, the personal and professional rewards are extremely useful, sustainable, and release lots of endorphins into our bloodstream. Conversely, when we do not *gel*, the effects can make us ill. Much of how well we perform in our professional lives links back to how well we work with others and how well others cooperate with us.

We are all familiar with the fatigue that comes with working alongside stakeholders with whom we just cannot seem to get along. Regardless, we had better find ways to cultivate a working relationship—and shame on us if we cannot make it work.

The more ways in which people are different from each other, the more effort will be required to achieve a productive outcome. Personality and behavior interact to create and maintain interpersonal relationships. Others see and respond to our behavior, and we respond to theirs. The following text describes the four Merrill & Reid social styles illustrated in Figure 3.1.

Controller

Also known as drivers or *A-types*, controllers are quick thinkers, quick to temper, and prefer to make decisions quickly and decisively. Controllers tend to grow impatient when they come across stakeholders who do not appreciate their way of doing things. Drivers are passionate and enthusiastic; they prefer to be in control. They like quick action and using information that is readily accessible. Their discourse is forceful and they prefer discussing concerns verbally. Controllers see themselves as *leaders of men* and will seek out others whom they feel show strong leadership. Drivers will often build mentor/protégé relationships with people they feel would benefit from their knowledge and experience.

Controller Decision Making

- The time frame is now
- Information gathering is pre-conceptive, based on experience and current facts
- Information processing is systematic, concerned just as much with the approach as the conclusion
- The comfort zone focuses on facts, logic, results, action, and risk taking
- Will reject inaction

Controller Typical Behavior

- Swift reaction and decision making
- Maximum effort to seek control of situations, minimum concern for relationships

- Limited body language, controlled movement and facial expressions
- Leans forward during discussions and holds eye contact

Working with Controllers

Always be a leader, be on time, make direct eye contact, get down to business quickly, be clear and precise, and follow an agenda. Be sure to follow the facts and show what they mean. Never be too chummy, linger, or engage in small talk, unless invited. If you need help from a driver, ask for it. They are usually happy to lend a hand and will respect you for your courage. When meeting with controllers, present your facts and supporting evidence, then draw conclusions and present recommended next steps with alternatives and a risk assessment. Once the meeting has ended, close the discussion cleanly, express appreciation for their time and input, and leave with minimal additional interaction. Table 3.1 provides some simple *DO*s and *DO NOT*s for working with controllers.

Table 3.1 Controller DOs and DO NOTs

DO	DO NOT
Focus on the now	Take circuitous path to the point
Be brief and efficient	Give too much detail
Quickly get to the point	Be ambiguous
Be results-oriented and give options	Limit options and omit results
Give them the control	Be adversarial
Refrain from too much socializing	Become too personal
Focus on the matters at hand	Backdown from a position

Promoter

Promoters, as the name suggests, tend to be outgoing in their emotive style, perhaps even a little resplendent. They are sometimes called *expressives* because of their need to express themselves as much as possible. Similar to controllers, promoters are very assertive, but with a people-oriented approach. As you might expect, they enjoy the center spotlight. When promoters are resting peacefully within their comfort zone, we see them as personable, stimulating, enthusiastic, dramatic, and gregarious take-charge leaders. Unfortunately, when pushed (or when they allow themselves to be pushed—depending on your philosophy) into anxious situations that are outside of their comfort zone, we may receive them as emotionally taxing, excitable, undisciplined, and quick to temper.

Decision Making

- The time frame is in the future
- Information gathering is *preconceptive* based on *instinct*
- Information processing is intuitive—a sense or a hunch (the information processes in the subconscious)

- Comfort zone tends to be about feelings and relationships, dreams and intuition, action and involvement
- Will reject inactivity, nonparticipation, and neutrality

Typical Behavior

- Rapid reaction and decision making
- Maximum effort to involve others
- Little concern for procedure, routines, process, and policy
- Seeks attention and the spotlight
- Promotes and enjoys the competitive spirit
- Will seek out and even push for conflict
- Animated speech and body language, with many anecdotes
- Emotive, exaggerated facial expressions and gestures
- Will not shy away from feelings, emotions, and opinions

Working with Promoters

Always be on time, make direct eye contact, smile, and show a personal interest beyond the business. Be warm, outgoing, and communicative. Take requisite time for socializing. Be sure to use anecdotes when providing information but keep the accounts focused and short. Engage in a debate but know your facts. Don't be neutral, inflexible, or too task oriented. Keep a strong emphasis on what needs to get done while maintaining an eye on the needs of those doing it. Focus on value and benefits and be a champion; share the dream. Table 3.2 provides a list of *DOs* and *DO NOTs* for working with promoters.

Table 3.2   Promoter DOs and DO NOTs

DO	DO NOT
Look to the future	Get right to business
Use stories to share ideas	Give too much detail
Seek input	Expect a linear path to solutions
Be big picture focused	Dwell on minutia
Have personal interest/involvement	Be impersonal or distant
Express your creative self	Be embarrassed to be yourself
Let them stand out	Try to take the spotlight

Supporter

Supporters are very personable and value the *social aspects* of project management over the project work itself. They tend to be less assertive than promoters. Supporters are not as comfortable with expressing themselves and do not crave the spotlight. However, their emotional intelligence (EI) may be as high if not higher than controllers or promoters. Also known as socializers and *amiables*, they are very supportive, friendly, respectful, and dependable—if they like you. Supporters may take some time to let you into their circle of trust, but when they do, it is a nice place to be. Just remember to stay on their *good* side. At times, supporters vacillate—waver between opinions or actions. Supporters tend to follow the strongest opinion leader.

Decision Making

- Time frame is now
- Information gathering is receptive
- Gathers information, then makes a decision
- Information processing is intuitive, influenced by relationships over data
- Comfort zone is with friendship, feelings, people, group affiliation, and teams
- Will reject conflict, hurt feelings, and group tension

Typical Behavior

- Quick to emote
- Maximum effort to relate and listen actively
- Supportive in words and actions over data
- Immediate effort to preempt conflict

Working with Supporters

Focus on supporting the team and its relationships. Listen and be responsive. Do not schedule critical deadlines—avoid the critical path. Try to schedule deliverables that require social interaction, such as workshops. Show a relaxed posture and an unhurried time frame. Engage in small talk and share personal feelings. Show sincere interest in the people involved in the project. Find a common interest and show how the business goal will help the people within the organization. Don't rush into tasks and goals and don't be reserved or formal. Drivers and supporters make up a large part of the social spectrum, so let's take a look at a few more ideas:

- Ask a lot of *how* questions
- Be patient and draw out opinions
- Avoid a strong expression of your opinions
- Don't debate about facts and figures
- Present your case in a non-threatening manner
- Go slow and give time for feelings to develop
- Demonstrate the link between business and people and goals and priorities
- Provide personal guarantees only if you can promise

Supporters are more likely to use a referent power base than any other social style. (French and Raven's Five Forms of Power—a person's perceived attractiveness, worthiness, and right to others' respect.) Remember to always leave a meeting with feelings of goodwill and friendship. Table 3.3 provides a list of quick *DOs* and *DO NOTs* for working with supporters.

Table 3.3 Supporter DOs and DO NOTs

DO	DO NOT
Be traditional	Get straight to business
Be flexible	Be detailed oriented
Accept a social connection	Expect things to be easy
Be relative, emotive, and listen	Dig into the details
Be courteous and receptive to courtesy	Be impersonal and distant
Ensure a safe environment	Try to take the spotlight
Protect the social construct	Excuse your creative method

One last bit of advice: the emotions and ideas of supporters can intertwine. Their brains are not as compartmentalized as directors and *logicals*. Be careful with criticism; express your views in a supportive manner; try not to argue solely from a position of logic. Carefully crafted predictions may get lost in fallacious thinking. Calling a supporter on a mistake may degrade the discussion into a fight, reinforcing or strengthening the fallacy. The same applies to expressive people, although not to the same extent.

Analyzer

As you might expect, an analyzer or analytical or logical is your data-oriented, perfection-geared team member. Analyzers try to figure out the equation, the *math of it* (so to speak)—quality over quantity, details, or summations and substance over flash. Analytical stakeholders may feel uncomfortable in social situations and may go to the back of the room where they feel safe and can observe. We tend to see analytical people as persistent and displaced, but they may also seem petty and picky when they are out of their comfort zone.

Decision Making

- The time frame tends to be historical, with a focus on discipline not urgency
- Information gathering is receptive—gathers extensive data and double checks for accuracy and completeness
- Information processing is calm, methodical, deliberate, and objective
- Comfort zone is with reasoning—predictions that build to a logical conclusion using verifiable facts, logic, principles and policy, rules, regulations, rights, and analysis
- Will reject personal involvement where commitments center on feelings, hunches, or poor and inconclusive data

Typical Behavior

- Slow, but deliberate and decisive
- Maximum effort to organize logical thinking structure
- Minimum concern for relationships
- Cautious with actions until all alternatives are carefully considered and expressed

Working with an Analyzer

Always be on time, logical, and have an orderly agenda. Stick to business and be sure to respect physical space. Show low emotion, strong passion may cause anxiety. Do not fake data or dismiss your research. Avoid introducing personal feelings or opinions based on anything but verifiable facts.

When presenting to an analyzer, proceed from the past through the present, adding measurable facts, and then proceed into the future. Remember to be mindful of the data and the information it conveys. Attempting to persuade an analytical through emotions or personal appeals will likely fail and result in a loss of credibility and trust. Table 3.4 provides a list of quick DOs and DO NOTs for working with an analyzer. Last, it is important to recognize the difference between data, information, and value, when working with a logical person. Data is raw material, like the parts of your computer. The information would be your computer assembled (in context) and value is the useful things you can do with your computer—essentially, the decisions you can make.

As you can see, the top half of the Merrill & Reid model would work well with each other, as well as the bottom half and each of the sides. Conflict arises when we move from corner to corner—such as supporters and controllers. Behavioral flexibility, or *flexing*, is our ability to meet the social style of our working partner. The capacity to meet the style needs of others is crucial for decreasing tension and increasing trust, credibility, responsiveness, and cooperation, not to mention persuasion and negotiation.

In the 2009 book, *People Styles at Work . . . And Beyond: Making Bad Relationships Good and Good Relationships Better*, Bolton and Bolton remind us that all social types are equally prone to stress and tend to have the same tolerance, more or less; however, we *deal* with our anxiety in different ways. Research shows that how we deal with the stresses of everyday life and project work corresponds to our primary and secondary social styles. For example, an open and expressive promoter might manifest as a controller, directing and forcing change because he is not *getting his own way*.

In another example, a stakeholder may be an analyzer in her default quadrant, but mostly a controller-analyzer. Their first avoidance of a stressful situation might go unnoticed; only when we observe continued escalation of anxiety does the behavior become noticeable and express more of the controller response modes. We would then begin to see the unreasonable and autocratic behavior indicative of controllers who are out of their comfort zone. Moreover, it is possible that stakeholders might oscillate between their primary and secondary social styles, in an attempt to reestablish healthy behavior. Although there is an

Table 3.4 Analyzer DOs and DO NOTs

DO	DO NOT
Focus on past, present, and future	Get straight to business
Focus on just the facts	Ask or be detailed oriented
Focus on the details	Be forceful or confrontational
Be linear, logical, and organized	Be quick to change
Provide specific direction	"Attack" ideas
Allow for consideration	Try to take the spotlight
Be aware of personal boundaries	Argue from a position of logic

element of randomness, for the most part, we can predict responses with a degree of accuracy. As we begin to move away from our comfort zone, these predictions are as follows:

- *Controllers*: will become energized, assertive, and attempt to acquire control of a scenario. Under extreme stress, the autocratic behavior may derail others.
- *Promoters*: rise to the challenge, for a time, but begin to *check-out* as pressure increases. As stressors intensify, the promoter's behavior increases; lashing out, sarcastic, condescending, and offensive habits become the norm.
- *Supporters*: will stay out of the way and avoid stress as much as possible. When caught up in it, however, supporters may increase their social behavior in an attempt to self-sooth. If the situation continues, we could see a submissive behavior as the stakeholder turns inward and *walks away*.
- *Analyzers*: could withdraw into themselves and focus on small details or repetitive activities, again, in an attempt to self-sooth. As project conditions worsen and team stress rises, that inward retreat becomes more intense to a point where this stakeholder may *check out* of the project altogether.

Styles overlap all the time. Finding gaps and frequent overlaps will help us avoid conflict and build rapport, trust, and credibility. In these circumstances, one or both stakeholders will have to adjust their style to accommodate the other's needs—easier said than done, right? If only one of us is willing to be flexible, there will be tension, but at least work can continue. This approach requires us to be mindful, aware of ourselves, our triggers, and how to avoid and deal with them. In many cases we assume it is the other person who must change, not us. So, we try to change our coworkers, our friends, or our partners to fit our idea of how they should behave. Ideally, we should temporarily modify our behaviors so that our stakeholders can easily relate. Since it is we who need them, then we must initiate—this is flexing.

Style flexing or blending should only be used reservedly, however. Frequently changing our behavior to mirror another's can create distrust. We do not want to be seen as a sycophant, always acting politely to gain an advantage. How do we know when to be flexible? It is at this point our EI comes into play—*the capacity to be aware of, control, and express one's emotions, and to handle interpersonal relationships judiciously and empathetically.*

Consider how social flexibility can help our communication styles. For example, are you mostly expressive, effusive, sequential, literal, or some variation? I will wager you can almost see the model from Figure 3.1 as you read the four basic types below. Expressive communicators use language to convey feelings, moods, or ideas. They will often use metaphors and allegories to evoke an emotional reaction. Their focus is not on conveying data, but rather feeling.

Using language to explain, and explain, and explain some more, effusive people communicate in an unrestrained, excited manner. They will sometimes include all relevant data. The message tends to include multiple topics that are sometimes directly related and at other times tangentially related. Often expressed as a deliberate web of ideas, you will not hear or read a clear-cut path to their point. Effusive communicators often ask their listeners or readers to spend time reflecting on and absorbing the ideas they have conveyed.

Sequential communicators make fantastic technical writers, assuming their grammar is well formed. Sequential communicators start at one central point and use all remaining paragraphs to logically step through the supporting detail. The best requirements artifacts will often come from sequential communicators. Which social style would you imagine is being expressed here?

Free from exaggeration or distortion, literal writers tell only the facts. There is no stylistic embellishment, descriptive words, or ideas not related to the main point. Literal thinking takes words and ideas as absolute; we understand their usual or most basic sense without metaphor or allegory.

There is a direct correlation between archetypical communication means and social styles. Similar to the communication paradigm, we often refer to these as *mother models*. As we continue through this chapter, review how we can use EI as a means to improve not just ourselves, but how we can more effectively interact with our stakeholders.

EMOTIONAL INTELLIGENCE

We live in a scarcity-based society, and our projects are no different. The funds we want, the solutions we require, and the stakeholders we need are always in scarce supply. Scarcity creates value, but it also creates anxiety and frustration. In my experience, a significant amount of project tension is rooted in cycles of project shortages. I call this the economics of project management. I have observed an anecdotal correlation between the cycles of supply and demand for project resources and the emotional health of stakeholders. Achieving equilibrium seems to be the obvious solution, but when supply seldom meets demand, we must look to our EI as a means to improve how we interact with others when projects and stakeholders reach their lowest point.

Ostensibly, there once lived a belligerent Samurai, who demanded a Zen master to tell him of heaven and hell. The warrior barked, in a voice accustomed to instant obedience, "Teach me about heaven and hell!" With utter disdain, the monk replied, "Teach you about heaven and hell? I could not teach you about anything. You are dumb. You are dirty. You are a disgrace, an embarrassment to the samurai class. Get out of my sight. I cannot stand you." His honor attacked, the Samurai threatened to kill the Zen master where he knelt. He pulled his katana from its scabbard and held it inches from the monk's neck. Looking directly into the Samurai's eyes, the monk breathed, "That is hell." Befuddled and ashamed, the Samurai sheathed his sword, closed his eyes, and began to calm himself. Feeling transformed by the master's wisdom he bowed and thanked him. "And that," announced the monk, "is heaven." (a Zen parable, adapted from Kofman, 2013).

This parable applies to all of us. We are all slaves to our base emotions from time to time. It reminds me of Aristotle, and the Nicomachean Ethics: "Anyone can become angry—that is easy. However, to be angry with the right person, to the right degree, at the right time, for the right purpose, and in the right way—this is not easy."

What is EI, how does it work, and why should we apply it to the business analysis profession? We define EI as the ability to identify, understand, and manage our feelings, and appreciate, interpret, and influence the feelings of others. Our patterns and emotions drive our behavior and impact the behavior of others.

Learning how to manage these emotions (and our response feelings), in ourselves and others, especially when we are under extreme project pressure, will go a long way to keeping the economics of project management less volatile—or at least *feel* less volatile.

Often considered the father of modern educational psychology, Edward Thorndike first described the concept of *social intelligence* as the capacity to get along with other people (Kihlstrom and Cantor 2000). It was not until the innovative dissertation by then-doctoral candidate Wayne Payne that the term EI became part of our vocabulary. Since then, Peter Salovey and John D. Mayer have led research on EI. In their influential article called "Emotional Intelligence," they define it as:

> *"The subset of social intelligence that involves the ability to monitor one's own and others' feelings and emotions, to discriminate among them and to use this information to guide one's thinking and actions."*

Psychologist Daniel Goleman popularized EI in his internationally best-selling book, *Emotional Intelligence: Why It Can Matter More Than IQ*. He presented the argument that noncognitive skills such as empathizing with others can matter as much as, if not more than IQ. Unlike personality and intelligence, which are more or less genetically fixed, self-awareness, self-management, social awareness, and relationship management improve with effort. Freedman et al. expresses it best:

> *"Emotional intelligence is a way of recognizing, understanding, and choosing how we think, feel, and act. It shapes our interactions with others and our understanding of ourselves. It defines how and what we learn; it allows us to set priorities; and it determines the majority of our daily actions. Research suggests it is responsible for as much as 80% of the successes in our lives."*

Authors Travis Bradberry and Jean Greaves took EQ a step further with their 2009 step-by-step book, *Emotional Intelligence 2.0*. Bradberry and Greaves present the idea that we can affect our EI by improving the competencies seen in Figure 3.2. According to them, EI expresses two central concepts—personal and social competence.

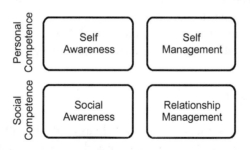

Figure 3.2   EI model (© The New BA, Ltd.)

PERSONAL COMPETENCE

Competence is a harmonization of the elements needed to do something successfully or efficiently. When we are personally competent, we are able to manage our behavior in most situations and be accountable for our actions. Personal competence focuses on individual skill sets within two subsections: self-awareness and self-management. The following text examines some of these skills.

Self-Awareness

Self-awareness is a foundational skill through which we develop other skills. Self-aware individuals understand the *ripples in the pond* effect. We affect our environment with our actions; self-aware individuals know how their ripples affect other people's ponds. The higher your self-awareness, the further your awareness of the ripple effect extends. Self-aware individuals:

- Trust their intuition and know what they do well
- Recognize what they need to work on
- May keep a project or personal journal
- Understand what motivates and satisfies them
- Are aware of which people and situations trigger negative emotional responses
- Can pull themselves out of the moment, slow down, and ask themselves why they are feeling a certain way

Self-Management

When we are managing ourselves well, we know when to act and when not to act; we can control our emotions and impulses. We control our emotions; our emotions do not control us. We are keenly aware that no one can make us angry. If we do become angry, we have allowed ourselves to get angry by what has happened or how someone has acted. Self-managed people:

- Think before they act
- Regulate themselves well in most situations by directing behavior in positive ways
- Have a high level of personal accountability
- Have a strong set of values, stick to them, and defend them
- Are thoughtful, considerate, respectful, and comfortable with change

SOCIAL COMPETENCE

Social competence is an externalized set of skills that help us to identify all the nuances of human interaction, then take what we know of ourselves and navigate and manage our relationships effectively. Socially competent people understand that they cannot get their message across without first building trust and credibility. When we are socially responsible, we can change our behavior to accommodate the needs of others, even if we disagree with their position. Socially competent people have achieved what is called social awareness.

Social Awareness

- Good at active listening
- Set emotions aside and consider other perspectives
- Treat people with respect and dignity, regardless of personal attitudes
- Put aside feelings during a discussion and focus on the matter at hand
- Have a high capacity to observe and understand complex social interactions
- Stay focused, absorbing critical information
- Able to remove distractions, when addressed, to give full attention to others

Social Management

- Effectively manage conflict
- Build lasting, meaningful relationships
- Have a strong sense of social responsibility that extends beyond their local community
- Maintain a relationship and frequency of contact, even in times of high stress
- Will challenge themselves to improve interactions and stay away from old habits

Different experiences create neural connections, which produce different patterns altering emotions and their corresponding feelings. The more we use those models and have those feelings, the stronger those pathways become. Scientists refer to this as neuroplasticity; a standard *umbrella* term used to describe the changes our brains undergo throughout our lives. Recently, this term has become popular with online brain games. Many aspects of our minds remain flexible well into our adult lives. As we learn new tasks, pick up new habits, or develop new belief systems, neuroplasticity provides the mechanism (Pittenger and Duman, 2008). Our ability to be emotionally resilient and reasonable minded works the same way.

Understanding how some stakeholders behave in given situations may help us get them back to their comfort zones, but how they got there in the first place is a much broader question. We can examine each situation in and of itself or we can look at the broader picture of behavioral patterns. This level of understanding brings us into a world that psychologists call normative social influence. We are all hardwired for social validation (some more than others), but at some level, we all need to be accepted by social groups. When we believe we are not gaining acceptance, we begin to express primitive emotions, which manifest as fear, anger, and sometimes hostility. We need to determine what is prompting this and how we can help our stakeholders and ourselves overcome it.

Neurobiologists have observed that we express emotions and that those emotions influence the decisions we make before we are even aware of it (Gigerenzer 2008). This ability served us well thousands of years ago but can be dangerous in some current project situations. Resisting the urge to react and analyze our feelings while we are having them, as we have already seen, is referred to as EI. We need to learn how to make use of this skill and understand how it works. To understand social intelligence, its influence, and its behaviors, we must first understand what neural mechanisms create these phenomena in the first place.

MINDFULNESS

Our brains evolved to learn quickly from bad experiences but slowly from the good ones. Throughout our evolutionary development, different parts of our sympathetic nervous system served different purposes. The sympathetic nervous system and the parasympathetic nervous system constitute our automatic responses to stimuli. Our ability to create patterns and the traditional flight, fight, or freeze/fawn response are just a few examples. These traits create problems in our modern and intricate cultural landscape.

> *"Mindfulness is a state of active, open attention on the present. When you're mindful, you observe your thoughts and feelings from a distance, without judging them good or bad. Instead of letting your life pass you by, mindfulness means living in the moment and awakening to experience."*[1]

> *"If your emotional abilities aren't in hand, if you don't have self-awareness, if you are not able to manage your distressing emotions, if you can't have empathy and have effective relationships, then no matter how smart you are, you are not going to get very far."*—Daniel Goleman

Specific neurotransmitters such as norepinephrine trigger an acutely stressed state whenever we feel threatened (Ciofoaia et al. 2011). This reflex served us well in our early development but now seems to cause more trouble than it solves. As we view the world around us, sensory data is first evaluated by our thalamus, which assesses the raw data and assigns its meaning. If this meaning is threatening, then a signal is sent to our amygdala so it can create the appropriate emotional responses. The amygdalae are small hemispherical structures located close to the hippocampus, in the frontal portion of the temporal lobe.

Amygdalae evolved to process many emotions and allow us to mirror them in others. Emotional mirroring, also known as empathy, helps us to keep tensions under control in stressful project situations (Rizzolatti, Fogassi, and Gallese 2001). Recent studies have discovered that at least part of the message from the thalamus is sent directly to the amygdala. This research explains our tendency to become hot-tempered in an otherwise benign situation. When we are in a *heated discussion* or feel as though we or our ideas are under attack, it is our amygdalae that are actively decreasing our ability to reason. The release of the stress chemicals epinephrine (also known as adrenaline), norepinephrine, and cortisol, from our brain's point of view, means that we must be ready for the fight of our lives. Depending on your current overall health, it could take an hour or a few days to return to a normal resting state (McEwen 2008).

Our brain cannot tell the difference between a heated discussion about the priority of a deliverable or a tiger chasing us through the tall grass.[2] Chemically, these events are identical to each other (Davis 1992). In this anxious state, we lose much of our working memory—the transient part of our brain that is partly responsible for processing new information. Working memory also plays a significant role in reasoning, comprehension, and learning (Phelps 2004). The more upset we get, the more unreasonable we become. We are biologically unable to carry a conversation based on logic until these chemicals have had a chance to subside. This narrow-mindedness could derail weeks of project effort in just a few minutes.

"The politics of fear appears to dominate daily life in Western societies." In his book, *The Politics of Fear*, Frank Furedi is referring to the broader post-9/11 political landscape—but in our ever-changing organizational setting, there is a notion of truth here. As project professionals, we live with a sense of dread and panic when it comes to meeting our deadlines. As a result, all manner of quality suffers. In earnest, we try to defend against these cultural biases; this leaves us irascible, showing a tendency to quick temper. Feeling this way creates dissonance in our minds. No matter how useful the idea is or how important it is for the conversation to occur, the brain has difficulty processing these extraordinary events when it is in this state.

Conversely, when we welcome the ideas of others, our brains release dopamine and create dopamine pathways, one of which plays an influential role in our reward-motivated systems and which affects so much of our primate behavior. Building a reward-based feedback system within project teams offers the opportunity for a more efficient and creative environment. These rewards, however, cannot be mere platitudes or trivialities used to patronize each other, masking our fears, apprehensiveness, and general mistrust. We must embrace each other. A project is a microcosm of our organizational culture. It is a chance to create something better; at least for a short time. Due to its importance, the amygdalae connect to many other parts of our brain, as well. When we are mindful of its potential dominance over us, it becomes clear that understanding how different stakeholders deal with these fundamental emotions will help us understand how to work with them in times of stress and bring them back to their comfort zone.

The more mindful we are about ourselves and those around us, the better equipped we are to realize what these fight/flight responses are—functionless holdovers from a time when having the ability to make life and death decisions quickly was critical to our survival. Social validation increases the levels of serotonin and dopamine in our brains and helps us to become more self-aware, calmer, and more open to the ideas of others. Serotonin is considered by some researchers as the chemical that is accountable for managing our emotional balance. A deficit of serotonin leads to depression (Lesch et al. 1996). When we are not aware of our feelings, we tend to fly on autopilot, creating patterns for this that are both real and imagined.

When we are intensely aware of ourselves and others, we can alter these misplaced emotions, nipping them in the bud, as it were. Observation and reflection strengthen our self-regulating neocortical regions of our brains, building new patterns of better, more constructive interactions with our teammates. Every time we take a moment, breathe, and not react prematurely to a potentially destructive situation, we are strengthening our emotional resilience and becoming more rational, thereby paving the way for critical thinking.

Our mirror neurons play a significant role in our ability to feel empathy for others. When we experience an emotion, perform an action, or imagine ourselves doing a thing or feeling a certain way, as you would expect, many neurons fire allowing us to do these things. Recent discoveries in neuroscience have found that many of the same neural pathways fire when we watch someone else performing the same actions or having what we perceive to be the same emotions, almost as if we were performing the actions ourselves.

This self-reflective system allows us to feel great empathy for others and is an integral part of our EI. Mirror neurons cannot tell the difference between us and others; to them it is all the same, hence our dependency on social validation (Ramachandran 2012).

When we are not mindful and reflective, most of what we do is impulsive. Our brain is making decisions below our ability to perceive them. We fall into our old behaviors, fights begin, decisions are quick, and project risks increase. The thought of randomly navigating through a project by making reactive rash decisions is frustrating and builds further mistrust, fear, and anxiety.

Our brains reconcile our behavior with ideas such as *we did not have time to plan, this was the only choice we could make,* or *our project culture does not permit us to proceed in a logically planned fashion.* These patterns become part of our memories, and we believe we were acting rationally the whole time—never realizing that it was fear that was leading our decisions.

As we continue to justify why we behave irrationally, we reinforce negative patterns within our minds, which then repeat themselves project after project after project. These harmful effects of erroneous thinking and false patterns plague our projects and often our personal lives. Thomas Gilovich,[3] the Irene Blecker Rosenfeld Professor of Psychology at Cornell University, writes about the fallacies of everyday life in his book, *How We Know What Isn't So: The Fallibility of Human Reason in Everyday Life*:

> *"When examining evidence relevant to a given belief, people are inclined to see what they expect to see, and conclude what they expect to conclude. Information that is consistent with our pre-existing beliefs is often accepted at face value, whereas evidence that contradicts them is critically scrutinized and discounted. Our beliefs may thus be less responsive than they should to the implications of new information."*

I remain stupefied at the number of illogical decisions made every moment of every day in organizations across the country and other places using poorly constructed cognitive patterns. The big decisions might contain sound judgment, but what of the little ones that happen on projects every day? They add up!

COGNITIVE PATTERN

The term *cognitive pattern* refers to recurring templates that we use during problem-solving/reasoning activities. For instance, a diagnostic pattern guides our efforts when we attempt to discover the cause of a problem. Design patterns, as used in the object-oriented community, are generally more detailed and would in many cases represent cognitive patterns.

Belief (in what we think we can do) and reason (what we are best suited for) are irreconcilable. We tend to build false patterns within our minds and make poor decisions from those trends. Why is this important? As part of understanding our stakeholders, within the context of the Belbin model, we also need to know which of them may tend to exhibit this phenomenon so we can manage them accordingly.

Let's think ahead to causality or cause and effect and how it relates to a root cause analysis, project rites, and rituals. Do you have any silly habits that you do every day (like turning the door handle three times to make sure it's locked) or do you plan your day in an unconventional way because you believe it will help keep you organized? I do—my life is full of rituals. I know that these unique things I do have no causal relation to anything, and yet I do them. Why? Assigning cause to something is in our nature. Our brains just cannot deal with the idea that *stuff happens.* As part of building an effective engagement strategy, I want to know which of my stakeholders may have the propensity to assign importance to random events or to events where an action is not immediately noticeable.

Imagine yourself traveling back in time to what is now present-day Europe. It is the Paleolithic era: the African Sahara is wet and fertile, and you live in a time when lions ruled France. You are about to bless the rains when you hear a rustle in the tall grass. What could it be? If it is a predator and you do not run—well, that will be it for you. Assigning causality where there is none, in this example, would only cost you some energy. Important, but not life-threatening. Assigning causality in every instance has kept us alive, but it has had a serious consequence in our modern lives. Our minds have developed two types of cognitive patterning errors, something Psychologist Michael Shermer calls *patternicity* (Shermer 2002).

Type-I Cognitive Pattern Error

This is also known as a false positive. A Type-I error is our tendency to believe in a pattern that does not exist; the phenomenon is neither measurable nor repeatable.

Type-II Cognitive Pattern Error

This fallacy is also known as a false negative. A Type-II error is the opposite of a Type-I. We tend to *not* believe in a pattern when in fact it is a measurable and repeatable phenomenon.

Assessing the difference between Type-I and Type-II errors is time-consuming, problematic, and cognitively expensive; thus, we have evolved to assume that most patterns are real. Enter your amygdala; it hijacked your brain. Coined by Goleman, an *amygdala hijacking* is an immediate and overpowering asymmetrical emotional response to a stimulus. It is disproportional because the perceived threat far exceeds the real one.

Our propensity to assume that all patterns represent real and important phenomena are easy to relate to our concrete jungle lives when we consider that the cost of making a Type-I error is less costly than a Type-II error. Also, there is little time for careful deliberation in the split-second world of predator-prey interactions. Natural selection favored animals that were most likely to assume that all patterns are real.

This theory explains causation failures in our cognition. Cognitive Scientist Jennifer Whitson, University of Texas at Austin, in her study called *Lacking Control Increases Illusory Pattern Perception*, has demonstrated that in a business culture, those who suffer from uncertainty or lack a sense of control in their environment have a propensity for increased illusory pattern perception. Whitson defines this as the *identification of a coherent and meaningful interrelationship among a set of random or unrelated stimuli*—a Type I error or false positive (Whitson and Galinsky 2008). Participants who lacked control were more likely to perceive a variety of illusory patterns, seeing images in random noise, forming illusory correlations in stock market information, business decisions, projects, and other business-related phenomena; and stakeholders were likely to perceive conspiracies and develop superstitions about changes within the workplace.

As it turns out, that rustle in the grass was just the wind—this time. When a pattern error between the grass and the wind befalls us, we associate activity, regardless. In this example, the agent is unseen and perceived to be dangerous, even though there is nothing there. This explains why causality was so critical to the development of our cognition. These patterns are hardwired and tough to overcome. They result when the cost of making a Type-I error is less than the cost of making a Type-II error. This theory becomes important to us when we consider fallacious thinking.

A fallacy is an exchange that accepts poor reasoning as its basis for a formal or informal argument. Fallacious statements tend to be misleading because the logic in the argument itself is flawed. An argument can be fallacious whether or not its conclusion is correct. In the business world, we are bombarded with false arguments all the time; and far too often we make decisions based on those seemingly logical reasons.

If these patterns are flawed, then any choices we make from them are also flawed. In the J. M. Beach blogspot article, *The Power and Danger of Fallacies: The Double Ad Hominem*, in March 2012, Beach writes, "in a fair and honest argument, the participants focus on making claims and defending each claim with both substantial and credible evidence and also logical reasoning."[4] This scenario, based on honesty and fairness, tells us that each participant's goal is to reach the truth—whatever that truth may be. Fallacious arguments, on the other hand, are dishonest—the intent is to win the argument at whatever the cost.

Beach goes on to write, "In an unfair argument, the person who wants to win usually does not use evidence at all. Instead, they use fallacies. Fallacies are rhetorical statements that often appear to be evidence, but in fact, are tricks designed to manipulate an audience." In all fairness, many of the fallacies that I have come across over the years were honest mistakes, poor judgment, or just plain rhetoric. There are times, though, when arguments become an attack on the person and not the idea.

Now that we have taken the time to understand our stakeholders from an organizational and behavioral perspective, we are ready to assemble our requirements team. Requirements management spans the entire scope of the project. If we do not have an effective requirements team, needs will be missed, and purpose and value will remain unfulfilled. The relationships that team members establish with each other is every bit as important as those you establish. As we begin to create our team, we will pay close attention to the ways in which our requirements stakeholders can effectively work together. We always look for ways to improve cooperation, trust, respect, and communication. In the next chapter, we consider some of the elements required to assemble the right people to do the right jobs.

REFERENCES AND ADDITIONAL SUGGESTED READINGS

Adriaens, Pieter R. and Andreas De Block. 2011. *Maladapting Minds: Philosophy, Psychiatry, and Evolutionary Theory* (*International Perspectives in Philosophy and Psychiatry*). Oxford University Press.

Alessandra, Tony and Michael J. O'Connor. 1998. *The Platinum Rule: Discover the Four Basic Business Personalities and How They Can Lead You to Success.* Warner Business Books.

Bolton, Robert and Dorothy Grover Bolton. 2009. *People Styles at Work and Beyond: Making Bad Relationships Good and Good Relationships Better.* AMACOM.

Bradberry, Travis and Jean Greaves. 2009. *Emotional Intelligence 2.0.* TalentSmart.

Churchland, Paul M. 1996. *The Engine of Reason, the Seat of the Soul: A Philosophical Journey into the Brain* (Bradford Books). The MIT Press.

Ciofoaia, Victor, Mark Metwally, Seth Gross, and FACG Norwalk. 2011. "Clinical Vignettes/case Reports-Esophagus."

Davis, Michael. 1992. "The Role of the Amygdala in Fear and Anxiety." *Annual Review of Neuroscience* 15, no. 1, pp. 353–75.

Freedman, Joshua, Anabel L. Jensen, Marsha C. Rideout, and Patricia E. Freedman. 1998. *Handle With Care: Emotional Intelligence Activity Book*. Six Seconds.

Furedi, Frank. 2005. *Politics of Fear*. A&C Black.

Gigerenzer, Gerd. 2008. *Gut Feelings: The Intelligence of the Unconscious*. Penguin Books.

Goleman, Daniel. 1995. *Emotional Intelligence: Why it Can Matter More Than IQ*. Bantam Books.

Grann, D. 2008. *The Chameleon: The Many Lives of Frédéric Bourdin*. The New Yorker 11.

Hare, Robert D., Timothy J. Harpur, A. Ralph Hakstian, Adelle E. Forth, Stephen D. Hart, and Joseph P. Newman. 1990. "The Revised Psychopathy Checklist: Reliability and Factor Structure." Psychological Assessment: *A Journal of Consulting and Clinical Psychology* 2, no. 3, p. 338.

Kamler, Howard. 2002. "Self-Identity and Moral Maturity," In *Personal and Moral Identity*, pp. 123–46. Springer.

Kihlstrom, John F. and Nancy Cantor. 2000. "Social Intelligence." *Handbook of Intelligence* 2, pp. 359–79.

Kofman, Fred. 2013. *Conscious Business: How to Build Value through Values*. Sounds True.

Lesch, Klaus-Peter, Dietmar Bengel, Armin Heils, and Sue Z. Sabol. 1996. "Association of Anxiety-Related Traits with a Polymorphism in the Serotonin Transporter Gene Regulatory Region." *Science* 274, no. 5292, p. 1527.

Mayer, John D. 2004. *Emotional Intelligence: Key Readings on the Mayer and Salovey Model*. National Professional Resources, Inc./Dude Publishing.

McEwen, Bruce S. 2008. "Central Effects of Stress Hormones in Health and Disease: Understanding the Protective and Damaging Effects of Stress and Stress Mediators." *European Journal of Pharmacology* 583, no. 2, pp. 174–85.

McLeod, Saul. 2014. *Attitudes and Behavior*.

Merrill, David W. and Roger H. Reid. 1981. *Personal Styles & Effective Performance*. CRC Press.

Phelps, Elizabeth A. 2004. "Human Emotion and Memory: Interactions of the Amygdala and Hippocampal Complex." *Current Opinion in Neurobiology* 14, no. 2, pp. 198–202.

Pittenger, Christopher and Ronald S. Duman. 2008. "Stress, Depression, and Neuroplasticity: A Convergence of Mechanisms." *Neuropsychopharmacology* 33, no. 1, pp. 88–109.

Ramachandran, V. S. 2012. *The Tell-Tale Brain: A Neuroscientist's Quest for What Makes Us Human*. W. W. Norton & Company.

Rizzolatti, Giacomo, Leonardo Fogassi, and Vittorio Gallese. "Neurophysiological Mechanisms Underlying the Understanding and Imitation of Action." *Nature Reviews Neuroscience* 2, no. 9, 2001. 661–70.

Shermer, Michael. 2002. *Why People Believe Weird Things: Pseudoscience, Superstition, and Other Confusions of Our Time*. Holt Paperbacks.

———. 2008. "Patternicity: Finding Meaningful Patterns in Meaningless Noise." *Scientific American* 299, no. 5.

Von Hippel, William and Robert Trivers. 2011. "The Evolution and Psychology of Self-Deception." *Behavioral and Brain Sciences* 34, no. 01, pp. 1–16.

Whitson, Jennifer A. and Adam D. Galinsky. 2008. "Lacking Control Increases Illusory Pattern Perception." *Science* 322, no. 5898, pp. 115–17.

ENDNOTES

1. Mindfulness | Psychology Today, https://www.psychologytoday.com/basics/mindfulness (accessed July 02, 2016).
2. In certain studies, researchers have directly stimulated the amygdalae of patients who were undergoing brain surgery and asked them to report their impressions. The subjective experience that these patients reported most often was one of imminent danger and fear.
3. Tom Gilovich. gilovich.socialpsychology.org. Social Psychology Network, http://www.socialpsychology.org/ (accessed July 17, 2016).
4. Dare to Know: The Power and Danger of Fallacies: The Double Ad Hominem. http://jmbeach.blogspot.com/2012/03/power-and-danger-of-fallacies-double-ad.html (accessed July 17, 2016).

4

CREATING A GREAT TEAM

"There is an amazing beauty and strength in diversity. Everyone has something special to offer, everyone has a gift that can add value to the organization, community and even the world. People with different tribe, race, religion and nationality can come together and accomplish something extraordinary. The key is the culture of unity and team work."
—Farshad Asl, *The "No Excuses" Mindset: A Life of Purpose, Passion, and Clarity*

Workplace culture is the center of all success within an organization. A small, devoted team is greater than a large, indifferent one. With growing complexity and geographical diversification, the need for increased team collaboration has risen tremendously. At every step of the project, the stakeholders wish to be well informed about the progress, success, and failures. This change in behavior requires a sophisticated group dynamic. The most effective leaders build their relationships out of trust and loyalty, rather than fear or the power of their positions. As we continue to develop our requirements team, let us review some fundamental concepts:

- Embody the attributes of servant leadership
- Remove roadblocks like the sweeper of a curling team
- All ideas have value
- Be mindful of yourself and others
- Consider unspoken feelings
- Set the tone for open, sensitive, and honest behavior
- Become a harmonizing influence
- Look for opportunities to mediate and resolve disputes; reach continually toward a higher set of values and conduct
- Always encourage transparency, trust, and collaboration
- Studies show that we need nonwork conversations and bonding; allow for teams to grow together outside of the project
- The relationships that team members establish among themselves are every bit as important as those you develop with them
- Determine methods for consensus

- As the team begins to take shape, pay close attention to how team members work together and take steps to improve communication, cooperation, trust, and respect in those relationships
- Delegate minor issues and problem-solving opportunities to the team; allow them to help themselves

We could go on for pages, but I think that captures a lot of the arguments presented up to this point. The internet is littered with blogs, papers, and articles on what makes a good team. Regardless of the author, they all seem to center around the following themes: commitment to team success and shared goals; interdependence; social skills and emotional intelligence (EI); open, honest communication and immediate reciprocity; set and understood social boundaries; compensation (not just money!); and commitment to team processes, leadership, and accountability. In my experience, one of the most effective tools to help us with these concepts is the Belbin team inventory.

TEAM INVENTORY

Formal project management requires us to identify the right people for the right deliverables, work packages, activities, and tasks. All too often, however, we get what we get and we don't get upset. Requirements management runs the entire length of the project's life cycle. It makes sense, therefore, that we take the time to build a well-balanced requirements team. Groups of people who are not aware of how to match different deliverables with various team roles trip over each other and themselves engaging in heroic delivery. Poet Maya Angelou once said, "I've learned that people will forget what you said, people will forget what you did, but people will never forget how you made them feel."

Best case scenario—the project will spend most of its time and money fixing defects, processing change requests, and not meeting stakeholder expectations because people spent too much time working on activities for which they were ill-suited. Worst case—the same will happen, but the stress will be extreme, the project will go into recovery mode, resources may leave, the project manager (PM) may get replaced, total failure may occur, and everyone will look unprofessional, lose credibility, and end up hating each other.

When a team's full value becomes realized, it is usually because the roles and responsibilities were well defined; skills determined; motivation and excellent leadership were present; and stakeholders communicated well and have a clear understanding of the project's objectives. There is trust, transparency, personal and professional commitment, respect for each other, and a strong sense of collaboration. Despite all of this, however, if we are not aware of our interdependence on each other, including our strengths and weakness, we may still fall short of our full potential.

Maybe some of our stakeholders do not participate as we had hoped. Despite assurances, some may not be as flexible with their time as we need them to be. Alternatively, incongruence may arise because stakeholders do not agree with each other's approach to problem solving. Our team roles are assigned but are they the right ones? An exercise known as Belbin's team inventory can help clarify our behavioral preferences (adopted from Belbin 2010). Belbin defines a team role as "*a tendency to behave, contribute, and interrelate with others in a particular way.*" For a team to be successful, it needs to have access to each of the nine Belbin team roles. Typically, most people have two or three team roles that they are most comfortable with; a few others that they can manage to cover if they need to; and finally, the rest that they prefer not to adopt at all.[1]

Dr. Meredith Belbin et al. studied teams for more than ten years to determine what makes them effective. The research on this theory is extensive and in-depth. Briefly, Belbin and his team observed that if left to their own devices, people would cluster around nine different team roles. A decade of research yielded a model that has:

- Nine distinct and identifiable clusters of behavior
- A higher probability of success when all nine areas of contribution are present and balanced
- An understanding of each role and whether it is preferred, not preferred, or simply manageable by each team member

Each role, named for how they contribute, has a list of behavioral traits and allowable weaknesses—my personal favorite. The Belbin model suggests we can manage ourselves effectively and be more productive on a team because we work to our natural strengths and weaknesses—as seen through the model, of course.

"People are more engaged and productive when they play to their key strengths. Belbin empowers individuals to fulfill their potential at work, and helps organizations to bring together the right people to form high performing teams."[2]

If a team is made up of comparable strengths, the likely outcome is competition over deliverables, rather than cooperation. Teams may also experience an imbalance if all the members have similar behavior or social styles. Likewise, the same applies if we share the same weaknesses. The model requires a balance on the team. The team must be arranged to allow each member to express his or her true teamwork strengths and social styles. The combined advantage of this approach is that we can address potential behavioral tensions or weaknesses among our requirements team members before escalation is required.

BELBIN MODEL GROUPS

The Belbin model groups into three classes: action-oriented, people-oriented, and thought-oriented. Each role characterizes behavioral and interpersonal strengths and allowable weaknesses. There is an expectation that the team member and whomever they report to would work together to improve any known weaknesses. Within the three categories there are nine team roles, as featured in Figure 4.1, and listed below:

- Action-oriented (doers)
  - Shaper (SH)
  - Implementer (IMP)
  - Completer/Finisher (CF)
- People-oriented (feelers)
  - Coordinator (CO)
  - Team worker (TW)
  - Resource investigator (RI)
- Thought-oriented (thinkers)
  - Plant (PL)
  - Monitor evaluator (ME)
  - Specialist (SP)

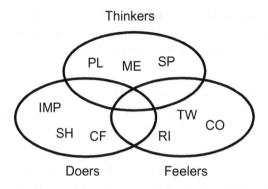

Figure 4.1   Belbin's team roles

Action-Oriented

Shaper

Shapers want the team to be on an improvement curve, always. They will challenge the team at every turn. Shapers are dynamic and usually thought of as extroverted. They enjoy stimulating others to think on their feet and will even push people outside of their comfort zone to get the very best out of them. Shapers dislike complacency and might look to shake things up for the sake of it. They may be unconventional, but it is that unconventionality that keeps things exciting and *edgy*. As you might expect, shapers have strong personalities and may easily offend.

Individual Characteristics

- Is seen as dynamic, driven, and outgoing
- Expresses strong leadership
- Is comfortable with confrontation
- Is always ready for a challenge

Contributions to the Team

- Leads in difficult situations
- Can make hard decisions and overcome obstacles
- Provides direction, delivers results
- Can set and meet goals and objectives

Allowable Weaknesses

- Provocative or aggressive
- Very task focused

Non-Allowable Weaknesses

- May become too argumentative and perceived as a bully
- Easily provoked and irritated

- Becomes impatient and may hurt feelings of others
- Tends to think that he or she is always in the right

Implementer

Implementers like to *get-r-done*. Every plant and shaper need an implementer. In fact, this role is recognized by the International Institute of Business Analysis (IIBA) as the implementation subject matter expert (SME) (IIBA 2015). PMs also make good implementers when they turn the team's intentions and thoughts into realistic plans and deliverables.

Typically, well organized, conservative, and disciplined implementers work systematically and efficiently. Commitments, deliverables, tasks, and timelines—all valued by implementers—cause a tendency to be inflexible and somewhat resistant to change.

Individual Characteristics

- Is loyal and action-oriented
- Is well organized, systematic, and always practical

Contributions to the Team

- Is hard-working and disciplined
- Can turn ideas into practical solutions
- Likes to follow the rules, which makes him or her conservative
- Can go the distance—has endurance
- Is very reliable

Allowable Weaknesses

- May become inflexible and slow to see possibilities
- Tends to become too conservative
- Responds slowly to new ideas

Non-Allowable Weaknesses

- May obstruct change
- Could become a barrier to project success

Completer/Finisher

Every implementer needs a completer/finisher who will make sure everything is completed *thoroughly*. Testers often make good completers/finishers because they want to ensure there have been no defects or omissions and that there is full traceability. As you would expect, completers/finishers are detail oriented and very concerned with deadlines. They have what it takes to encourage the team to meet a deadline, but as a consequence, they may worry unnecessarily. They have a difficult time delegating work to others.

Individual Characteristics

- Seen as a perfectionist, which could also be a weakness

- Conscientious toward others
- Results oriented

Contributions to the Team

- Has an eye for detail, defects, omissions, and quality
- Is orderly and exacting but urgent
- Is painstaking and methodical

Allowable Weaknesses

- Will require more time for perfection, quality, etc.
- Exhibits undue worry and anxiety
- Is unable to stay focused on a larger picture
- Spends too much time mired in the *weeds*
- Is uncomfortable delegating work

Non-Allowable Weaknesses

- Tends to be seen as nit-picking over irrelevant details
- May be prone to obsessive-compulsive spectrum behavior
- Interrupts the work with obsessive needs
- Can be overly negative and pessimistic

People-Oriented

Coordinator

Although shapers are outgoing and express strong leadership, it is not at the team level, leaving the space open for coordinators to fill the role of team leader. This function is sometimes known as the *chairman of the board* (or just *chairman*). Coordinators are comfortable with guiding the group to what they perceive are the project's objectives, and they delegate well.

Coordinators are active listeners and can spot talent, recognizing the value that each stakeholder brings to a requirements team. Coordinators are calm and good-natured, but watch out, they may resort to manipulation to get what they want.

Individual Characteristics

- Has a strong sense of objectives
- Projects confidence and is quietly charismatic
- Communicates well and listens actively

Contributions to the Team

- Focuses well and delegates effectively
- Leads through empowerment and promotes team contribution

- Promotes decision making and delegates readily
- Is effective at chairing meetings, committees, workshops, and events

Allowable Weaknesses

- Is not particularly creative
- Might manipulate, but is within reason and not destructive

Non-Allowable Weaknesses

- Could rely too heavily on the team
- May delegate his or her work to others and then take credit for it

Team Worker

Supportive and flexible team workers will always want the team to get along and work effectively with each other. Supporters will naturally fill the role of a negotiator, and they tend to be quite flexible. Popular and capable people, supporters value team cohesion and need everyone to get along. This internal need for coherence and unwillingness to *rock the boat* makes for indecisive behavior and a neutral position during discussions and decision making.

Individual Characteristics

- Is social, felicitous, well-suited, and pleasant
- Acts as a conciliator and enjoys counseling others
- Is seen as supportive, diplomatic, and encouraging
- Is uncompetitive, with a sensitivity to team undercurrents

Contributions to the Team

- Helps with intra-group conflict and communication
- Acts as the cheerleader and fosters team spirit
- Builds on the suggestions of others

Allowable Weaknesses

- Tends to be indecisive for fear of upsetting the group
- Avoids conflict and anxious situations
- Is not very dynamic or comfortable with change

Non-Allowable Weaknesses

- A capable person but competes for visibility
- Values the social connection over the work
- Can have ostentatious behavior characterized by vulgar or pretentious displays designed to impress or attract notice to him/herself

Resource Investigator

Innovative and also naturally curious, resource investigators develop contacts with vendors and are adept at negotiating for resources. They will explore all of the options before making an informed choice. Resource investigators express enthusiasm for the project and are optimistic (sometimes overly), outgoing, and extroverted. Their enthusiasm may be short-lived, however, when another curiosity catches their eye.

Individual Characteristics

- Is seen as being an excellent communicator, popular, and inquisitive
- Is extroverted and enthusiastic—building on the ideas of others
- Responds well to challenges
- Is aware of what is going on outside of the team

Contributions to the Team

- Develops contacts to acquire and negotiate for resources
- Recognizes opportunities and can exploit them
- Can fix errors in a crunch

Allowable Weaknesses

- Is not very critical
- Has a relaxed nature when the pressure is off
- Is liable to lose interest
- Tends to be overly optimistic
- Needs positive feedback

Non-Allowable Weaknesses

- May let stakeholders down by not following through
- Can be too externally focused
- Requires positive feedback and validation

Thought-Oriented

Plant

In nature, plants are born of seeds, and that is what the Belbin plant provides to the team. The plant is the creative innovator with new ideas and approaches on how to solve problems and take advantage of opportunities. Plants take much pride in their work and love praise. Criticism, on the other hand, is not easy—their trade is very personal. Unable to communicate well, plants are often introverted and prefer to be away from the central group. Their ideas can be unconventional, which can make them impractical and out of scope. Plants focus on maximizing their utility.

Plants often feel that they can ignore rules, policies, or procedures because of their creative *genius*. However, as an actual creative *genius* and theoretical physicist was once attributed to having said, "Everybody is a genius. But if you judge a fish by its ability to climb a tree, it will live its whole life believing that it is stupid" (attributed to Albert Einstein).

Individual Characteristics

- Is thought of as a creative *genius* and original thinker
- An individualist and loves to generate ideas
- Uses unorthodox methods in his or her approach—such as thought experiments

Contributions to the Team

- Exhibits appreciative inquiry, strong inference, and problem solving
- Uses dimensional thinking, innovative, unconventional approaches, and imagination
- Is focused on the big picture—building ideas for strategic and tactical goals and objectives

Allowable Weaknesses

- Is absentminded, not focused on the here and now
- Would not make a good leader despite their intelligence quotient (IQ)
- Has a disregard for practicalities and people

Non-Allowable Weaknesses

- Has very strong ownership of his or her ideas, refusing help or cooperation
- Excludes others, which can derail efforts
- Will only focus on his or her ideas, disregarding additional ideas

Monitor Evaluator

Every plant needs water, sunlight, and micronutrients—and of course, a great monitor evaluator. Monitor evaluators are born analyzers. They evaluate the ideas of other people—usually plants. Monitor evaluators, thought of as shrewd, objectify a plant's abstract ideas into practical, concrete forms. Monitor evaluators are natural force-field thinkers, weighing the forces for and against a change before making an informed decision. Their decisions stem from data, not emotion. This reasoning makes monitor evaluators appear detached and unemotional. You would not expect to see a monitor evaluator as a motivational speaker, nor would you see them as an instigator; they prefer to sit back and react, as needed.

Individual Characteristic

- Is a stable, careful, and objective personality
- Is analytical, shrewd, fair, and balanced

Contributions to the Team

- Is discerning and will question things and results
- Can seek out threats and plan responses
- Can see many options and exceptions
- Helps to defuse an over-enthused team with practical means and applies reason to their work

Allowable Weaknesses

- Is seen as uncreative and uninspiring
- Is a bit detached and also somewhat skeptical

Non-Allowable Weaknesses

- Displays pessimistic attitudes and general skepticism that may turn into self-interested cynicism

Specialist

Ah, finally we meet our SMEs—saved the best for last, eh? Many of your stakeholders will be specialists, but they may also be two or three other roles such as supporters, plants, or chairpersons. Of course, specialists are just that—experts with data, information, and knowledge that you need. With a specialist comes a deep sense of pride. They have worked long and hard to gain their wisdom and will protect it if they feel threatened. These experts tend to have at least one professional designation, often more. The specialist's team role is to be an expert and defer actual decisions to others.

Depending on their personality and other Belbin roles the specialist may fall into, this could be a conflict of interest and a source of arguments. Specialists must understand their role, as a stakeholder, in this context. It falls upon us to manage this relationship and be sure they know that their function within the team is to speak for and be an authority of their domain and to commit themselves fully to their area of expertise. This reality limits their contribution, and again, depending on their personality, may also lead to a preoccupation with technicalities at the expense of the project's scope.

Individual Characteristics

- Is recognized as an expert in a domain
- Tends to be very single-minded
- Is dedicated and very professional

Contributions to the Team

- Tends to ignore factors outside his or her domain unless there is a conflict in personality or other Belbin team roles
- Will keep up-to-date on recent trends, technology, etc.
- Is credible and trustworthy and provides accurate information
- Will inform the team when technical circumstances change

Allowable Weaknesses

- May have a narrow vision
- Does not see or is disinterested in the larger picture
- Tends to have little interest in other people or their work
- Limits his or her contributions and time

Non-Allowable Weaknesses

- Can be too narrow-minded

- Will ignore project elements that are outside of his or her domain
- Can become distracted by unrelated specialized or personal interests

Applying the Belbin Team Inventory

We must be aware of and manage our allowable and non-allowable weaknesses at all times. If you are a shaper, you are going to hurt some people's feelings. It is who you are; it is in your nature. The Belbin model is at its best when there is a balance between all of its elements; this includes the weaknesses.

Remember, some *negative* behavior is allowable. If a plant forgets to come to your workshop or is there but not participating, do not be alarmed and lash out. The shaper comes by their behavior as a result of their personality; they mean no disrespect. However, if the behavior persists, this is a matter of EI, controlling one's behavior, and must be addressed. We all have our weakness; that is the beauty and elegance of the Belbin model. It asks that we accept each other for who we are, within reason.

When negative patterns continue and move into the non-allowable range, corrective action is needed. So how do we use this behavioral model? Working with the Belbin team or a trained and licensed consultant will give the best results. If you want to implement this theory at the organizational level, then I indeed suggest that be your course; however, for the rest of us, all we need is some reasoning and much observational analysis.

Over the period of a few weeks, observe the people you need on your requirements team. Watch their natural behavior: Who comes to your meetings late? Who is willing to accept tasks right away? Who is in the back corner? Look for clues that will help you determine into which Belbin team role your stakeholders may fall. Keep in mind that the importance of each role varies by project phase. Avoiding corrective action or escalation during your observations is necessary. You are looking for natural tendencies and attitudes. Document what you observe and follow the information I have provided in this chapter. What are each person's characteristics, requested contributions to the team, and allowable and non-allowable weaknesses? Look for word opposites that best suit each stakeholder's personality, like the examples provided in Table 4.1.

Table 4.1   Sample Belbin-style key words

Ambitious or Harmonious Cheerful or Reserved Consensus or Caring	Coordinating or Autonomy Curious or Respectful Diligent or Conscientious Disciplined or Task-focused	Energetic or Skillful Extrovert or Independent Fantasize or Convey Gregarious or Challenging
Imagine or Listen Impatient or Sensitive Innovate or Analyze Intelligent or Worrisome	Networking or Controlling Objective or Specialist Orderly or Communicative Organize or Improvize	Practical or Critical Prudent or Driven Rational or Concerned Restless or Friendly
Scientific or Impulsive Sensible or Agreeable Serious or Open-minded	Sober or Emotional Systematic or Diplomatic Talk or Study	Troubled or Defensive Visionary or Expert

You might also consider value statements for which there are ranges from *strongly agree* to *disagree*, such as:

- I like debating ideas and solutions with other people rather than working on my own
- When solving issues, I prefer working with my team rather than on my own
- I am happier when I am working with others than by myself

My motivation is highest when:

- I work alone
- I work mostly on my own
- I collaborate with a team
- I have no preference

Different team roles are in the spotlight at various points within the project life cycle. For example:

- We need shapers and coordinators during project initiation to set the project's direction and establish strategic goals and objectives
- Plants and resource investigators are critical for identifying creative solution options to meet the organizational needs, which will be used to define the charter and scope statement

During the discovery, iterative, and definitive portions of project planning, the monitor evaluator and specialist will be in demand. To ensure that all plans complete on time and that we can meet all stakeholder expectations, the team needs the talents of the completer/finisher and implementer.

When it is time for solution analysis and logical and physical designs, the monitor evaluator and specialist's time will be in even higher demand. We will also need to call upon the team worker, coordinator, and implementer. The implementer or coordinator should keep the team organized and on scope.

As you might expect, the solution builds and release to operations requires the expertise of the specialist again, but also the completer/finisher, the implementer, the coordinator, the resource investigator, and perhaps even the team worker and the monitor evaluator—*all hands on deck*. If your project is dealing with a significant number of outside vendors, the resource investigator and team worker roles should be present at all times.

Once you have completed your analysis, compare the research to the information in this chapter, noting the primary and secondary roles that best describe each stakeholder. It is at this point where things get tricky and a little outside the scope of this chapter. Your goal is to establish a balanced set of team roles. I have provided some samples and guidance, but in the end, you will have to be the judge. Table 4.2 illustrates a sample hypothetical analysis of a requirements team.

Scored from one (strong) to nine (weak), we can see that the product owner, for example, has a strong preference for the completer/finisher, team worker, and shaper roles. Moreover, they do not have a desire for the plant, implementer, or coordinator positions. Ideally, the team should have at least 1, 2, or 3 in each of the roles—but not too many for any position.

Table 4.2   Sample Belbin-style team results

	Product Owner	Business Analyst	Systems Analyst	Lead Designer	Lead Developer	Lead Tester	Release Manager	Super User	SME (1)	SME (2)	SME (3)
Requirements Management Team											
% on Project	75%	100%	87%	70%	85%	75%	25%	75%	50%	50%	50%
PL	7	7	2	4	9	8	7	2	9	5	4
ME	4	2	4	1	4	2	7	4	7	3	6
SP	5	3	5	5	8	1	5	4	3	7	2
SH	3	1	1	2	7	3	5	5	1	6	6
IMP	8	4	9	8	3	2	5	4	7	2	4
CF	1	1	7	9	6	6	7	5	6	6	5
RI	6	5	8	8	9	2	3	5	7	2	6
TW	2	6	7	6	1	7	1	6	4	1	9
CO	9	8	3	3	3	4	7	2	8	4	7

These reports do not tell us how strong someone is at performing within a team role. For example, in Table 4.2, SME 1 and 2 both scored a six for completer/finisher. The Belbin model does not predict which of them will be a better completer/finisher. Neither does it indicate the *distance* between the roles. Team members may only have a few percentage points separating their top team role preferences, while others have one that dominates over others.

If the team is unbalanced, identify roles that are not covered and see if there are opportunities for other members to fill in the gaps. Also, anticipate possible areas of conflict. If there are too many shapers on the team that rank equally in your stakeholder salience analysis and their expectations must be met, it is possible that they may each try to take the requirements team in different directions. Last, observe how the team roles relate to how stakeholders behave when they are in or out of their social style comfort zones. Many of the conflict issues that beset our requirement teams resolve through efficient use of a combination of social styles and the Belbin approach.

The Belbin team inventory, based on more than a decade of observation and research into interpersonal styles, informs individual and group work habits. The Belbin approach is a prudent theory; however, even Belbin will argue that aspects of our behavior within the model are situational. It relates not only to our natural working style but also our personal and professional relationships with others, and the work we perform (Belbin 2010). This links us back to EI and our need to be adept at managing our personal and social competencies. Remember to include all the principles that I have mentioned, do not depend on one over another, and temper any conclusions that you make with common sense.

Regardless of whether you use the Belbin model as intended or as a loose guide for building a requirements team, just knowing its approach can bring greater team harmony, increased job satisfaction, and the knowledge that various methods apply in different situations.

INFLUENCE WITHOUT AUTHORITY

Leadership does not need authority—this is my belief. I share this position with (among others) Ken Blanchard, PhD, "The key to successful leadership today is influence, not authority." I have always been of the mind to reason that a leader is someone whom other people *choose* to follow.

Ken Blanchard is an American author and management guru. He has written over 60 books and is widely considered to be an expert on the subjects of management and leadership consulting. If you have not read *The One Minute Manager*, I strongly suggest you make it part of your business analyst (BA) toolbox. I am sure you can find it in one of its 37 languages. Another equally prominent leader in this domain, Stephen Covey, the man who brought us *The 7 Habits of Highly Effective People*, believes:

> *"True leadership is moral authority, not formal authority. Leadership is a choice, not a position. The choice is to follow universal timeless principles, which will build trust and respect from the entire organization. Those with formal authority alone will lose this trust and respect."*

I am a fan of leaders who understand the behavioral and social connections of leading a team to lasting success. Covey's seven habits are:

1. Be proactive
2. Begin with the end in mind
3. Put first things first
4. Think win-win
5. Seek first to understand, then to be understood
6. Synergize
7. Sharpen the saw (self-renewal)

There is no shortage of books and blogs on this subject—some more authoritative than others. I struggled over this section for some time. Leadership is an essential tool for a BA, and the odds are that we do not have any authority to back it up. According to the gurus, though, we do not need any; sure, tell that to our requirement's stakeholders who will do almost anything to avoid our workshops, and complain, ironically, when their needs remain unfulfilled. After careful consideration, I believe I have selected a few tools that suit our needs quite well. As we continue to build an effective team charter, we will discuss the Cohen-Bradford influence model and Vroom expectancy motivation.

Cohen-Bradford Influence Model

The Cohen-Bradford influence model forms off of a deep-rooted psychological concept known as the *Law of Reciprocity*. Reciprocity is just responding to a positive action with another affirmative action based on an agreed-upon exchange which is/should be fair to both parties. Social psychologists call it a law because it is believed to be hard-wired into our social nature. Without trust and equitable trade, reciprocity focuses on the unequal profit obtained from the concept of reciprocal concessions. Delayed reciprocity is a little more complicated, in that it asks for something now in exchange for something later, sometimes much later, or much, much later!

The Cohen-Bradford influence model, developed by Allan R. Cohen and David L. Bradford (2005), concludes that the term *authority* can be problematic. This conjecture is consistent with Blanchard, Covey, and other well-regarded leaders. Just because you have the power to assign stakeholders to a task does not mean that you have their support, commitment, or motivation. In fact, in my experience, I see the opposite—fear and anxiety over (perceived) unreasonable demands—and the impact on project and diminished requirements quality becomes noticeable.

The Law of Reciprocity fulfills a deep need within us to repay others as a means of reinforcing social bonds—it is a form of social grooming (Hamilton, 1964). Stakeholder analysis, lists, maps, registers, and personas help project professionals understand a stakeholder's relationship to the project with respect to their influence, interest, urgency, and required participation; however, as with many concepts in project management, that's just the tip of the iceberg. We need to dive into that cold black abyss if we want to understand our stakeholders and build lasting relationships.

The Cohen-Bradford model relies on fair exchange. The process is as follows:

- Assume anyone can help you
- Take the time to identify what matters to you—why and what specifically you need
- Understand the stakeholder's current situation, workload, status within the organization, and what's important to them
- Recognize who they are as people and professionals

As you can see, we have already covered many of these ideas in our investigations of social styles and EI. We use the model under the following conditions:

- We need something from a stakeholder whom you are not authorized to direct
- We do not know the stakeholder well; there is resistance, conflict, or a relationship strain
- This stakeholder will not tolerate persistent requests from you

Assuming that everyone can help you is not just a state of mind; it is part of social science. Prosocial behavior, a term used by psychologists, describes actions intended to help others. Acting *selflessly* in most situations is a path to group membership and acceptance. Doing things for other people ultimately services our sense of self. We help others because it makes us feel good about who we are—we are what we do. In this regard, no act can be truly selfless.

I have concluded that we are incapable of acting selflessly beyond our line of sight. This changes if our line of sight includes a social group of which we wish to be a member. I am not likely to donate my time or money to a cause or group that I care nothing about or through which I do not wish favor. A sad truth, but one we must accept. Our capacity to care deeply for others rarely extends beyond the members of our group or the groups of which we want to be members.

We know that reciprocity can help us influence others. What we do not know is how probable it is that we will receive assistance when we need it the most. Understanding our stakeholders is a recurring theme in business analysis and project management. According to the influence model (Cohen and Bradford, 2005), we must be sensitive to the following:

- What are the organizational culture and subcultures like?
- Does the stakeholder belong to cliques and groups?

- What are the stakeholder's primary responsibilities?
- What is generally expected from the stakeholder—from peers, supervisors, and bosses?
- How is the stakeholder's performance measured?
- As far as we know, is our stakeholder performing within expected tolerances?
- Are tolerances sufficient?
- What personal or professional pressure is our stakeholder currently experiencing that may draw them away from their comfort zone?
- What motivates our stakeholder?
- What factors does the stakeholder value most about working?

Concerning which factors our stakeholders value most, Cohen and Bradford identified five types.[3]

Personal

There is nothing more personal than a personal appeal—assuming it is sincere. Your honest and heartfelt gratitude will go a long way, even in times of stress. Stakeholders who are sensitive to the personal approach must be free to make their own choices; they must not feel rushed or hassled. Accept what they are willing to offer and do not try to bargain for more. In their mind, they are doing you a favor. When you appeal to these stakeholders, do so through their appreciation for honesty and integrity.

Relationship

These are people who value connections and kinships with their teammates; they want to belong and feel a great sense of pride in these relationships. As we have already seen in the social styles model, they tend to value their affiliations over their work. When you appeal to these stakeholders, you do so through their desire to build close personal relationships. Be an active listener, take the time to connect with them, and listen to their challenges. Offer emotional support and understanding, sincerely. If you are fake, they will know it, and they will cut you off without hesitation. Remember to be thankful and positive. The stakeholder who gets into this circumstance may not be able to separate their self-identity from the work they produce.

Inspiration

Stakeholders who find meaning in what they do are intrinsically motivated and value accomplishments as rewards. These stakeholders value morality and business vision and take pride in personal strength. Don't be surprised if one of these teammates goes out of his or her way to help you because it is the right thing to do. Their sense of self, shaped through service to others, lends itself well to this philosophy and set of management practices known as servant leadership.

Dating as far back as China, 570–490 BCE and attributed to Lao-Tzu, the greatest form of leadership is one in which the people are barely aware (Chanakya 2016). The concepts behind servant leadership weave their way throughout history in many cultures and religions. The Gospel of Matthew in the Bible makes mention of servant leadership: "Instead, whoever wants to become great among you must be your servant, and whoever wants to be first must be a servant of all" (Matthew 20:26).

We are meant to learn something here. I often wonder why this philosophy is not a universal policy. When you appeal to stakeholders, do so through their sense of morality, integrity, and virtue. Help them be the servant leader they want to be. Explain the value of your needs and how their support will contribute to the larger picture.

Position

Stakeholders who relate to *position* want recognition for their accomplishments in contrast with inspirational stakeholders who are in service to the work as an end in and of itself. Position-oriented stakeholders treat the work as a means to an end. In this case, the end is reputation, visibility, and another rung on their perceived ladder of success. We might argue this as service to self, as opposed to service to others. When appealing to position-related stakeholders, use the WIIFM model—what's in it for me? Offer these stakeholders something they will value, such as public recognition for helping you, a high-profile luncheon, or increased project visibility.

Task

If your currency is the fair exchange of resources, supplies, time-in-lieu, or the almighty dollar, then you relate to what Cohen and Bradford call *task*. Negotiating with these stakeholders is straightforward. Their thoughts and motives are practical and economical. If you have something they need, an exchange is possible. This worldview is neither good nor bad; we are who we are, it is how we act on our policies which determine our effect on others. You must know what you have to bargain with—such as your time, expertise, or position—in order to influence other stakeholders to offer their time or expertise. If you are willing to trade for your time and knowledge to accomplish tasks and get what you need, then you are a valuable commodity to most organizations.

When you are negotiating for something—anything, from anyone—regardless of their position, currency preference, or motivational triggers, you much always know your best alternative to a negotiated agreement (BATNA). First used by Roger Fisher and William Ury in 1981, BATNA refers to the position you take if the other person will not negotiate with you (Fisher, Ury, and Patton 2011). You must have your BATNA well defined before you enter into any consults with anyone, ever! Your BATNA is your best option, assuming you do not get the help you need. Without this predetermined and unchanging standard, you cannot make an informed decision.

With this simple idea, Fisher et al. were able to help us understand some of the logic that drives negotiations. If your BATNA is less than the presented offer, then you should probably continue negotiating. If the presented offer is greater than your BATNA, this might be a good time to stop and accept; and if you find yourself in an unyielding situation, an endless loop, well, at least you have your BATNA, and are no worse off than you started.

Since we have already covered many aspects of the influence model in other theories, I will stop here and move on to Vroom. In keeping with the theme of the Requirements, Elicitation, Planning, Analysis, and Collaboration Framework™(REPAC®) source superset, just because you do not need to feel significant, be acknowledged, or feel admired doesn't mean that no one else does. Keep an open mind, anticipate the needs of others, treat your stakeholders as people, not resources. With that, let's move on to Vroom.

MOTIVATION

The Vroom expectancy motivation theory fits well with our discussions because it assumes that behavior follows from intentional choices among alternatives whose purpose it is to maximize pleasure and minimize pain. Vroom asserts that effort, performance, and motivation are inexorably linked. Described in Figure 4.2 and propositioned in Equation 4.1, the concept variables, expectancy, instrumentality, and valence create an algorithm, which defines how we are motivated.

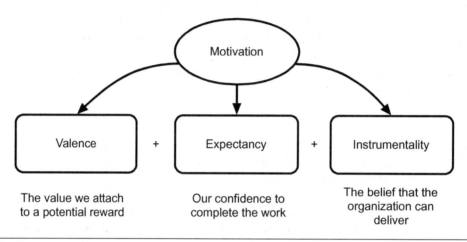

Figure 4.2   Expectancy theory process

Making Sense of the Expectancy Theory Equation

$$MF = (E \to P)(P \to R)V(R)$$

[Eq. 4.1]

Where:

- MF is the motivational force directing specific behavioral alternatives
- E is expectancy and P is performance; an attitude held on the perceived likelihood that more effort leads to greater performance
- P is performance and R is the reward; this leads to instrumentality—an attitude held on the perceived likelihood that performance will result in desired rewards
- $V(R)$ is known as valence; the value some people place on expected rewards

The equation makes use of arrows ($\to$). If you recall from the REPAC equation, an arrow in math is just a material implication, conventionally compared to an *if/then* in English; although it does not specify a causal relationship between the variables like its English counterpart. In mathematics, we read the statement as: "if E then P" or "E only if P." In Equation 4.2, "I" refers to instrumentality, the belief that we receive rewards when we meet performance expectations. Let's take a look at the model in closer detail.

$$MF = E\ I\ V$$

[Eq. 4.2]

Before we begin to negotiate for rewards from our PM and sponsor, we need to understand each stakeholder's valence. Valence is how we interpret the importance and significance of the rewards of an outcome. We base this on our needs, goals, objectives, desires, morals, ethics, patterns, preferences, and motivational preferences. Equation 4.3 illustrates the formula for valence.

$$-1 \rightarrow 0 \rightarrow +1$$ [Eq. 4.3]

Where:

- −1 represents our desire to avoid the outcome
- 0 represents our indifference to it
- +1 represents our desire to seek it out

As much as possible, provide rewards that our stakeholders will value. This application is subjective because different people value different things. Valence is rooted in our individual principles, standards, patterns, and judgment about what, for us, is most important. Keep in mind the Cohen and Bradford social styles and EI to understand in which currency your stakeholder will deal. Our stakeholders must believe that we have the ability, granted to us from our PM or sponsor, to provide rewards based on performance.

Linking effort to performance ($E \rightarrow P$) requires us to consider three factors. First and most important, we need to make sure that the level of difficulty matches the stakeholder's abilities. If the results are believed to be unattainable, then the expectancy will be small. Next is self-worth, which ties directly into the level of difficulty.

Self-worth is the belief that we can achieve our deliverables. We balance this with our stakeholders by ensuring that they have the skills they need, the necessary information at hand, the confidence to move forward, and the courage to make mistakes. Next, we need to make sure that our stakeholders have the permissions and controls they need to complete their deliverables. If our stakeholders do not believe they can influence, their expectancy and motivation will be low.

When it comes time to link performance and rewards ($P \rightarrow R$) we consider instrumentality. Instrumentality is our belief that rewards will be released once performance reaches its threshold. As mentioned earlier, if we do not do the groundwork and make sure we have the authority to provide rewards, the model will fail. Factors to consider are trust, credibility, control of the compensation discretion, and written policies which clearly state the correlation between performance and outcomes.

The product of expectancy, instrumentality, and valence is motivation. These elements act as a motivational force, which causes us to act. Motivational forces get us up each morning. Since we are pleasure-seeking beings, we select a motivational force between $0 \rightarrow 1$ and avoid ones between $-1 \rightarrow 0$. Let's take a look at a scenario.

Our PM tells us that we can have next Thursday and Friday off if we complete the business requirements document no later than Wednesday at 4:00 p.m. We value this proposal because our vacation scheduled for the following week will give us a perceived four more days. However, it is already 3:30 p.m. on Monday; the day is almost over. No matter how much effort we put into the work, there is virtually no chance it will be complete in the given time frame. Using the Vroom equation, Figure 4.3 illustrates how our motivational force is affected.

As you can see, even though both I and $V(R)$ are positive, we will not be motivated to complete the task. Our belief that the work will be complete within the allotted time is zero. In this example, expectancy is

Figure 4.3 Expectancy theory scenario

not valid; therefore, we cannot achieve performance, $(E \rightarrow P)$ and MF = 0. Sorry, no extra vacation time. This scenario is a simple example, but if we replicate it over many deliverables, assuming any instrumentality offered and the valence for it will always equal one, we are still unlikely to see any motivational force because of a persistence of insufficient time.

So, how do we influence and motivate? To paraphrase Einstein, we want things to be as simple as they can be, not simpler. However, the psychology of influence is a complicated field; indeed, we are all complicated people, and we do not understand ourselves very well. There are many motivational theories—Vroom is just one of them. Vroom's model centers on the idea that the intensity of our work depends on whether we believe our efforts will lead to the desired outcome. The minute that changes, motivation is affected. Poorly assessed stakeholders, a weak sense of purpose, lack of time, inefficient planning, and inadequately assigned roles and responsibilities are the chief contributing factors to motivational loss. If we want to increase the links between effort and performance, performance and reward, and reward and goal, we should remember these simple things:

- We must be sure to maintain credibility, honesty, and transparency so that our stakeholders will continue to believe that their increased effort will lead to the desired outcome and that we can provide the promised rewards
- We conduct assessments on efficient and effective team and stakeholder interplay
- As project conditions change we can ensure our rewards match each person, as carefully as possible
- We must arrange for training and other skills improvement options, as often as needed, to make sure that rewards will be attainable
- The causal link between reward and performance must be clear, understood, and accepted by all team members and other stakeholders
- We must continue to assert self-interest in the connection between rewards and performance

SALIENCY

In this context, saliency is the quality of being particularly prominent, essential, or influential to the success of the project. Boxer Mike Tyson reminds us that "everyone has a plan until they get punched in the face." This quote is not just funny but lends itself well to our studies on EI, social styles, fallacies, and the like. Our policies tend to go out the window at the first sign of trouble, but that does not mean we have to take it on the chin, as it were.

Former United States President Dwight Eisenhower once said, "In preparing for battle I have always found that plans are useless, but planning is indispensable."[4] Having the ability to be nimble, agile, and responsive to change, in near real-time, is critical for maintaining quality requirements and, by extension, project success. We cannot accomplish this without a great group of stakeholders to back us up—to have our backs.

There is no point in doing a stakeholder assessment if we are not going to use it, enforce it when needed, and escalate it if necessary. Risks to relationships notwithstanding, our stakeholders must always believe that we have their best interest at heart, despite how a stakeholder grid may present it. Always be sure to check and recheck your facts, assumptions, and theories. Take the time to get to the heart of their real issues and concerns. Managing stakeholders well, all day, every day, is the *only* way to deliver a successful project. Before we analyze and rank our stakeholders, however, we must find them. A stakeholder analysis along with its subsequent stakeholder register is the cornerstone of an effective project—requirements elicitation and analysis, planning, requirements management, risk analysis—everything. Sponsors and product and project managers are always a good place to begin. We approach the task of building our stakeholder list in the following manner:

- Identify stakeholders and stakeholder groups
- Establish stakeholder typology
- Define stakeholder ranking strategy
- Recognize social styles, influencers, and power bases
- Define motivations and expectations
- Assemble the stakeholder engagement model

IDENTIFY STAKEHOLDERS AND STAKEHOLDER GROUPS

Stakeholder theory or putting stakeholders first is a discipline that helps ensure a project's success. This approach does not mean we sacrifice constraints such as quality, time, and cost; in fact, a stakeholder approach assures us that we meet demands because we manage expectations from the stakeholder's point of view of scope, quality, time, and cost, not the project's. It helps them ensure that their projects succeed where others fail. We build our requirements management plan with our requirements stakeholders—they are our partners. A well-executed engagement plan identifies opinion leaders, influencers, power bases, supporters, and resistors, among others.

Projects are a microcosm of the organization and an opportunity to affect a positive influence on its culture. Through communicating with stakeholders early and frequently, we ensure that they fully engage and understand what we are doing and the value we bring as professionals. Obviously, we need the support of our PMs and sponsors, who, of course, are stakeholders themselves, and as such we will manage them as we manage others.

Most of us use something called a stakeholder onion diagram when we begin to visualize our stakeholders. A quick image search on your web browser will return multiple images. Mine is a little different; I split mine into two separate models—the stakeholder project life cycle (PLC) onion diagram and an operational version. Each must communicate different information in very different contexts; for me, it makes sense to separate them. Figures 4.4 and 4.5 illustrate how I envision stakeholders on the project and the certified solution.[5] Figure 4.4 illustrates the traditional stakeholder salience groups as they relate to the project. Although I have shown the classic impact and influence approach, this method may also apply to the stakeholder salience model, which we will examine later in this section. It is imperative to remember that our stakeholder's salience will change as the project progresses and as different issues and risks present themselves. Figure 4.6 illustrates this example.

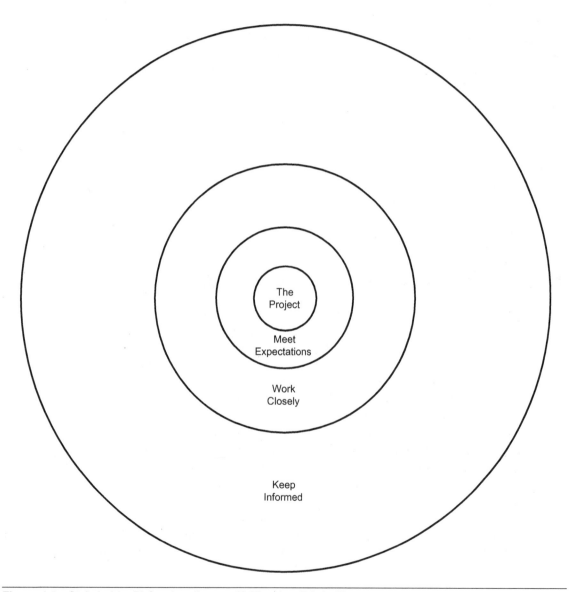

Figure 4.4   Stakeholder PLC onion diagram (© The New BA, Ltd.)

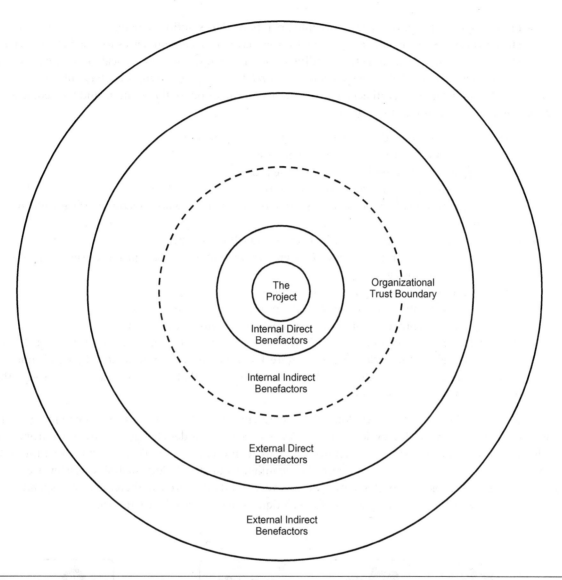

Figure 4.5   Stakeholder operations onion diagram (© The New BA, Ltd.)

The onion diagram changes once we move into operations. The solution remains in the middle, but the project stakeholders are no longer in the picture. Now we have to concern ourselves with stakeholders who are receiving or providing value directly or indirectly. Remember, whenever we speak of the solution, we are stating *the solution and all of its components as they relate to the people, processes, and tools/technology/ stuff triad*. This model infers all artifacts that are about, come in or out of the solution, and the people who handle them. I divide this into three groups:

- *Direct beneficiaries*: include internal stakeholders who directly:
    - Provide raw materials (input) to the process
    - Perform activities (end users) within the process
    - Sample the process for performance metrics
    - Provide technical or mechanical service or aid to those who directly interface with the process
- *Indirect beneficiaries*: include internal stakeholders who indirectly:
    - Receive value from the process through outputs that the process produces such as products, services, or data
    - Provides supportive services for the process
    - Manages or authorizes any or all of the processes or its components
    - Regulates the processes or audits it against regulations, without contact
- *External stakeholders*: include the attributes of the two previously mentioned groups, but I have placed them behind the circle of trust in Figure 4.5. Either directly or indirectly, these stakeholders are providing or receiving value to or from the solution, but that value must exchange through the organization's secure trust boundary.

As you can see in Figure 4.6, the black dots, which represent stakeholders, move around depending where they are within the project life cycle. Also, the BA may see the model change as they move from one analysis activity to another or from one process activity to another. We should not assume that the configuration is static at any point in the project. We reconfigure our stakeholder analysis every few weeks or as needed. The stakeholder impact analysis grid is a very standard approach; therefore, I will spend time discussing the lesser known, but equally useful technique, stakeholder salience model.

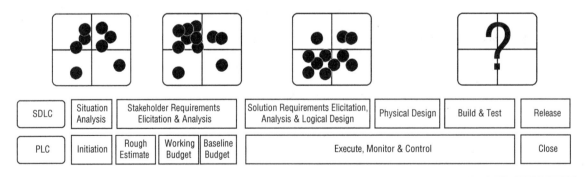

Figure 4.6 Impact influence grid PLC alignment

Establish Stakeholder Typology

Establishing stakeholder typology is a useful way to place our members into meaningful categories for further analysis and management. Some possible classifications include (there might be some overlap, but you'll get the idea):

- Acceptors, signatories, managers, supervisors, and owners
- Competitors and direct and indirect influencers
- Contractors, vendors, and suppliers
- Customers, clients, and direct and indirect users
- Environment, media, and special interest groups
- Internal and external governance
- Observers, opinion makers, and the general public
- Providers, consulters, general staff, and supporters

This list is also useful for identifying stakeholders. I often begin with document analysis, looking for stakeholders within process diagrams, policy statements, rules, use cases, data maps, and anything else I can get my hands on. After I begin my interviews with the stakeholders, I find the artifacts within. After each interview, I always ask for more potential sources.

Define Stakeholder Ranking Strategy

Once we are confident that we have a solid list of requirement stakeholders, it is time to rate them regarding their importance to our requirements and the influence they have over those requirements. Some of our considerations include:

- *ADKAR*: ADKAR refers to the stakeholder's *awareness* of the project, their *desire* to engage, the *knowledge* they have about the change, any *abilities* they have or require that will help with the change, and how we will *reinforce* new behaviors and compel cooperation, if necessary.
- *Value*: What will the stakeholder bring to the project? How valuable is this knowledge, expertise, or counsel? Are they a signatory, if so, for what, and when will they be needed?
- *Legitimacy*: How reasonable are the stakeholder's claims on the project and solution scope?
- *Necessity*: How dependent are we on this stakeholder? Will we need a backup if this person ranks high in necessity but low in engagement?

Other considerations include:

- How will we communicate (who, what, when, where, why, and how) and manage expectations?
- What are their concerns, assumptions, threats?
- What are they doing, how much will it cost, what is the effort, how efficient are they, how long will it take?
- What do I need to know to understand them as a resource?
- What do I need to know to understand them as a person?
- What are their needs as a project resource?
- What are their needs as a person?

- What can I do to help them?
- How can I win and maintain their support?

We must also consider how stakeholders will influence other stakeholders. For example, if *Stakeholder A* can affect the scope, how will that affect *Stakeholders B and C*. We document this relationship in a stakeholder map. "Stakeholder maps are diagrams that depict the relationship of stakeholders to the solution and one another" (IIBA 2015). Figure 4.7 illustrates an example of a simple stakeholder map.

Mendelow's Power/Influence Interest/Impact Grid

Since time immemorial this technique has been a standard almost everywhere. The Mendelow Matrix, as it is also known, was developed by Aubrey L. Mendelow at Kent State University in 1991. The model uses two dimensions—the level of power or influence that a stakeholder has over the project and its objectives, and the level of interest and impact they have on the project scope. Figure 4.8 represents a standard power/interest grid.

As you can observe, we only need to meet the expectations of the stakeholders who score within the top half of the grid. Figure 4.9 provides the standard key.

- Score = 20–25: high power and high interest. We must keep these stakeholders satisfied and meet their expectations (project objectives and stakeholder needs, issues, concerns, constraints, and the like). Their involvement is critical to success. These stakeholders must commit their time to the project. These stakeholders are usually the project's decision makers and typically own the project and solution scope. We may have one or two stakeholders from this group on our requirements team.

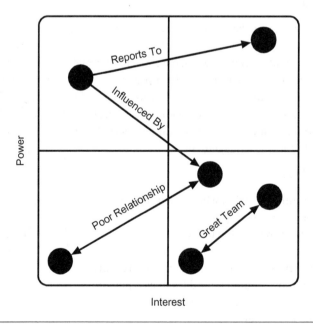

Figure 4.7   Stakeholder map example

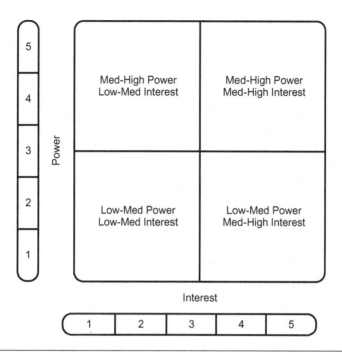

Figure 4.8   Mendelow power/interest grid

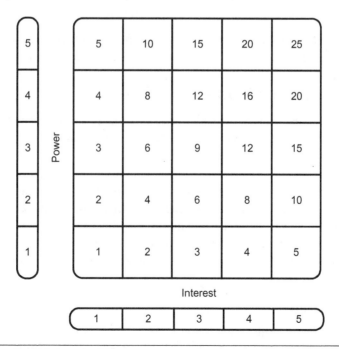

Figure 4.9   Mendelow power/interest grid key

- Score = 11–19: med-high power and med-high interest. Scoring second highest, we must do our best to meet these stakeholder's expectations only when they do not interfere with the stakeholders who scored higher. Project involvement is paramount to success. These stakeholders are usually team members. This group will make up the bulk of your requirements team.
- Score = 5–10: low-med power and med-high interest. We can expect to see some of these stakeholders on our requirements team. Their involvement is important but not critical to success. We should maintain regular communications and provide feedback on requirements status, as needed.
- Score = 1–4: low power and/or low interest. Scoring the lowest on the Mendelow Matrix, these are indeed stakeholders, but they do not have much of an impact on the project. Keeping them on a distribution list should suffice.

Mendelow's approach is the most commonly applied stakeholder classification technique used in project management. Next are some other ideas that I believe are worth sharing.

The Stakeholder Circle® Method

The Stakeholder Circle is a proprietary 5-step methodology that was developed by Lynda Bourne and Derek Walker. It is part of a larger stakeholder relationship maturity model (SRMM) developed by Stakeholder Management Pty Ltd. (Bourne and Walker 2008).

> *"The Stakeholder Circle is designed to manage the essential stakeholder engagement process needed for the success of a business change initiative, a project or a program. The methodology and tools focus on the integrated management of stakeholder relationships at all levels including project, program, portfolio and corporate to deliver value whilst meeting organizational CSR and sustainability objectives."*[6]

This model uses a radar metaphor to help identify and classify stakeholders in much the same way as most other models have done. Figure 4.10 shows us how the radar metaphor is applied.

The Stakeholder Salience Model

We understand organizational salience through social psychology and motivational theory. Within the context of requirements and project management, I organize salience in the following manner.

Psychological Salience

BAs must help their stakeholders focus the excessive demands on their perceptual and cognitive resources. It behooves us to help our stakeholders stay concentrated on the most pertinent information at the most suitable time. Stakeholders are very busy, and we must respect their time. "The hippocampus participates in the assessment of salience and context using" memories to filter new incoming stimuli by "placing those that are most important into long-term memory."[7] Therefore, we must take the time to filter information for our stakeholders.

Requirements Team Salience

Ronald K. Mitchell, Bradley R. Agle, and Donna J. Wood (1997) first used the term salience in project management in an article for *The Academy of Management Review*. Unlike the power/interest or

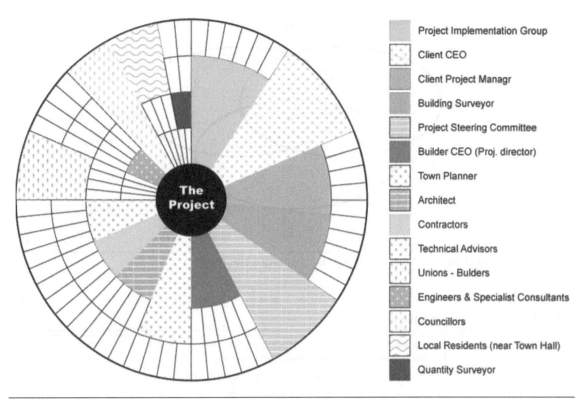

Figure 4.10   The Stakeholder Circle method (© 2010, Dr. Lynda Bourne)

power/influence grids that appear in both the *BABOK®* and *PMBOK® Guides*, the more complex salience model uses three measures to organize stakeholders: power, legitimacy, and urgency. Using set theory, each parameter, defined as follows, provides a multidimensional way of understanding project salience.

Power

Power describes the ability a project stakeholder has to influence the outcome of an organization, its goals, or its projects, and project scope/deliverables.

Legitimacy

Legitimacy is the actual authority or level of involvement that project stakeholders have on a project.

Urgency

This third parameter—urgency—is the time expected by project stakeholders for responses to their expectations. Adding this third dimension helps BAs understand how to organize their elicitation activities, how to approach issues, and what potential roadblocks stakeholders may put in the way. Figure 4.11 and Table 4.3 illustrate and describe the eight different salient types. Figure 4.12 shows us how stakeholders move locations on the model based on project conditions, stage, timelines, and other criteria.

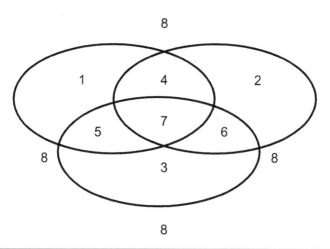

Figure 4.11   Project salience Venn diagram (© Mitchell, Agle, and Wood)

Table 4.3   Project salience table of terms

1	Core	These are the critical project stakeholders. As a BA, we need to provide focused attention to these stakeholders. Expectations must be met.
2	Dominant	Stakeholders with power and legitimacy, but do not have urgency.
3	Dependent	Project stakeholders with no real power on the project. Dependent stakeholders may align themselves with other more important interested parties and thus must still be managed.
4	Dangerous	Stakeholders who have power and urgency, but no legitimacy. These stakeholders may force their views on the project. Keep them suitably engaged and satisfied.
5	Latent	Latent stakeholders are present but not visible, apparent, or actualized until an event pulls them in, such as the project entering recovery mode.
6	Demanding	As the term suggests, demanding stakeholders believe their needs require immediate attention; careful management is required. BAs must be sure to identify claims before they become issues.
7	Discretionary	Discretionary project stakeholders require little more than regular status updates.
8	Non-stakeholders	Non-stakeholders cannot affect or are not affected, and thus are not stakeholders. We still need to know them, however, because they may become stakeholders later on.

Among all the stakeholders, regardless of which model you use, the ones for whom we are doing the project will always be your front stakeholders. Do not confuse that with the end users. They are consumers of our efforts. Indeed, they do receive and provide value, but the project is not for them, the project is for our highest influencers, impactors, the largest in legitimacy and the like—ultimately, the stakeholders formally receive and authorize the release of the project into production.

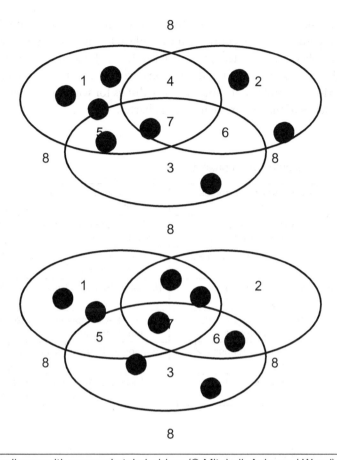

Figure 4.12   Project salience with mapped stakeholders (© Mitchell, Agle, and Wood)

Defining Expectations

We used to say a project was done well if it delivered on all of the (agreed to) requirements, finished on time, and stayed on budget. Things are much easier now (he writes with sarcasm)—all we have to do is meet our stakeholder's expectations, which implies meeting all of the (agreed to) requirements, finishing on time, staying on budget, and rules of engagement. The following is a list of conditions every project stakeholder must agree to:

- Accessible to me
- Courteous to me
- Responsive to me
- Prompt for me
- Well-trained and experienced
- Manage my needs, escalations, and exceptions/constraints and their changes and follow-up with me responsibly

Stakeholders certainly have expectations of us, but what about us of them? With the aid of stakeholders (remember this includes other members of the team), Table 4.4 provides a numbered list of all the activities that a BA is responsible for on a typical project (IIBA 2015). Table 4.5 illustrates stakeholder responsibilities. Based on Table 4.5 and many of the discussions we have had throughout this book so far, Table 4.6, in no particular order, is a joint list of expectations—things for which we are equally responsible. This accountability is the essence of the requirements team charter.

Table 4.4   BA responsibilities on a typical project

1. Plan Business Analysis Approach	2. Conduct Stakeholder Analysis	3. Plan Business Analysis Activities	4. Plan Business Analysis Communication
5. Plan Requirements Management Process	6. Manage Business Analysis Performance	7. Manage Solution Scope and Requirements	8. Manage Requirements Traceability
9. Manage Requirements Risks	10. Prepare Requirements Package	11. Communicate Requirements	12. Define Business Need
13. Assess Capability Gaps	14. Determine Solution Approach	15. Define Business Case	16. Prioritize Requirements
17. Organize Requirements	18. Specify and Model Requirements	19. Define Assumptions and Constraints	20. Verify Requirements
21. Validate Requirements	22. Assess Proposed Solution	23. Allocate Requirements	24. Assess Organizational Readiness
25. Define Transition Requirements	26. Validate Solution	27. Assist with Transition	28. Evaluate Solution Performance

Table 4.5   Stakeholder project responsibilities

1. Provide Input for Business Case	2. Define High-level Scope	3. Participate in Stakeholder Analysis	4. Provide Input to BA Activities
5. Provide Current State	6. Provide Target State	7. Provide Input for Proposed Solution	8. Assist with Requirements Work Breakdown Structure
9. Participate in Requirements Team Charter	10. Provide Communication Needs	11. Provide Input on Requirement Risks	12. Help in Preparation of Requirements Package
13. Provide Input for Change Management Plan	14. Approve Specified and Modeled Requirements	15. Provide Input for Assumptions and Constraints	16. Provide Input for Baselining Requirements
17. Provide Input for Change Requests	18. Approve Change Requests	19. Assess Proposed Solution through UAT	20. Provide Input for Organizational Readiness
21. Provide Input for Transition Requirements	22. Provide Input Data for Solution Performance	23. Provide Final Acceptance of Project Deliverables	24. Assist BA with Transition

Table 4.6   Joint requirements expectations

The business analyst as the requirements lead	Get involved in the business case process	Use a controlled range of requirements success	Participate in the stakeholder analysis process
Respect team roles and responsibilities	Each deliverable has its own RACI	Respond to requests in a timely manner (3-day e-mail triage)	Respect the requirements process and provide all possible input, upon request
Respect the issue escalation process	Respect the communications plan	Respect the change management process	Attend meetings marked as *required*
Get involved in the planning process early	Take advantage of a shared requirements portal	Allow for training, as needed	Take part in acceptance testing, as needed
Make time for the requirements process	Use a shared list of *to-dos* such as Kanban	Rely on our intrinsic ability to motivate ourselves	Make ourselves available for learning and training
The project is important and deserves our time	Reach consensus on all decisions, whenever possible	Show each other our work in small bits, as it progresses	Collaborate as much as possible
Give honest non-judgmental feedback to each other	Meet daily to discuss accomplishments, objectives, and roadblocks	Approve requirements incrementally and often	Assist with transition to operations

If our stakeholders expect a unicorn riding a magic carpet and holding Aladdin's lamp, then it is our fault! A requirements team charter forms the foundation through which we manage our stakeholders and lead them to the success they depend on us to deliver.

Our requirements team charter will help us develop the team, set and manage all expectations, establish a unified direction, create boundaries, set communication channels, and motivate the team to get involved often and early. Investing the few days it may take to assemble a charter like this will reduce confusion, provide a sense of purpose, and clearly establish what the stakeholders expect of us and what we must expect of them. The result is a functioning team spending less time on rework and change requests and more time providing quality requirements. This is the foundation of an adaptive team.

REFERENCES AND ADDITIONAL SUGGESTED READINGS

Belbin, R Meredith. 2010 Management Teams: Why They Succeed or Fail. Taylor & Francis.

Bourne, Lynda. 2009. *Stakeholder Relationship Management: A Maturity Model for Organisational Implementation*. Routledge.

Bourne, Lynda and Derek H. T. Walker. 2008. "Project Relationship Management and the Stakeholder Circle." *International Journal of Managing Projects in Business* 1, pp. 125–30.

Chanakya, Kautilya. 2016. *Kautilya's Arthashastra*. CreateSpace Independent Publishing Platform.

Cohen, Allan R. and David L. Bradford. 2005. "The Influence Model: Using Reciprocity and Exchange to Get What You Need." *Journal of Organizational Excellence* 25, no. 1, pp. 57–80.

———. 2005. *Influence Without Authority* (2nd Edition). Wiley.

Darboe, Kebba. 2002. *An Empirical Study of the Social Correlates of Job Satisfaction Among Plant Science Graduates of a Mid-Western University: A Test of Victor H. Vroom's (1964) Expectancy Theory*. UPA.

Eerde, W. Van and H. Thierry. 1996. "Vroom's Expectancy Models and Work-Related Criteria: A Meta-Analysis." *Journal of Applied Psychology*.

Fisher, Roger, William L. Ury, and Bruce Patton. 2011. Getting to Yes: Negotiating Agreement Without Giving in. Penguin Books.

Hamilton, W. D. 1964. Genetical evolution of social behaviour I & II. *J Theor Biol*. 7, no. 1, pp. 1–52.

Heneman, H. G. and D. P. Schwab. 1972. "Evaluation of Research on Expectancy Theory Predictions of Employee Performance." *Psychological Bulletin*.

IIBA. 2015. *A Guide to the Business Analysis Body of Knowledge (BABOK Guide®)*. International Institute of Business Analysis.

Isaac, R. G., W. J. Zerbe, and D. C. Pitt. 2001. "Leadership and Motivation: The Effective Application of Expectancy Theory." *Journal of Managerial Issues*.

Mitchell, Ronald K., Bradley R. Agle, and Donna J. Wood. 1997. "Toward a Theory of Stakeholder Identification and Salience: Defining the Principle of Who and What Really Counts." *Academy of Management Review* 22, no. 4, pp. 853–86.

Project Management Institute. 2015. *Business Analysis for Practitioners: A Practice Guide*. Project Management Institute.

Van Eerde, W. and H. Thierry. 1996. "Vroom's Expectancy Models and Work-Related Criteria: A Meta-Analysis.," *Journal of Applied Psychology*.

Vroom, Victor H. 1994. *Work and Motivation*. Jossey-Bass.

Vroom, Victor H. and Philip W. Yetton. 1973. *Leadership and Decision Making*. University of Pittsburgh Press.

ENDNOTES

1. Belbin Team Roles | Belbin, http://www.belbin.com/about/belbin-team-roles/ (accessed June 26, 2016).
2. Home | Belbin, http://www.belbin.com/ (accessed July 04, 2016).
3. The model refers to these five items as related factors. I like to think of them as currency. Some people trade in things that will inspire them, others want recognition, and still others desire an exchange of something practical, such as time off or money.

4. *Plans Are Useless, but Planning is Indispensable.* https://stickybranding.com/plans-are-useless-but-planning-is-indispensable/ (accessed July 20, 2016).

5. The REPAC model itself is also a good tool for finding stakeholders. Each of its set members are themselves stakeholders.

6. *Stakeholder Management—Stakeholder Engagement Analytics.* http://www.stakeholdermapping.com/index.php (accessed July 22, 2016).

7. Salience (neuroscience)—Wikipedia, the free encyclopedia, https://en.wikipedia.org/wiki/Physical saliency (accessed June 22, 2016).

5

COMMUNICATING FOR CLARITY

"The way a team plays as a whole determines its success. You may have the greatest bunch of individual stars in the world, but if they don't play together, the club won't be worth a dime."
—Babe Ruth

Communication, communication, communication! Where to start? I could fill dozens of books three times the size of this one and still not scratch the surface. Not to put things too lightly, but our entire civilization depends on this one word. When we begin our exploration of the depth of perspective—in particular, qualitative analysis—much of what we discuss here will directly associate with how we analyze communication in all its forms. Although there is much more we could consider, I believe that these choices cover most of our profession. Before we dive in, however, let us dispel a few myths about non-colocated teams.

From a conceptual standpoint, there is no significant difference between how virtual projects and traditional projects manage. We still need to track progress, meet objectives, and satisfy critical stakeholders. Virtual teams do, however, present unique challenges that we must address. It was reasoned that virtual teams could not match the productivity of colocated teams, but more recent studies indicate that virtual teams (with proper preparation and management) can match or even exceed the productivity of face-to-face groups. A virtual team's success cannot depend solely on the skill level of its members. Assembling a unit of the best and the brightest isn't enough to guarantee success. Team members need to know how to communicate, collaborate, and make decisions as a team. Many virtual organizations benefit from targeted training in these areas early in the project. Some challenges include:

- Lack of face-to-face meetings and informal chats
- Cultural differences add complexity
- More time is needed for virtual team members to get started, trust one another, and feel a sense of belonging
- Members often depend on communication technologies

Our need for tactile experience diminishes the sense of *realness* for some stakeholders. We mistakenly put our trust in advanced technologies, fallaciously believing that these tools will solve our communication issues. While a certain amount of technology is necessary for virtual teams to succeed, the human element is far more critical. Managing virtual projects requires a lot of communication, expectation setting, self-organization, and problem solving. A group of people who work interdependently, dedicated to breaking boundaries with a shared purpose, can be satisfied across any amount of space or time. As with any team, non-colocated teams require:

- Defined roles and tasks
- Extensive quality checks and balances
- A step-wise mindset
- An effective means to mediate conflicts and reduce issues
- An agreed-upon approach toward problem solving and decision making
- Open and dependable lines of communication that are available at all times
- Operating and social norms
- Ongoing performance assessment

As with the agile mindset, virtual teams must first establish a set of attitudes before they engage in non-colocated project work. Effective teams have a core group of individuals that do not frequently change over the course of the project. Virtual units work better if they are smaller due to the added layer of virtual communication. Selecting the right team is critical. Members must be comfortable working alone for extended periods without direction and be self-motivated. When assembling your team, in addition to experience and skill level, consider potential team members' communication skills, work ethic, and ability to make decisions for themselves. Strong team members are:

- Very sensitive to peoples' needs and cultural differences
- Effective communicators and collaborators
- Fair, brave, transparent, and honest
- Considered to have a servant leader mindset
- Deemed to have a high degree of emotional intelligence (EI)
- Loyal about listening to and respecting their teammates' feelings and ideas
- Participative and critical thinkers with an open mind
- Trusted to share responsibility and pick up the slack without question
- Faithful to respect and attend all meetings on time and then end all meetings on time
- Committed to coming to meetings prepared to work and solve problems
- Efficient and effective managers of tasks, resources, and time
- Comfortable with working independently
- Very comfortable with communication technology
- Of a mindset that embraces adaptiveness and trust

A team must form a highly developed culture that facilitates trust and openness. Teams that maintain an environment of trust and focus on behaviors (as opposed to personalities or stereotypes) tend to be more efficient. If you have not noticed by now, the elements discussed for virtual teams are just as relevant to colocated teams. In fact, I led into the previous bulleted list with "Strong team members are:" A team member is a stakeholder, thus I could have just as easily led into that list with "Strong stakeholders are:" Regardless, we must all understand the fundamentals of communication.

CLASSIFICATIONS OF COMMUNICATION

Projects, in their simplest form, are just people exchanging words and deeds. Almost everything starts with communication. The five basic types of communication and what they mean to us are elaborated on in the following subsections.

Rhetorical

As project professionals, we use rhetoric as a means to persuade and motivate our stakeholders. Since rhetoric is a type of discourse intended to drive and impress an audience, we sometimes see it as lacking in sincerity or meaningful content. This means we have to combine our rhetoric with critical analysis. When we speak in small bits and only have a short amount of time to get our point across, we sometimes use rhetorical statements to emphasize our message.

Business or Technical

The most common communication style that we use is classified as business or technical communication. This book is a mixture of academic, business/technical, and a dash of interpersonal for good measure. Although these are different classifications, I will include socio-psychological and socio-cultural communication, as we rely on them in our daily conversations with our stakeholders.

A large part of our lives as project professionals is working with stakeholders in a social and behavioral manner. We need to understand how our stakeholder's thoughts, feelings, and behaviors are influenced by the actual, imagined, or implied presence of others, and how they affect the processes and systems that they work on daily. Socio-cultural communication is relevant to us as we try to understand and work with social orders of other cultural groups.

Semiotic

Equally important to us as project professionals is semiotic communication. Each time you draw a process diagram, use case design, or some other model you are using signs, which is the core of semiotics. In fact, the process of semiosis is a preferred way to convey requirements. Words can often be confusing and misunderstood, whereas symbolic languages such as Unified Modeling Language and Business Process Modeling Notation both offer organizations the capability to understand circumstances, procedures, and transactions in a standard (and globally accepted) graphical method.

Phenomenological

As we attempt to uncover the objects of direct experience that lead to business matters such as reductions in process quality or poorly executed projects, we find ourselves struggling to identify empirical relationships between cause and effect.

Cybernetics

The last classification important to us is cybernetics.[1] I am not referring to the *Terminator* series' Cyberdyne Systems or ". . . a cybernetic organism, living tissue over a metal endoskeleton."[2] For us, cybernetics is concerned with the comparative study of automatic control schemes, as in mechanical-electrical communication systems. Cybernetics, in project management and business analysis, is transdisciplinary, meaning it crosses many domain boundaries. In a simple example, we may want to understand how a group of users interact with a complex rule-based information management system within a highly predictive organizational culture shifting to an adaptive mindset. In this small example, four disparate disciplines—regulatory analysis, information theory, human interfaces, and organizational psychology—interact, creating a holistic communication approach. Cybernetic communication provides a means for examining the design and function of any system, including the social networks that govern organizational management. Our purpose is always focused on increasing efficiency and effectiveness.

COMMUNICATION MODELS

Communication models help explain the processes we go through as we try to exchange information through a medium. Regardless of speech, intent, or form, the communication process is essentially the same:

- First, we express the intent to communicate
- Then, we cognitively form the message
- Next, we encode the message into a medium—such as speech or symbols on a page
- The message is then transmitted through the medium as a series of bytes

Once the message has been received, the receiver cognitively reconstructs the message and attempts to understand it as intended. As with many things, the *devil is in the details*.

Linear Communication

Anything linear follows a straight path; this includes communication. Discussion follows known cycles or step-by-step progressions where a message takes the form of a packet. The packet, once received by a listener, is processed based on myriad factors, some of which include their relationship to the sender and their own *worldview* up to that moment in time and physical noise that might degrade the message. Once the receiver processes the message, they usually respond in kind.

We can find the application of linear communication in the Socratic method, which is a form of inquiry and debate between two or more people with opposing ideas. Each participant asks and answers questions to stimulate rational thought and illuminate ideas; therefore, it follows that: if a = b, and b = c, then a = c—it's that simple!

The Sender

Communication is a two-way method that begins with a sender. The responsibility is on the originator to provide clarity and precision. Too often, however, what is said is not always what we *hear*. A good communicator remembers to:

- State one idea at a time
- State ideas simply
- Not act superior or patronizing

- Explain when appropriate
- Repeat if appropriate
- Encourage feedback

The sender must also take into account:

- *Effective communication skills*: traits such as diction, cadence, enunciation, clarity, listening, presentation, reading, and writing are the beginning of a valid message packet. If not, proper discourse cannot occur. We are accountable every day as professionals to adjust our patterns to suit all stakeholders.
- *Attitudes*: also an important factor in communication. The views of the members involved create positive or negative responses. This is part of the behavioral context.
- *Familiarity*: the subject of the message must be at a reasonable level of understanding. Also, we must consider cultural differences, social factors, values, beliefs, laws, rules, and context.

The Message

The message is solely the information that the sender wants to communicate to the receiver. To reduce potential problems, the sender should:

- Use correct terminology (standard commands)
- Speak clearly
- Send the message at a time when the receiver will be able to listen

Messages should come across as imperative. Even when asked in the form of a question, the question should be structured to motivate an immediate response. Picking an appropriate time to send the message is important; we want to be relevant to the receiver, not a distraction.

When forming a message, ensure that it is inclusive and informative. Inclusively constructed messages refer to the content—everything the receiver needs to understand and act upon in the message. Informative messages are things that the receiver should know or needs to know. The key factors affecting the message are:

- Content and the contexts previously discussed
- Elements of nonverbal gestures, morae (syllable weight), rhythm, signs, phonological patterns, and phonemes
- Treatment of the message, such as volume, tone, impact, and conveyance, in order to make an impression, feeling, or idea known, understandable, and impactful
- Structure and arrangement of the sounds and words of a logical and grammatically accurate packet
- The encoding or form the message packet takes—text, voice, video, or some other combination

The Channel

A message may use one or more mediums simultaneously. In today's business environments, media include mostly electronic devices such as texting and e-mail. We may consider organizational channels in the following groups:

- Face-to-face (meetings, interviews, and workshops)
- Corporate games

- Broadcast media (posters, banners, newsletters, and magazines)
- Mobile, electronic, written
- Hybrid channels that combine different media

The Receiver

Active receivers verify their understanding of the message. They consider words, tone, and body language when they give feedback. Forms of feedback include:

- Acknowledging that the message has been received
- Using our mirror neurons to mimic behavior
- Parroting—repeating back verbatim the words of the speaker
- Paraphrasing or rephrasing in your own words the content of the sender's message to the sender's satisfaction
- Confirming that the message was decoded and understood

The receiver needs a clearly delivered message in order to be effective. Moreover, the receiver must also be a good listener. Regrettably, most people find listening difficult. Receivers should exert control over the communication process since they are the ones who must act on the message. On some level, the sender and the receiver must be on the same page on understanding. When this is not the situation, it is incumbent upon the sender to deliver the message in a way that it will be understood. We sometimes call this *speaking to the lowest common denominator*. I have never liked this expression.

Barriers and Filters

Sometimes communication noise is just that—noise. Often, however, barriers and filters come from other sources including internal biases or organizational concerns such as a poorly evolved corporate culture. I classify communication noise, filters, and barriers as follows:

- Organizational
- Personal
- Semantic
- Physical

Organizational barriers include negative climates or inadequate support from management. Highly structured functional environments where policies are either very restrictive or unknown may also contribute to ineffective communication. In severe cases, information may be intentionally filtered, implying the willful distortion of facts. Sadly, some stakeholders use their status and power to affect changes. In most cases, this does not engender trust—making communication ineffective.

Personal barriers, such as the ones we experience within ourselves and with others, are a major contributor to failed communication. It can be tough to insulate yourself from how you feel about the information or the person giving it. This requires mental training. We process information differently and at different rates. If we inundate our stakeholders with too much, too soon, their anxiety will rise causing them to generate barriers as a means of protection. Without proper care and training, we create faulty expressions to our stakeholders. The message fails to convey your intended meaning to the receiver. Lack of clarity, vague terms, poorly expressed knowledge, or a complex organization of ideas are some causes of faulty expressions.

Also, we all have unique perceptual differences that may clash. We cover perception later in the Requirements, Elicitation, Planning, Analysis, and Collaboration Framework™ (REPAC®) as a means to address this very problem. I have mentioned fear and anxiety a few times already as a major contributor to communication issues. I have also seen stereotyping, the halo effect, and general intention as barriers. The halo effect cognitive bias is one in which we allow ourselves to become influenced by our feelings rather than reason or logic.

Semantic distortions—deliberate or accidental—arise when misunderstandings stem from the different ways in which we interpret words and symbols. Cultural differences will often mix with semantic issues. An example where I have seen this as a barrier and a filter in many requirements documents over the years would be: *The system will allow the end user to enter information faster than before*. Before what?

Physical barriers are just that; the noise either preventing someone from hearing the message or cognitively distracting us from decoding and processing the message.

Enhancers to communication are considered attributes. These include such things as speaking with enthusiasm, describing appealing results, and adjusting how you communicate to match your listener's reactions, message by message. This is not easy. Learning how to be an effective communicator takes time and dedication.

EFFECTIVE COMMUNICATION STYLES

Consider thinking about your discussions, interviews, workshops, focus groups, requirements documents, and other artifacts as objects filled with discrete *bits*. Each sentence becomes an individual packet of data. As a stand-alone object, what must be contained in that packet so that the receiver can understand it? Deconstruct your thoughts into bits and build each piece into sentences that inexorably link to each other, creating a coherent set of concepts. Work on communicating the absolute minimum number of words needed to get the point across.

Communication theory maintains that there are only three elements needed for basic linear communication—a transmitter, a channel, and a receiver. If I send you an e-mail asking you to come to a requirements workshop, I am the transmitter or message source; the e-mail and server are the channels or media; and you, of course, are the receiver. As a transmitter of information, I am only able to send a finite number of messages per communication cycle.

Getting back to our requirements workshop example, let us imagine that I, the source or sender, only have one agenda item to cover—one message. The chance that you, the receiver, will receive this message through the medium of the workshop is 100%. As I continue to add bits of information to the workshop, the uncertainty that all messages will be correctly received and understood increases. Too much information increases the risk of high dissipation of the intent of our message. We should use as few bits as possible to convey the most information in a single bit.

Complicated messages are difficult to decode and understand. Reduce your meetings, workshops, business requirements documents, and other project communications to small, easy-to-transmit bits that are fully encapsulated within their context. Keep your information in the bull's-eye, not spread all over the target. You can do this by using a simple marketing technique that is designed to get a message across in a few moments.

Former director of talent and casting for CBS Television, Milo Frank (1922–2004), is best known for his book *How to Get Your Point Across in 30 Seconds or Less*. He identified a very useful way to compress your communicative intentions into easy-to-understand bits, as we have been discussing. These established techniques give us the ability to share information quickly, precisely, and powerfully. Before you speak or write something, ask yourself:

- What SMART (specific, measurable, actionable, realistic, time-bound) objectives do I want to convey for every message bit?
- Have I researched my need thoroughly?
- Can I answer questions, if challenged?
- Have I researched my listener thoroughly?
- Can I address my listener's needs?
- What is my central theme?
- Which words will best convey the importance of my need?
- Is my request reasonable?
- Can I build a convincing case around my needs?
- Is this a stand-alone request or will it lead to other bits coalescing into an overall thesis?
- How do my needs relate to the listener?

Whether you are writing an e-mail, conducting a workshop, negotiating for a resource, building a requirements specifications package, or just engaging in a simple conversation, this is an invaluable training tool because it focuses on the minimum number of bits necessary to make a point. Each statement becomes a self-contained, fully structured thought that is designed to motivate action.

NONLINEAR COMMUNICATION

Nonlinear communication is a way of using language in a creative rather than logical way. Some believe that nonlinear thinkers create a mental picture as a means to understand the messages they are receiving. An example of this phenomenon might be: you are talking to someone and when they say something, it creates an image in your mind and you focus more on the picture in your mind to come up with a response instead of responding to the words that were contained in the message.

VAK Communication and Learning Style

Many people are visual learners, but not all. Thus, we must determine which style works best with which stakeholder. We use all three modalities to understand information. However, according to the VAK or modality theory, one or two of the theory's styles plays a dominant role in our learning.

Developed by educator and author Walter Burke Barbe and his colleagues, the VAK theory[3] provides a guide to the three basic styles of learning—visual, auditory, and kinesthetic/tactile (Barbe, Milone, and Swassing 1988). According to the theory, we want to present information using all three styles. This allows all stakeholders the opportunity to become involved, no matter what may be their preferred style. VAK theorists break the model into three forms:

- *Visual*: a visually-dominant learner uses pictures, diagrams, and charts as a means to absorb information—think semiotics
- *Auditory*: an auditory-dominant learner responds to voices, workshops, lectures, or group discussions
- *Kinesthetic*: the kinesthetic-dominant learner likes the *hands-on* approach

Visually-Dominant

Visually-dominant stakeholders:

- Use visual language ("I can see what you're saying")
- Remember images and charts quickly (spatial)
- Enjoy watching and observing (spatial)
- Quickly remember what they read (linguistic)
- Prefer to write down directions (linguistic)
- *See* words (linguistic)

Trigger words for visually-dominant stakeholders include the examples that can be seen in Table 5.1. When communicating with visual stakeholders try to:

- Use graphs, charts, illustrations, or other visual aids
- Emphasize key points that will cue them when to take notes
- Eliminate visual distractions
- Leave white space in handouts for note-taking
- Encourage questions to help them stay alert in auditory environments
- Post flip-charts to show what will come and what has been presented
- Encourage stakeholders to create their own diagrams
- Ask stakeholders to envision the topic
- Ask them to act out requirements scenarios

Table 5.1   Visual communication cues

Appears to me	It's right under your nose
Clear cut	Let me paint you a picture
Getting a mental picture	Look at what happened
I can see it now	My perspective on this
I see what you mean	Now see here
I see where you are going	See eye to eye
In light of	See what I mean
It appears more clear now	Sight for sore eyes
It's a little foggy	You can plainly see

Auditory-Dominant

Auditory-dominant stakeholders:

- Tend to talk to themselves as they work through problems
- Are often Socratic (systematic doubt and questioning toward truth)
- May move their lips when reading to themselves
- Tend to have a busy internal monologue
- Make great listeners
- Remember who said what and when
- Conclude with a summary rather than specifics
- Prefer to listen or read rather than watch and participate

Trigger words for auditory-dominant stakeholders include examples from Table 5.2. When communicating with auditory stakeholders try to:

- Set up what you plan to say, say it, then follow up
- Speak clearly and accurately
- Provide detailed verbal instructions
- Create connections between them and the project
- Review material before, during, and after a meeting
- Use auditory language (*be loud and clear*)
- Allow time to *talk* through problems and tasks

Table 5.2   Auditory communication cues

Get a hold of yourself	Listen to what I am saying
As clear as a bell	Little voice in my head
Bite your tongue	Pay more attention
Break the silence	That rings a bell
Describe in detail	Within hearing range
Hold your tongue	Giving me an earful
In a manner of speaking	You sound confused

Kinesthetic-Dominant

Kinesthetic-dominant stakeholders:

- Do best while touching and moving
- Tend to lose concentration if there is little or no external stimulation or movement
- Get the big picture first, then look for details
- Typically use color highlighters and take notes by drawing pictures, diagrams, or doodling
- Enjoy physical contact
- May feel overwhelmed in a verbal conflict

Trigger words for kinesthetic-dominant stakeholders include the examples found in Table 5.3. When communicating with kinesthetic stakeholders try to:

- Use activities that get the stakeholders up and moving
- Play music, when appropriate, during activities
- Use color markers to emphasize key points
- Provide toys to give them something to do with their hands
- Guide through a visualization of complex tasks

Table 5.3   Kinesthetic communication cues

Get a hold of yourself	Keep your shirt on
Hard as nails	Let's move away from that
Hot headed	My gut is telling me
I feel this is right	Sharp as a tack
I sense that	Starting from scratch
It boils down to	They go hand in hand
It slipped my mind	When push comes to shove

No one person has a single mode of communication, but we each have our preferences. When communicating to a broad audience, it is important to have a little of something for everyone.

If you, for example, retain information primarily by visual and kinesthetic, then you remember things better when you see it—but even better when you do and *feel* the thing you are trying to remember. The business analyst must be able to optimize their communication style to other people. After you get an understanding of your personal communication/learning style, you can apply the same concept to help communicate effectively to others.

Being able to coordinate with the other person's primary communication style allows you to be a more effective communicator. For instance, if a person has a high visual modality, then using effective gestures and facial expressions will help get the message across. Alternatively, if the individual has an active auditory modality, then having a clear voice and tonal variety will be your best bet.

EFFECTIVE COMMUNICATION MANAGEMENT

Feelings of loyalty, enthusiasm, and devotion among stakeholders comes from effective communication. Effective communication is rooted in a deep understanding of ourselves and each other. It's not rocket science. Being mindful and sensitive to the cues given to you by others will help avoid conflict in most situations. Taking a page from the Myers-Briggs Type Indicator® (MBTI®), Table 5.4 gives us some hints on how to communicate with different personalities.

The MBTI bases its theories on *the four personality archetypes*, and both base their ideas on the opinions of the founder of analytical psychology, Carl Jung (1875–1961). Although there are dimensions in the MBTI, the ideas are more or less the same.

Table 5.4 Tips for effective communication across personalities

Introvert to Extrovert	State your issues openly. Do not leave others to guess what you might be thinking.
Extrovert to Introvert	Take time to listen and give introverts the time they need to think and reflect before they respond.
Sensors to Intuitives	Personal experience tends to make sensors overconfident in their opinions and conclusions. Don't overgeneralize; confidence is not the same as truth.
Intuitives to Sensors	Use facts, figures, and citations when expressing opinions. We gain their confidence when we use reliable information.
Thinkers to Feelers	Thinkers consider their reason and objectivity to be virtues. This may be seen as callous. Take the time to use empathy and appreciate other's emotive thoughts.
Feelers to Thinkers	Get to the point! Remember thinkers do not like a lot of time-consuming conversation.
Judgers to Perceivers	Do not jump to conclusions. Judgers tend to make fast decisions and then move on. The need for closure can cause premature decisions.
Perceivers to Judgers	Do not be vague. Perceivers prefer to keep options open, as a just in case. However, lack of decisions can present issues for the project. Judgers see this as unpreparedness.

Resolving Conflict Constructively

There is nothing wrong with conflict. Life is rather dull without it. Conflict is just opposition arising from incompatible expectations. It is neither good nor bad, but it must be managed to achieve a successful outcome. Stakeholders base their arguments on their patterns and belief systems—all of which we have thoroughly explored. You already have the tools to manage conflict but what do we do when our best efforts are unsuccessful and we cannot handle an emotional situation? Should we disengage—avoid? Remember, that is a lose/lose response. We need to figure out what barriers are preventing reason and discourse.

Barriers are determining factors that hinder or break down a continuous communication loop. Based on myriad factors, they may obstruct, misrepresent, or modify the message package. Using all the theories, models, tips, and such that we have discussed thus far, we can identify the barriers and apply countermeasures, reopening the flow of message looping. Communication breakdown is the leading cause of unhappiness and dissatisfaction in the workplace.

Table 5.5 gives us a small sample of workplace communication barriers; naturally, the list goes on. A stakeholder's entrenched logic often limits behaviors, thus forcing responses such as, "It has always been

Table 5.5 Workplace barriers to communication

Non-/Too-assertive behavior	Inappropriate priorities
Task preoccupation	Organizational culture
Anger or frustration	Distractions
Personal bias	Tunnel vision
Team diversity	Interruptions
Lack of training/confidence	Rank differences
Poor planning	Poor management

done this way." Organizational culture reinforces prescribed ways of thinking about situations and people and the ways in which we should respond. Putting all of this together creates a fascinating model that I like to call *From Data to Wisdom: An Information, Knowledge, Understanding, and Wisdom Processing System* (IKUW), as seen through our external and internal world, and detailed in Figure 5.1.

Communication comes in the form of data packets. Data informs us once we perceive the context. Barriers such as physical, biological, cross-cultural, social-psychological, organizational, and others affect how we conceive the data packets. Contextual elements often present as obstacles. Reason, understanding, knowledge, and wisdom help us understand contextual frameworks and the world around us. Entropy—often described as the degree of unpredictability, disorder, or randomness in a system—interferes with the transformation of data into information through natural degradation of the scheme and its inability or unavailability over time to provide useful work for the receiver. The older the data, the more entropy it has experienced. Naturally, this process, although mechanically the same for all of us, is very different when we consider the knowledge one has and the general personality one carries that affects that experience. Two monologues do not a dialogue make!

Within the cognitive subsystem, there is a cognitive bias known as illusory superiority. We observe this as the Dunning–Kruger effect. This bias is vital since it can derail an entire dialogue in a single blow. This phenomenon was first noted and studied by Psychologists David Dunning, professor of psychology at the University of Michigan, and his then graduate student Justin Kruger, now of New York University. The Dunning-Kruger effect has an affect on those whom we might refer to as *low-ability*. This theory is not about intelligence, but rather a lack of knowledge, experience, and wisdom. The bias creates false superiority. We tend to assess our ability as much higher than it is.

> *"The trouble with ignorance is that it feels so much like expertise."*

> *"We Are All Confident Idiots"*

> *—David Dunning, Pacific Standard*

The Dunning-Kruger effect is a general incapacity to recognize our ineptitude and evaluate our competence accurately.

We all suffer from this to some degree. We lessen its effects through careful evaluation of data and the building of accurate citable knowledge and wisdom. The research also suggests—and I admit, I am immensely guilty of this—that those with high abilities may underestimate their own competence and assume that tasks that are easy for them are also easy for others. According to the research that I have done, this bias seems to stem from the illusions and assumptions we create about ourselves, the judgments we place on others (teasing and blaming), and our inability to trust and be honest with each other and each other's knowledge and abilities.

The less you know, the more you think you know—or, a little information can be harmful. Conversely, the more we learn, the more we identify with how little we know—and the more we cannot understand why others don't *just get it*. As a Socratic paradox, we might joke, "I know that I know nothing" or "I know one thing; that I know nothing."

The more ways that people are *different* from each other, the more effort will be required to communicate and achieve a productive outcome from interpersonal relationships. Personality and behavior interact to create and maintain interpersonal relationships. Others can see and respond only to our behavior; we can see and respond only to theirs.

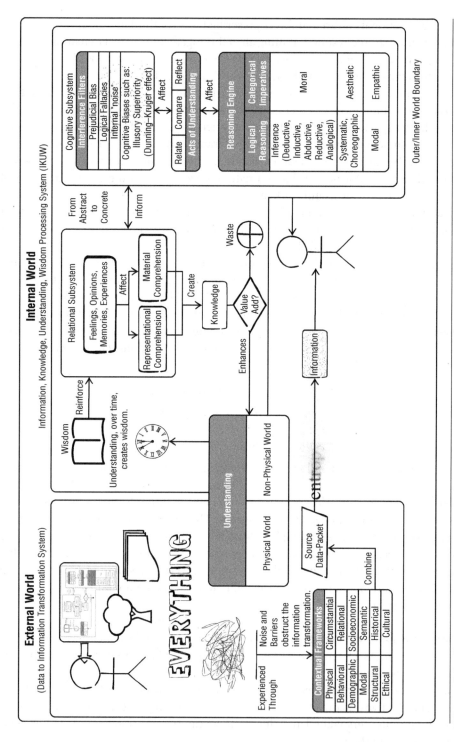

Figure 5.1   From data to wisdom: an IKUW (© The New BA, Ltd.)

We have spent the last several chapters taking a critical look at our stakeholders and requirements team. In our next chapter, we will assemble the document that will carry us through the rest of the REPAC Framework—the requirements team charter.

REFERENCES AND ADDITIONAL SUGGESTED READINGS

Barbe, W. B., M. N. Milone, and R. H. Swassing. 1988. *Teaching Through Modality Strengths: Concepts and Practices.* Zaner-Bloser.

Dennis, Richard. "Notes from "How to Get Your Point Across in 30 Seconds or Less" by Milo O. Frank."

Frank, Milo O. 1990. *How to Get Your Point Across in 30 Seconds or Less.* Gallery Books.

Littlejohn, Stephen W. and Karen A. Foss. 2010. *Theories of Human Communication.* Waveland Press, Inc.

Mehrabian, Albert. 1971. *Silent Messages: Implicit Communication of Emotions and Attitudes.* Wadsworth Publishing.

Mehrabian, Albert. *Nonverbal Communication.* Aldine Transaction, 2007.

Thompson, Jeff, PhD. 2011. "Is Nonverbal Communication a Numbers Game?" *Psychology Today* Blog, Beyond Words.

ENDNOTES

1. Cybernetics is the scientific study of how people, animals, and machines control and communicate [data and] information. (Cybernetics | Definition of Cybernetics by Merriam-Webster, http://www.merriam-webster.com/dictionary/cybernetics (accessed August 15, 2016).
2. Terminator 2: Judgment Day—Wikiquote, https://en.wikiquote.org/wiki/Terminator2 (accessed August 19, 2016).
3. Visual, Auditory, and Kinesthetic Learning Styles (VAK), http://nwlink.com/.

6

THE TEAM CHARTER

"The greater the loyalty of a group toward the group, the greater is the motivation among the members
to achieve the goals of the group, and the greater the probability that the group will achieve its goals."
—Rensis Likert

Rensis Likert (1903–1981) was an American psychologist primarily known for developing the 5-point Likert scale, a bipolar psychometric model. If you have ever completed a survey, you have seen this scale in action. Do you: strongly agree or strongly disagree; neither agree nor disagree; agree or strongly agree?

Psychometrics or psychological measurement is a field of study concerned with the objective measurement of knowledge, abilities, attitudes, personality traits, and educational achievement. Likert's quote expresses a simple feedback loop. The greater we work together as a team, the better we will get along and the more motivated we become to achieve our objectives, which increases the odds that we will reach these goals—the greater we work together.

Although Likert was a psychologist, his contributions in organizational management encouraged managers to coordinate teams more efficiently. Likert established the theory of participative management, which has since become a way to engage employees on equal footing. Likert's techniques are also used to shape the field of social and organizational psychology. Many of my beliefs as a professional attribute to Likert, among others. Using Likert and others, I have created a social contract that has served me well over the years. Practically, we call it a *team charter*—a highly under-utilized tool in project management.

OUR TEAM'S CHARTER

The charter is developed by and for the team—the whole team—including all stakeholders who are responsible for, accountable to, supporting of, consulting in, or informed about the creation or delivery of any work, feature, function, or anything having anything to do with the project or any of its products or services! Are we clear? The charter's creation is a highly interactive process, and we must achieve consensus. We use this artifact to clarify the group's purpose and direction while establishing its boundaries. A team charter defines how a team will work together. Serving as a *roadmap*, it helps us start things off right by building a foundation for success. Regardless of what precisely you put in your charter, it should address the following concepts: duration, responsibility, collaboration, core values, purpose, objectives, communication, escalation, reporting, resources, and support.

Addressing as many of these concepts as you can speeds up the process of forming, storming, norming, performing, and creating a more efficient team in less time. I know this is a lot. Do not worry. Once you have a charter in place, it will remain useful for a long time. If your teams only come together for a short period, inserting a new group into a premade charter that rests at a departmental level will create more stability and a higher level of authority. Let's consider the charter's basic structure.

MISSION STATEMENT GOALS AND OBJECTIVES

What is the difference between missions, goals, and objectives? A mission statement is a statement of purpose—the very reason the team exists. Goals are qualitative statements that reflect project scope, while objectives are SMART (specific, measurable, actionable, realistic, time-bound) quantitative declarations that are intended to fulfill the goals; and the goals are always in line with the team's statement of purpose. Mission statements aim to be absolute, while both goals and objectives may change from project to project, depending on scope. If the team intends to solve a particular problem, then the objectives are specific statements outlining how the group will meet the stakeholders' needs. The goal must address what problem the team is addressing, the expected result, and why it is important. For example:

- *Mission*: our requirements management team exists for the sole purpose of delivering the best possible solution (and all of its components) to our core stakeholders in an iterative, cost-effective, and timely manner
- *Goals*: (1) build lasting value-add relationships with all of our stakeholders; (2) stand as a voice and advocate for the people, processes, and technologies that represent our stakeholders' solutions and all of its components; (3) establish an empowering, supportive, and fulfilling team culture; and (4) always question assumptions, think rationally, and iterate, as a matter of direction

A Checklist

Communicate the following checklist of business analysis activities to all stakeholders. Everyone involved needs to know how you and your team intend to conduct your work:

- Business analysis planning
- Elicitation and analysis
- Traceability, monitoring, and reporting
- Collaboration and communication
- Solution evaluation
- Delivery and support

TEAM STRENGTHS AND DEVELOPMENT REQUIREMENTS

Ensure that your requirements team and stakeholders have the requisite knowledge and abilities to complete their tasks. Where deficits exist, arrange for training as soon as possible. Once you complete training, follow up on the newly acquired skills often. Identified business analysis competencies include:

- Conceptual, logical, and physical thinking
- Servant leadership
- Data analytics
- Organizational theory
- Business principles and practices
- Personal accountability
- Reliable communication in all modes and techniques
- Facilitation and negotiation
- Organization-specific applications, where required

Roles and Responsibilities

One of the principal causes of confusion, conflict, and complete team failure is a lack of understanding regarding team composition, roles, responsibilities, and accountabilities. Teams reach a peak in effectiveness when:

- The right people are doing the right jobs at the right time
- Cross-pollination is possible
- There is knowledge sharing as a means to help with knowledge gaps and succession planning
- The team does not experience stress beyond their comfort zone for an extended period
- The team has not suffered loss concerning a disruption in members, scope, time, cost, and quality
- The team is not asked to multitask; work packages are scheduled consecutively (where overlap is necessary, time is taken from a contingency to account for the inevitable drop in performance and quality)
- The team is permitted to work iteratively utilizing scheduling techniques such as finish-to-finish or start-to-start
- There are sufficient members available for fair completion of deliverables
- Someone is working behind the scenes removing impediments and other threats
- They have support and representation from leadership
- They have the requisite support, representation, and collaboration from committed and involved teams, departments, divisions, or other relevant categories of stakeholder

Refer to the project's objectives when selecting the right people for the right roles, be they a subject matter expert (SME) or a systems analyst. Remember to use this and other reference material as a guide to assessing social styles and other important behavioral and organizational considerations. Some other factors include:

- What are the team's training requirements?
- Do the stakeholders understand what we expect of them?

- Do we know what their expectations are of us?
- How will we assure that the team charter is accepted?
- How will the team manage their day-to-day operations?
- How will we arrange support and assistance to individual team members?
- How will team status reports be assembled, and to whom are they addressed and delivered?
- Are they prepared to take on the duties required of a stakeholder?
- Who is the requirements team leader?
- How will the team communicate within itself and with the other stakeholders who are not part of the requirements team?

Be sure to identify roles and responsibilities at the team level and the work level. The preferred method for this is a work breakdown structure (WBS). A WBS is a hierarchical decomposition of the total scope of work to be carried out by the project requirements team to accomplish the project objectives and create the required deliverables (Project Management Institute 2013). Place an 'R' in front, and we have a requirement work breakdown structure (RWBS). Figure 6.1 illustrates a possible example of how business analysis work may decompose. I wrote *may decompose* because there is no right or wrong way to approach this useful tool. We need only follow these simple guidelines:

- Establish the milestones or major project deliverables
- Break each of them down into more manageable sub-deliverables or categories, if you like
- Continue to decompose the deliverables until you reach unique packages of work that will be completed by somewhere between 8 to 80 hours of uninterrupted effort
- Identify the activities and tasks that will repeat across the packages
- Assign roles and responsibilities for each work package

It is fair to say that if we forget to put something on the RWBS, we may forget it in delivery. Even if we do remember at some later date, work has already been assigned and scheduled, making it much harder to alter the project without negatively affecting its scope. The acronym known as RACI (responsible, accountable, consulted, and informed) is standard in responsibility management. I have modified it to *RASCIOR*:

- *Responsible*: the person performing the work
- *Accountable*: the person in charge of the performer
- *Support*: anyone who is helping deliver the work
- *Consulted*: SMEs required to provide knowledge
- *Informed*: any persons who must be made aware of the outcome
- *Observe*: persons such as designers, developers, and testers who should come to the workshop to remain *in the know* but observe only, thus preventing premature *solutioning*
- *Resolve*: a formal manager, product owner, project manager (PM), or sponsor who can address issues during an event and clarify matters of scope, in real time

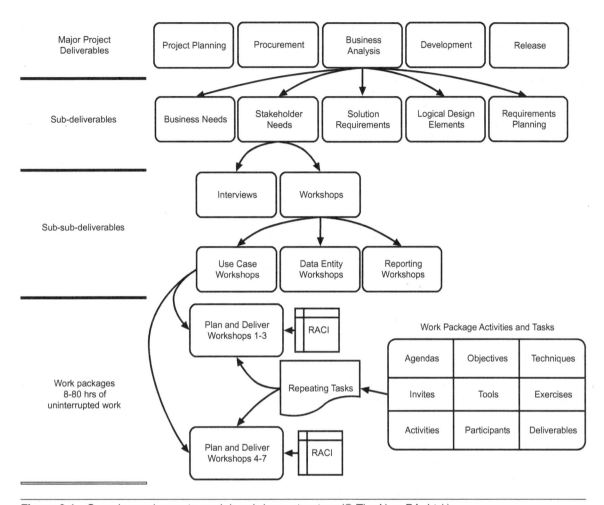

Figure 6.1   Sample requirements work breakdown structure (© The New BA, Ltd.)

TEAM AUTHORITY AND BOUNDARIES

The team's boundaries and levels of authority should address what the team can and cannot do to achieve its mission. Among these are a few considerations: the overall percentage the requirements team can allocate to their mission, the overall importance the requirements team's activities have over other ongoing project and operational activities, and the consideration for project areas such as contingency, new members, time, budget, and approvals. The following subsections contain some examples.

Leadership

The requirements team lead has the authority to direct and control the requirements team's work along with any of the stakeholders who were assigned to provide consulting services to the project for the duration of the requirements elicitation, analysis, and logical design phases of each project iteration, until release.

Solution Scope

The requirements team is permitted to adjust the solution scope without entering a formal solution change request under the following conditions:

- Team members have reached full consensus
- The extent of the solution change does not affect any other system or any component of the solution scope
- The magnitude of the modification does not change any other requirements
- The extent of the amendment does not affect any other processes
- The change does not affect thresholds established for solution quality
- The scope of the modification does not affect any other policies, business rules, etc.
- The extent of the change remains aligned with business objectives and does not conflict with any known stakeholder's needs
- The extent of the change can complete without altering the project's thresholds for resource utilization, budgets, and timelines

Project Scope

The requirements team is permitted to adjust the project's scope without entering a formal project change request under the following conditions:

- Team members have reached full consensus
- The extent of the project change does not affect any other system or any component of the solution scope
- The extent of the modification does not affect any other processes
- The change does not affect thresholds established for project quality
- The scope of the amendment does not affect any other policies, business rules, etc.
- The extent of the change remains aligned with business objectives and does not conflict with any known stakeholder's needs
- The extent of the change can be completed without altering the project's thresholds for resource utilization, budgets, and timelines

Threats and Opportunities

The requirements team is permitted to build project contingency for additional time and costs using qualitative and quantitative means. However, emergency funds are not to exceed ten percent of the project's total contingency budget for time and money.

Daily Operations

Among the criticisms I hear from the various students, clients, and other professionals whom I work with is feeling displaced on a day-to-day basis. That is, the team member or stakeholder understands the larger picture of what he or she is required to accomplish, however, day-to-day routines remain a mystery. This section is an attempt to quell this sensation and give everyone a set routine that can be modified as the need arises. Here are a few examples:

- Each team member is expected to provide a worst, best, and average estimate of work effort in uninterrupted hours—adjustments will be accounted for in the requirements management plan (please review the requirements plan for details)
- Each team member is expected to spend his or her day working on work packages to which they were assigned
- All non-package time, such as scheduled and unscheduled meetings, personal time, and random unplanned events, is anticipated as risk items in the requirements management plan
- Weekly goal setting takes place every Monday from 9:30 to 10:00 at a rotating meeting space (please check your calendar by 3:00 p.m. on Friday for location details)
- All out-of-office team members and stakeholders are required to be connected to the bridge at least ten minutes before the start of any meeting or workshop
- Please refrain from bringing distractions, such as mobile phones and laptops—this will help the meetings to proceed much faster
- Each morning, all team members and relevant stakeholders will meet at the lead business analyst's (BA's) desk for ten minutes to provide a quick status update—the BA will require responses to the following questions: (1) what tasks did you accomplish the previous workday, (2) what tasks do you expect to accomplish this working day, and (3) are there any threats, issues, or impediments preventing you from completing these tasks?
- The lead BA will work daily with all relevant stakeholders to respond to threats and remove issues and roadblocks
- At the end of each week, the lead BA conducts a full status update meeting with all relevant team members at a rotating location (please check your calendar by 3:00 p.m. on Thursday for location details)
- Each team member is expected to provide the lead BA with a short status report, no later than 4:30 p.m. on Thursday for the work packages that he or she is working on (please see the requirements communication plan for status report expectations)
- Each team member is required to familiarize themselves with the end-of-week status report before the actual meeting—this is necessary so we can focus our time on problem solving (meetings are more productive when we are all on the same page)
- If at any time, any team member is unable to perform his or her duties, including attending meetings, a notification must be sent to the lead BA and designated backup as soon as possible
- A summary of all status meetings will be published in the pre-designated project space by the lead BA no later than one full business day following the meeting

Bertrand Russell, from his *Unpopular Essays*, reminds us that, "Collective fear stimulates herd instinct, and tends to produce ferocity toward those who are not regarded as members of the herd." We have seen this in countless movies and read about this in numerous stories. Fear spreads faster than a cold in a tiny warm room! I cannot stress the importance of surrounding yourself with kind words, good thoughts, and good deeds. Allow yourself guidance and influence by those whom you admire. You will be surprised at how beneficial it is to identify those who can affect your character, development, and behavior. Even something as fundamental as a team charter would benefit from the wisdom you have gained through the years.

As the charter continues to evolve, we begin to see increasingly tricky subject areas, such as protocols for team negotiations and bargaining for time and resources.

NEGOTIATION AND AGREEMENTS

Our team charter should emerge naturally through fair discussion and negotiation. With the help of this book, you should be able to put the bones together in short order. The finer details may take a few weeks, but if you continue with negotiations, the end product will be a great accomplishment—something of which you and your team can be very proud.

In this section, you may want to identify how your team will conduct itself when it comes to negotiating for resources, budget, or other miscellaneous items. Having an established protocol will reduce ad hoc, at the moment, heroic delivery-type situations that cause conflict, descent, and general unhappiness. These three things are vital to the requirement team charter's success:

- Discussion between the team members, stakeholders, and the lead BA to make sure that the team charter is credible and authoritative
- Effective and efficient negotiation between the sponsor, the PM, and key stakeholders guarantee that the mission is achievable and that sufficient resources will be deployed as needed
- Full support from the sponsor, key stakeholders, and the PM to assure that the charter will be respected, served, and enforced if required

Ultimately, the team needs to understand what the objectives are and believe that management will support them and the charter in their efforts. To reach a high level of trust and credibility, several negotiation meetings may need to take place. The basic process for negotiation in almost any situation is preparation and planning. Here, groups organize and accumulate the data they need to validate their claims to the other. If you are asking for another ten days to spend on elicitation and another fifteen for analysis and logical design, you had better have a solid reason. You need to convince the team, the sponsors, the PM, and other key stakeholders of the correct thing to do; otherwise it will put the project at high risk of failure. Use the lessons learned from other projects in both qualitative and quantitative ways to illustrate percentages and other key factors. Also, we need to:

- Clearly define your goals, objectives, current situation, preferred situation, and your means to get there
- Determine who the decision makers are and arrange to work with them exclusively
- Determine what your goals are and how reaching them will provide value for you and the project
- Decide your approach and intentions, such as distributive negotiation, zero-sum game, integrative, or non-zero-sum game—are you competing or collaborating?

- Research, research, and research some more—always own the information
- Be prepared because situations may reach an impasse; save something in your back pocket—you may need it to clear up a situation
- Identify the interests and objectives of your negotiating partners
- Define the ground rules such as time limits per meeting, what topics are off the table, and what will happen if an agreement cannot be reached (remember your BATNA—best alternative to a negotiated agreement)

Discussions

After you have completed your plan, researched your position, and are ready to state and defend it, the discussions may begin. The key words here are clarification, justification, bargaining, problem solving, courage, dispassion, and above all, patience. Once you have stated, justified, and supported your initial position with substantial reason, facts, and figures, you should:

- Seek to understand all positions from their point of view and how they relate to you and your team
- Realize that what is important to you may be of no consequence to your managers, sponsors, or other stakeholders
- Build a foundation of trust and credibility as soon as possible (you might even informally open talks before the meeting), consider offering something that you know is important to whomever you are working with (something important to them, but something you could do without)
- Quickly seek to find common ground by spinning phrases such as *our mutual areas of interest . . .* ; *it would be beneficial to both of us if we . . .* ; or *our shared vision . . .*
- Keep in mind that while some minor issues can be resolved through e-mail, phone, or text, you need to be sure to have face-to-face discussions about the important issues—a web conference is better than the telephone
- Remember all you have learned and read in this book and other materials you have researched; effectively *reading* reactions gives you a significant advantage

Iterative Bargaining and Discussions

Once each member has stated his or her opening positions, continue to bargain and problem solve in good faith. Maintain clarity and justification and:

- Do not show all of your cards, give out what you have little by little in order from least to most precious
- Look for trade-offs but concede only when it is advantageous
- Do not burn through all of your research too quickly—inference, words, logic, and numbers are your weapons of choice
- Remember to stick to the matters at hand, own the data, and do not become emotionally involved
- If it seems as though you're at an impasse, pull out something that you saved in the planning phase to clear up the implacable situation in which you find yourself

Conclude the Discussions

Never commit to anything until you have met all of your objectives. One of your goals should always be that of the building and/or reinforcing of active and lasting relationships. Always bargain in genuine faith and look at the other side as partners in the process.

Iteration Protocols

The requirements management team uses a task planning and management method similar to the Kanban approach, regardless of which project method is already in place. Once the team has decomposed their deliverables into sub-deliverables, work packages, and tasks, the tasks will be placed on a board and divided into three basic categories, as seen in Figure 6.2. Kanban is a Japanese word that translates to *billboard sign*. The Kanban system was originally developed in the late 1940s by Toyota Motor Corporation as a result of studying supermarket supply chains. The interest was on how they apply their shelf-stocking techniques on the grocery floor. The ideas were then adapted and refined for inventory management. This method is also known as JIT or just-in-time delivery.

When we look at the supermarket supply chain, there is a high probability that what you need today will also be there tomorrow; thus, you do not need to *stock up*. This behavior is the essence of a Kanban board. Shoppers only buy what they need, when they need it—just-in-time. This technique allows the supermarkets to stock just enough produce and other items to get through the week, reducing costs considerably.

As an adaptation, our requirements team will use the Kanban approach to *hand off* tasks to each other in much the same fashion a runner hands a baton to another runner in a relay race. This method frees up resources as each one passes the baton—they can take another task off of the Kanban board. As a general rule, we take the highest priority task from the board and work it until completion. Always select tasks best suited to your abilities.

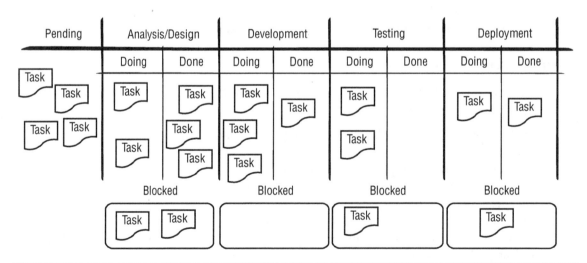

Figure 6.2   Example requirements management Kanban board (© The New BA, Ltd.)

CONFLICT MANAGEMENT AND TEAM ESCALATION PROTOCOLS

Despite our best efforts, stakeholders sometimes have different interpretations of the requirements and differing priorities causing them to resist participation in the requirements development effort. For these reasons, we need to write into the charter how we will handle conflict. Our first option should always be to *keep our dirty laundry in-house*. Occasionally, however, we cannot keep our conflicts backstage. These situations expose a need to invoke the escalation protocols documented in our team charter.

In principle, any escalation issue should focus on project-related items such as decisions, deliverables, accountabilities, or behaviors. The issue should always be specific and clearly defined. It should pertain to the project (not a broader generalization about an operating group, a person's role, etc.). The following list describes four levels of escalation that you may find useful:

- Level 1: Team member to team member—raise issues directly with each other first (one-on-one or with the entire team, as appropriate). The goal is for team members to resolve problems with each other. Team members may ask others to mediate.
- Level 2: Team member to PM—if the team is not able to resolve the issue among themselves, then escalation to the PM should occur. The goal is for the PM to address issues within the team or with the individual team members, as appropriate.
- Level 3: PM to client acceptor or project sponsor—if the issue remains unresolved through Levels 1 or 2, any team member may request that the PM formally escalate the issue to the project sponsor or designate. The PM can escalate a project issue to the sponsor if he or she has not been able to resolve it through Levels 1 or 2. The goal is to work with the PM and the team to address and settle the issue.
- Level 4: Acceptor/project sponsor to functional leaders or steering committee—the project sponsor works directly with operational leaders to resolve a particular issue or may decide to call a steering committee discussion. The goal is to work with the leaders and/or the steering committee to bring about a final consensus.

As I have mentioned, we can avoid many conflicts by taking the time to understand our stakeholders. This approach involves answering these fundamental questions:

- Who are the stakeholders?
- What are their needs, constraints, threats, and assumptions?
- How will I communicate with them and manage expectations?
- What is the influence and interest of each stakeholder?
- How can I win and maintain their support?

Team Building Exercises

There are many team building games available; too many to mention here. If you do not have the budget for laser tag or capture the flag, then organize a scavenger hunt. The only cost is some planning and a little time.

A scavenger hunt is always my first choice for collaboration, logical inference, and team bonding. Quests can be as simple or as complicated as you want them to be. You can write poems, riddles, or even math problems. I find it is always fun to include managers by hiding clues in their offices. Writing rhyming riddles is quite easy. Direction riddles are the easiest. Math riddles might provide the location to a meeting room or address.

Team Assessment

Assessing the requirements team is best done through a questionnaire using the Likert approach. Here are a few categories and sample questions you may want to include.

As a Member of this Team:

- I know my purpose, goals, tasks, and deliverables
- I feel excited to participate
- I do not feel dominated, subjugated, or prejudiced against
- My team accepts me for my talents and allowable weaknesses
- I feel professionally satisfied

As I Understand the Team's Foundation:

- Our team has a definite vision of what it is supposed to do
- Our team uses a clear team charter to guide our actions and behavior
- Our team members have the skills they need to accomplish their tasks
- Our team has adequate resources to achieve its goals
- All member roles have been clearly identified and well defined
- Our team can measure its performance accurately
- Our team understands our stakeholders' needs and expectations
- Our stakeholders have clear and understood expectations

As I Understand our Team Culture, Performance, and Operations:

- The team exhibits high morale
- The team is authoritative and has trust, transparency, and credibility
- The team works as a single unit and team members support each other
- The team resolves conflict quickly and from within
- The team feels free to express themselves professionally
- The team uses short-term iterative planning
- The team works well together and with other teams and organizations
- The team consistently meets the targets and tasks to which it is assigned

By creating a requirements team charter at the very beginning of the project, we set ourselves up for success. We ensure that everyone understands who does what, when, where, how, and why. We define our boundaries and permissions. Moreover, by creating the charter, all parties can shape the project so that it stands a good chance of victory. Charters are a great way of bringing dysfunctional teams back to a place of safety and satisfaction. Much of my career as a PM or a BA was spent fixing troubled projects or misaligned requirements. Once I had completed my research, I would bring all of the stakeholders and the rest of the team together, and we would write a charter from scratch—and the document would always look similar to what I have presented to you in one form or another.

Finally, we come to approval. All members of the team must now sign the charter and commit to its principles. Unless your charter is part of a larger statement of work with an outside vendor or vendors, this is largely a symbolic gesture intended to socially bind the parties to a way of conducting themselves within the boundaries of the project—hence the term, social contract. It also helps to create accountability to one another and the organization.

At present, we are focusing our thoughts on looking at business analysis, project management, stakeholder management, and requirements management through the lenses of communication and organizational and behavioral psychology. It is now time to shift gears toward more technical aspects of our profession. It is time to direct our lens toward *causal analysis*.

REFERENCE

Project Management Institute. 2013. *A Guide to the Project Management Body of Knowledge (PMBOK® Guide)*. Project Management Institute.

SECTION 2:
Reason Cause

7

CAUSES AND CORRELATIONS

There are no accidents in my philosophy. Every effect must have its cause.
The past is the cause of the present, and the present will be the cause of the future.
All of these are links in an endless chain stretching from the finite to the infinite.
—Abraham Lincoln

Business analysis, for me, was mostly a hunt-and-peck affair. Having come from the information technology (IT) world as a UNIX administrator and Oracle database administrator, my experience with various business units was limited. Feeling downcast early in my career and never knowing what conversations I should have, when, and with whom, I knew there had to be a better way. How should I identify requirements? Where do I start? In the early 1990s, there was little to no reference material available. That is when I began to create my materials and techniques, which I slowly developed and refined over the course of my career. My ideas have never been original, but my approach is. The words I use, the combinations, the mixing and matching of the old and the new—that's what makes it my own. My philosophy has always been that business analysis is primarily rooted in organizational and behavioral psychology, which is the science of the mind or mental processes—our organizational needs and how our personality relates to those needs. I also appreciate many other underlying competencies such as:

- Conceptual and visual thinking
- Organization and time management
- Accountability
- Adaptability
- Business methods, principles, and practices
- Communication and interaction abilities
- Systems and software awareness (IIBA 2015)

However, the root of it all are the stakeholders. We spend most of our time with people, listening to their professional issues, problems, dislikes, and anything and everything that is preventing them from reaching a sustainable level of productivity within their work environment.

Many of the issues I have identified over the years source back to cultural shortfalls—organizational habits that seem too insurmountable to resolve. Organizational and behavioral physiology, to me, has always seemed to be a good way to understand the needs of my stakeholders. It is for this reason that the Requirements, Elicitation, Planning, Analysis, and Collaboration Framework™ (REPAC®) uses very particular nomenclature such as *focus* and *source* in very distinct ways. I do not conduct a root cause analysis, per se; rather I work to find a genuine source.

Admittedly, I may have to employ traditional techniques in the process, but the emphasis is not on tradition, but rather on a more obscure way of thinking. We are not looking for a particular cause so much as we are looking for *causality*. As Abraham Lincoln reminded us, "All of these are links in an endless chain. . . ." It is our duty as professionals to identify causality. We must not be satisfied with mere Band-Aid solutions, casual symptoms, and easy fixes. If we think that there is something bigger going on in the background, we must not be reluctant to take action. We must have a deeper understanding of causation and its close cousin, correlation.

Causality, *agency*, and correlation are at the heart of source identification. Correlation does not always imply causation. We refer to this misconception as a questionable cause fallacy. Causality is known as cause and effect whereas correlation infers relationships. Both require independent and dependent variables. An independent variable is something that can affect, while a dependent variable is controlled or influenced by outside factors.

Agency is the actual thing that caused the action or intervention that produced the effect. For example, a book or article can sometimes change the way you think about a particular subject. In this case, the book itself played the role of the agent. Agents cause things to happen, and cause always has one or more effect. Sometimes we believe in *unseen* agents acting negatively. This scheme is a false correlation known as a false pattern. Our first step in identifying a source for our REPAC set is to determine if we are dealing with causation or correlation.

Correlation is a relationship between two sets of variables used to describe or predict data. If there is a correlation, we can sometimes assume the dependent variables change solely because the independent variables change. We may see a correlation and find causality, but not always. Correlations can be positive or negative. A positive correlation, for example, would be the number of help-desk tickets and the frequency of change requests for a particular system.

The dependent and independent variables increase or decrease together. Nonetheless, this arrangement does not imply causality. Conversely, in a negative correlation, the dependent and independent variables increase or decrease opposite from each other. In another example, a business analyst (BA) might notice that the more requirements there are on a project, the less time he or she seems to have to analyze and package them, but the more time he or she seems to spend on them. Once again, correlation does not imply causation. Upon closer examination, we may discover that although these issues correlate to one another, they neither cause nor affect each other. This idea seems counterintuitive since the examples given become cited as causal issues for project lateness, cost overruns, and the like. Misunderstanding the differences between correlative events and actual causation with *agency* are issues systemic in many projects.

Causation, on the other hand, is much harder to see. As a species, we tend to apply agency to events. In the social sciences, agency is our ability to make choices. When an agent is perceived to be unknown or unseen, we tend to see causality where none exists.

Because we are not wired to understand randomness, we tend to believe if two events happen in sequence, the first one must have caused the second. This belief system can be very challenging when we are trying to predict how long something will take. When event Q directly follows event P, our brains, by default, perceive a direct correlation to a third, often unseen agent. We then draw causation between the agent and the events. Is the relationship between poorly written requirements and defective solutions correlative or causality? Is there an unseen agent controlling the outcomes?

Let's look at another example. I recently backed my car into a garage and accidentally bumped the back wall. Later that day, I opened my trunk, and it would not shut. It would seem that my car's inability to latch the trunk was a direct result of bumping the back wall of the parking garage. I must have bumped it harder than I thought—enough to cause structural damage. If I want to establish cause and effect, I must find evidence to support the correlation.

If I were to do some quick calculations, I would discover that the required force needed to misalign the trunk latch was not necessarily enough to bend the steel as I had first related. At the time, I was merely coasting into position. My vehicle did not have anywhere near the required energy. This logic is an example of a questionable cause fallacy. Without imperial evidence, we cannot prove causality. The REPAC source set helps us understand correlations by identifying subsets of concepts that assist us in organizing our thoughts. These correlative events group in the following manner.

CAUSES

Linear Causality

Linear causality is one of the easiest to identify since cause usually precedes effect in a sequential pattern. Linear cause and effect tend to have a clear beginning and a clear ending. We know when the situation started, and we know when it ended. This relationship is binary, one effect traces to one and only one cause. Linear causality may move forward or in reverse, as observed in Figure 7.1.

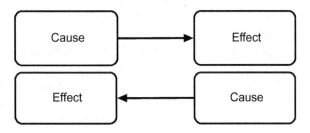

Figure 7.1   Linear causality

Sequential Causality

This type is known as cumulative, domino, ripple, or house of cards, as we can see in Figure 7.2. Sequential causation can be described as a causal chain of successive events that take place in close temporal proximity to each other. Consider my car again. When a short befell my poor electrical system, it caused a chain of electrical shorts which began to affect the car's basic operations. Cumulative causality usually provides a clear start and end point; however, sequences can break into more than one branch.

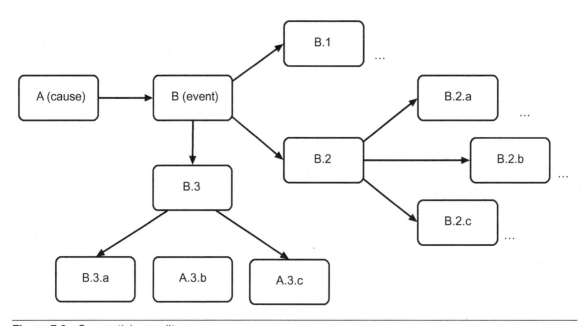

Figure 7.2   Sequential causality

Cyclical Causality

Cyclical causes impact one another, in turn. The first event affects the second event, which impacts the first or may impact other activities that affect others, eventually leading back to the first event. Cyclical implies repeating patterns and feedback loops. The pattern's beginning and end points are difficult to find, and the events may be sequential or simultaneous.

Many years ago, I was an operational BA working with SAP, an enterprise-level solution designed to manage business operations and customer relations. Each month a team of engineers would bill their clients for services rendered and each month they would make input mistakes, and each month I would have to fix those mistakes. This repeated itself month after month after month (exemplified in Figure 7.3). I was not permitted to identify correlation or causality. My function was to repair the errors for each month end, nothing more.

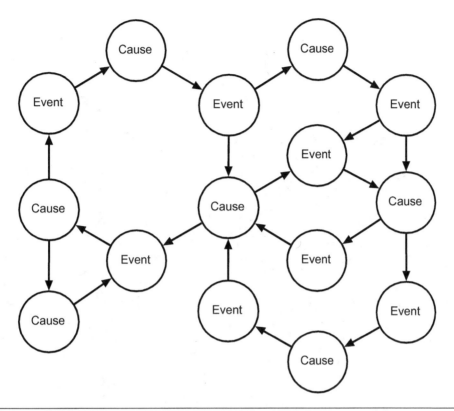

Figure 7.3 Cyclical causality

Spiral Causality

As Figure 7.4 illustrates, spiral causality is logically similar to cyclical causality except it is sequential, and there are clear beginnings and endings. We identify spiral causality through cascading frequency and/or amplitude. As each cause and event cycles, it decreases the time to the next cycle and/or increases the severity of the next cycle. We often call this causality *spiraling out of control*. Numerous branching, multiplied from a single cause in a small period, creates a sense of panic, which induces fear and anxiety. Our fight, flight, or freeze responses trigger and our ability to reason diminishes. Figure 7.4 exaggerates this concept by overlapping multiple spiraling vectors, all converging on a final event. Thinking back to my car, could the electrical shorts multiply eventually leading to cascading failure and costing thousands of dollars in repairs? Scenarios like these cause us to see patterns that may not necessarily be there.

Relational Causality

Organizations are complex systems. As we've seen, causality can also be complex. When two or more comparable causes converge on a single effect, the causation is said to be relational. We see this example diagrammed in Figure 7.5. The causes may relate to each other through balance, equivalence, similarity, or

Figure 7.4   Spiral causality (© The New BA, Ltd.)

difference. If one or more of the causes change, the relationship changes, thus the event will also change. These changes create a dynamic causal relationship with shifting variables; very challenging when we propose possible solutions. Always remember to look for the shifting variables in a dynamic system; any system involving people is sure to be dynamic. If the variables change, but the relationship does not, then the effect remains unaffected.

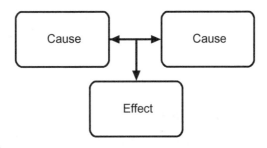

Figure 7.5   Relational causality

Mutual Causality

Illustrated in Figure 7.6, mutual causality, sometimes called chicken and the egg, is diabolically simple and difficult to resolve. Referring back to my days on SAP, the organizational culture where I worked did not support change. The input errors made by the engineers created other errors for other departments, which often created situations where event A caused B, which in turn caused A, ad infinitum. When two events are both cause and effect, the causation is mutual. "The impact can be positive for both, negative for both, or positive for one and negative for the other. The causes and effects are often simultaneous but may be sequential."[1] The phenomenon may be event-based or may be a relationship over time. Imagine a game of *Pong* where a computer plays both sides. Under the right conditions, a game like that might outlast us!

In many cases, we experience verification bias or confirmation bias, which is the tendency to evaluate new evidence as confirmation of our existing beliefs. Sometimes, though, there is no causality. Sometimes trouble happens; as in the absence of causality or a random convergence of events. In the absence of causality, events occur through random convergence. These types of events challenge many people. If we are to group minds into *skeptics* and *believers*, then it is the believers who argue the absence of causality.

Recall, I have discussed how evolution favored *agency* over detection. Believing a connection between things or agents is very hardwired. Our brain makes cognitive mistakes every day. Science, reason, logic, and mathematics are the only tools we have to defend ourselves against our cognitive evolution.

The asymmetry between organizational *agents'* causes and effects make for challenges to lasting change. When we consider causality as it relates to the alignment of IT and business strategy, we must ensure we make the right investments for the right reasons—the actual source of the matter.

The rise of business analytics as a means to help determine organizational goals and objectives has created a loose definition of causation and correlation. When we use these terms interchangeably without

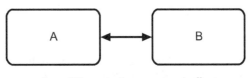

A and B are both cause and effect.

Figure 7.6   Mutual causality

understanding their phonetic placement or fundamental logic, we set ourselves up for spending millions of dollars on the wrong problems.

CORRELATIONS

Positive and Negative Correlation

Events that increase or decrease in frequency in the same direction express a positive correlation. Example: when solution defects increase, the time needed to repair those errors also rises. Events that increase or decrease in frequency in the opposite direction express a negative correlation. Example: when time spent on testing decreases, defects increase (remember this event is not the cause).

Linear and Nonlinear Correlation

Events that increase or decrease either positively or negatively at a constant rate are linear relationships; nonlinear relationships change at a curved rate. For example: for every missed systems test, there is one defect described as a direct or linear correlation; however, if the rates are uneven then it is a nonlinear association.

No Correlation

There is no relationship between the events. For example: My car's inability to fasten the trunk had nothing to do with bumping the back wall in the parking garage. It was, in fact, due to an electrical short that caused the trunk to think it had fastened. The reason or causation for the system short was a wire that had come loose. The wire had come loose because it had been caught on some debris while I was driving earlier that morning.

Causes and effects are sometimes distant in time and space. They may be inverse or converse, linear or nonlinear, sequential or nonsequential. Whatever the relationship, the REPAC source set helps us understand causality by identifying subsets of cause and effect.

REFERENCE

IIBA. 2015. *A Guide to the Business Analysis Body of Knowledge (BABOK® Guide)*. International Institute of Business Analysis.

ENDNOTE

1. Six Causal Patterns—www.cfa.harvard.edu/. https://www.cfa.harvard.edu/smg/Website/UCP/pdfs/SixCausalPatterns.pdf (accessed September 8, 2016).

8

THE REPAC SOURCE SET OF ELEMENTS

The best way to solve a problem has always been to avoid it in the first place; that is, plan, design, and test things so the problem is unlikely to occur. That said, organizational culture is imprecise; planning seldom allows for proper design and testing and missteps and mistakes often happen without proper resolution.

Determining a root cause can be a gigantic activity when we consider the different ways that cause and effect interact. All too often we focus on symptoms—issues with tissues, as I like to call them. Fixing symptoms is easy. It does not demand that much discipline and we feel some satisfaction afterward. Unfortunately, this behavior is self-deluding. The word *root* in *root cause analysis* refers to the underlying causality. We often see symptoms of a cause on the surface, much like a weed. Weeds, as we all know, have extensive root systems. Actual causation has the foresight to move past the obvious, beyond the surface, below the weeds, to the organization's underbelly.

As we glean information on the cause and effect of a situation, it is important to remember our sample size. Are we examining a large enough set element, including the right variables, conditions, instances, and the like to gauge the causation accurately? American astrophysicist and famed science communicator Neil deGrasse Tyson is fond of reminding us that if we dip a glass into the ocean and declare "there are no whales in the ocean" just because there are none in the glass, we have assumed a questionable cause, also known as an informal causal fallacy. Our sample size is incomparably small to reach such a conclusion. The same applies to business analysis. If we want to solve business problems, not only do we have to identify the right cause-and-effect relationship, but we also have to verify and validate the correlation through relevant unmistakable evidence that cannot be demonstratively proven incorrect. Remember, it is not *who* is right, but *what* is right that is of importance.

The Requirements, Elicitation, Planning, Analysis, and Collaboration Framework™ (REPAC®) helps us find correlative and causal evidence through the source set. These source elements identify potential reference points for further conversations and analysis. Think of the source elements as subjects. Does our problem have to do with capitalization? What communication or contracting or service interruption issues must we resolve? If we conduct a root cause workshop, the source elements will serve as the categories that branch out from the spine of an Ishikawa diagram (talked about next).

REPAC SOURCE SET ELEMENTS AND SUBSET ELEMENTS AND RULES

The REPAC source set elements are:

- Source = c, s, p where:
- *c* refers to the source causality type,
- *s* relates to a source subject, and
- *p* is the subject perspective.

The Subset Elements Are:

- Causality = linear, sequential, cyclical, spiral, relational, and mutual
- Subject = acquisition, assets, capitalization, communication, competition, consumer trends, contracts, environmental, expansion, innovation, interruptions, IPO, legal, liabilities, market trends, mergers, partnership, privatization, regulations, resourcing, safety, security, segmentation, social trends, suppliers, supply chain, and vendors . . .
- Perspective = opportunity, threat, opportunity-and-threat

The Subset Rules Are:

- When selecting a source causality, only one selection is permitted. Causation types are disjointed or mutually exclusive, meaning a cause-and-effect relationship cannot be cyclical and mutual at the same time.
- When selecting a source subject, the order does not matter, and repetition is not allowed. It would not make sense to build a REPAC source set with two or more of the same elements.
- When selecting source perspective, the order does not matter and repetition is not allowed. Subjects perceive as opportunities, threats, or both, simultaneously.

Now that we have a possible causal type and a source subject, what do we do with them? It is now time to problem/opportunity solve. Many business analysts (BAs) know how to use a cause-and-effect diagram, otherwise known as a fishbone diagram, and for some BAs, this is all they use or understand. It is a fine brainstorming tool, but it is not without its limitations. The fishbone or Ishikawa diagram, illustrated in Figure 8.1, was developed by Kaoru Ishikawa as part of Japan's first quality management innovations. Ishikawa was a Japanese organizational theorist and professor at the Faculty of Engineering at The University of Tokyo.

Ishikawa developed his technique to analyze industrial processes—and therein lies the problem. As you can see from the previous example, an Ishikawa diagram can only focus on the potential causes of a particular event—linear causality. It was never designed to handle the more complex causal relationships like what we reviewed in Chapter 7. It is for this reason that we cannot rely on this technique to the exclusion of other problem-solving devices. Figure 8.1 shows us a possible line of reasoning. Again, this method only allows for linear causality, which is typical in the manufacturing world—but not so much in ours, the world of knowledge workers. In a complex organization where people, processes, and technology interact, often in unpredictable ways, we must *up our game*, as it were, and develop a sophisticated set inference— conclusions reached from evidence and reasoning frameworks.

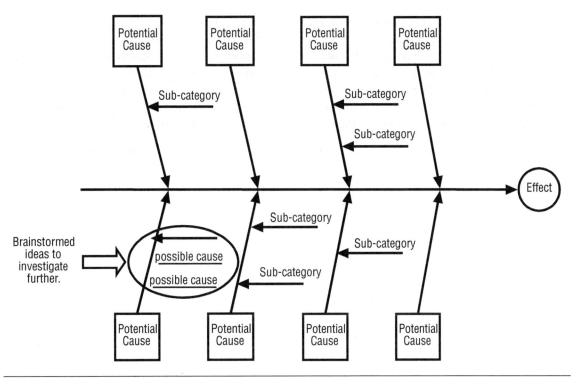

Figure 8.1   Ishikawa diagram example

Critical thinking is one of a BA's most powerful tools. Finding the source of a business problem involves no less than five types of mental frameworks: inductive, deductive, abductive, reductive, and fallacious reasoning. Inductive reasoning, not unlike analytics, starts with precise data and infers general conclusions. Deductive reasoning, on the other hand, begins with very general data and moves toward a logical hypothesis. Both approaches require testing. Remember to keep in mind that data in this context is the raw material we work with, whether that is general stakeholder discussions or actual electronic data. Once we understand the data, we call it information because it informs us.

Abductive reasoning requires us to determine a reasonable cause based on incomplete data. Tests would be inconclusive due to the nature of the source data. Reductive thinking starts with inference, and we attempt to support it by disproving opposing conclusions. Finally, fallacious arguments are a broken chain of logic that may or may not be deceptive, fraudulent, or just plain false. Fallacies tend to come from monological points of view. Monological, as opposed to dialogical communication, is one-sided. Typically, the communicator is not interested in exploring an issue through dialogue. I have mentioned erroneous thinking several times in this book, as I believe it is one of the most common causes of poor decisions made on projects. Fallacies may be formal or informal. Formal fallacies are a break in logical form while the more common informal are content related, such as when a premise fails to support its conclusion due to poor writing or research. Understanding fallacies is essential to critical thinking (see Chapter 17 for more on how they relate to projects and business analysis, and what to do about them).

Of the reasoning skills I have mentioned, inductive is my preference. I do not accept any raw data as factual, even if the provider is authoritative and *vouches* for its accuracy. I always quantize the data into its core elements, cross-analyze, and reference everything provided. This method helps me to reduce the amount of incorrect or out-of-date data that goes into my analysis. Before I can present my findings, however, I must test them. Rather than accepting the raw data, I challenge it—interrogate it. To take advantage of induction and other reasoning techniques, we need more sophisticated problem-solving tools. In the next chapter, we will examine many of these techniques and build a REPAC source set, applying it to an example problem scenario.

9

GETTING TO THE ROOT OF IT ALL

"Customers will never love a company until the employees love it first."
—Simon Sinek

The international bestseller, *Start with Why: How Great Leaders Inspire Everyone to Take Action*, by author and U.S. Military Advisor Simon Sinek, is a compelling book that helps us understand the power of the word *why*. In all things, there is no point in doing anything until you know why you are doing it. If I had a nickel for every project I have seen that did not have a clear sense of *why*, I would be very wealthy.

Even when we try to avoid bitter disputes over what we should or should not do or what we can or cannot do, we occasionally find ourselves arguing over irrelevant details. Sometimes even the smallest change to a process can have dramatic effects—as evidenced by one of my favorite anecdotes:

> *Two scientists walk into a bar. The first one says, "May I have H₂O please"? The second one says,*
> *"I will have H₂O too, please." The second one died after consuming his drink. The second scientist*
> *died because "H₂O too" (H₂O₂), or hydrogen peroxide, in large amounts is lethal. If we add an extra*
> *oxygen atom to water, we change the molecule entirely.*

If you add extra steps to a process, the effects can change or magnify, significantly. Small imperfections in the requirements management approach or initial causal analysis will set us off on the wrong path. Compound these first mistakes over months and the result is a solution that vastly differs from the stakeholders' expectations. Imagine a sharpshooter aiming at a target one mile or 5,280 feet away. If the initial aim is off by just one degree, the projectile will miss its target by as much as 92.2 feet.

Take a look at Figure 9.1; given that the angle of error, represented by the Latin symbol θ (the trigonometric function for cosine), is 1% and the adjacent distance to the target is 5,280 feet, the opposite side is 92.2 feet from the target. Imagine a pilot flying us across the continental United States. This 1% mistake would result in being 50 miles off course if we flew from New York to Los Angeles—I would not want to be on that plane! Relating these metaphors to a project, this "tiny" mistake would result in huge failure if you do not or are unable to make corrections.

These allegories are similar in concept to a burn-up chart. A burn-up chart is a tool that compares project progress to solution scope. You may already be familiar with a burn-down chart which tracks how much work remains. A burn-up chart compares the team's velocity (total number of story points

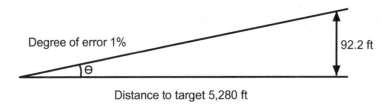

Figure 9.1   Small imperfections have lasting effects

or necessary work effort, in hours) or scope to the progression of work required to accomplish the project's goals. Figure 9.2 provides examples of each. The sniper's small 1% deviation to his target becomes larger and larger the further the bullet travels. In comparison, we notice scope changes immediately on a burn-up chart. If we add more or new work, the total work line (which should be flat and steady) will show an increase in scope and overall work, further separating the total story points or hours of effort from the total completed. Figure 9.2 shows us a burn-down and burn-up chart for the same project. The burn-down chart appears to report that the team did not produce much value around the middle of the project or iteration but in classic waterfall heroics, managed to finish all of the work on time. As you can see in Figure 9.2's bottom diagram, which represents a burn-up chart, the scope remaining line (expressed as a dotted line) is not flat. This chart shows us a scope that seems to increase steadily. Just like our sniper, the initial estimates were off, forcing the scope to decrease sharply during the last half of the project. Time

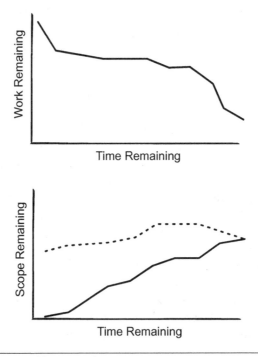

Figure 9.2   Example burn-down and burn-up charts

remaining and remaining scope do meet, but only because we decreased scope; had we not, who knows how far these lines would have diverged.

Scope creep is the bane of a business analyst's (BA's) existence. In the face of chronically missed targets, a burn-up chart can bring this problem to light, keeping changes under control. If you have ever adopted or viewed a burn-down chart, then you know that they can be misleading when trying to determine why the daily tracking of work does not match where the team should be or the budgeted cost of work scheduled does not line up to the actual cost of the work performed. A burn-up chart tracks the ebb and flow of scope and makes evident the deviations between performance and changes in solution scope. Using burn-up charts will show all stakeholders a clear causal relationship between missed deadlines and changes to scope. Burn charts can identify causal relationships among any number of measurable project variables, such as requirements and solution defects or the relationship between time estimated and spent on tasks. As useful as burn charts are at showing us where we are and where we may end up, they are only helpful when the project is in motion. Before we begin the project, we must make every effort to identify the actual cause of our stakeholder's issues; lest we end up like our sharpshooter friend—forever missing the target.

In this chapter, we focus on some analysis tools designed to help determine our stakeholders' root issue(s). There are many techniques; however, the following list contains some of my preferences:

- Affinity/decision analysis
- Soft systems methodology (SSM)
- Appreciative inquiry
- Constructive controversy
- Heuristics
- Appreciative inquiry
- 5-ways or why-why
- Fishbone diagram
- Causal loop diagrams
- Force field diagrams
- *T* charts (pro/con)
- Decision trees and decision tables
- Failure mode and effects analysis

AFFINITY ANALYSIS

Affinity analysis establishes similarities based on characteristics. Affinity diagrams bring together fragmented analysis results into cohesive groups of related information. We typically use brainstorming sessions to generate the potential causes of the problem and then group the results into categories or affinities. Not unlike a fishbone diagram, this technique is an effective way to organize our thoughts so we can focus on the potential causes while ignoring irrelevant data. The steps to producing an affinity/decision analysis are as follows:

- Present the problem
- Set duration for idea generation
- Ask participants to write on sticky notes as many ideas as they can about the topic at hand

- Once the time has expired, offer five-minute stretch/restroom break to the participants
- During the break, analyze the results and group everything into themes that describe the ideas expressed
- Remove duplicates
- Continue discussions until you reach your agenda

After creating our affinities, we follow-up with decision analysis, which "formally assesses a problem and possible decisions to determine the value of alternate outcomes under conditions of uncertainty" (IIBA 2015). Since we are perceptually stuck on the here and now, decision analysis depends on the personal, unbiased expertise provided by our stakeholders. *A Guide to the Business Analysis Body of Knowledge (BABOK® Guide)* goes on to point out a few variables that we must consider before we book a decision analysis workshop: ". . . the values, goals, and objectives that are relevant to the decision problem, the nature of the decision that must be made, the areas of uncertainty that affect the decision, and the consequences of each potential decision."

SOFT SYSTEMS METHODOLOGY

Some of the causal analysis tools, techniques, and methods we use can over-simplify things, leading to false premises. Complex causal relationships such as cyclical or spiral require tools designed to handle the messy business of our business. In situations where seemingly myriad factors contribute to a problem—and there are several perspectives to consider—it can challenge us when identifying the prime cause. In these situations, we may turn to a method designed to solve the multifaceted issues that face our complex business systems.

> *We cannot solve our problems with the same thinking we used when we created them.*
> —*Albert Einstein*

Peter Checkland was a British management scientist and emeritus professor of systems at Lancaster University. He developed soft systems methodology (SSM)—a type of organizational or business process modeling—after an extensive study of how a community of practices systems practitioners improved the way they addressed issues and solved problems (Checkland and Poulter 2007). Its primary goal is to address complex situations where there are divergent opinions and attitudes about how to define the business problem. The term *soft systems* refer to the issues themselves. An example of a *soft problem* or *system* (as in a business system or process) might be, *how can we reduce the number of quality errors in the requirements we produce for all of our projects*?

Systems thinking is a way to address problems by breaking the issues into constituent elements and looking at each part independently, as combinations and permutations, and as a whole. Checkland encourages us to stop thinking about *problems* that need to be *solved* by a *solution*. Rather, treat his technique as a problem-solving approach. Checkland suggests we focus on *problematical situations* and organizational improvements.

Complex organizational issues often have ill-defined, nonlinear relationships; for this reason, SSM is not a linear approach to problem solving. SSM is not a step-by-step process; its activities are not entirely defined. SSM tools closely resemble mind maps—they show relationships between possible causes, but they do not show a linear route through them. Conducting a causal analysis using the SSM method involves four considerations.

Our first goal is to explore the situation by creating a vibrant, textured *picture* of the issues at hand. Specifically, we look for connections between events—connections that cause patterns. This scheme represents the mind map of the current state. We also examine different perspectives. The Requirements, Elicitation, Planning, Analysis, and Collaboration Framework™ (REPAC®) provides many elements for this step.

Next, we must examine the value-add and non-value-add activities carried out by the stakeholders involved in the problem under analysis. SSM suggests two approaches for this goal. First, we may identify purposeful activities by just focusing on the six interrogatives (who, what, when, where, why, and how)—Checkland only offers three—what, who, and why—which he calls P, Q, and R, respectively (I added all six questions). The second approach is a technique called CATWOE (customers, actors, transformation, worldview, owner, and environment). Each approach allows us to integrate the issue and provide responses to the words associated with either technique. The activities we document will focus on the three Es of process management—efficacy, efficiency, and effectiveness.

Third, we discuss each purposeful activity. We must identify ways to improve the problematic situation. Some questions to focus on are:

- Do the events represent reality for all users?
- Do the dependencies and relationships between activities exist in reality for all users?
- How efficacious, efficient, and effective is each activity?
- How is each of the activities performed?
- How long does each activity take?
- How much does each activity cost?
- Have we covered each of the interrogatives?

Last, we define actions to enhance the current state. The mindset here is not to *fix* the issue, but rather *improve the problem* until it is no longer a threat or is below our risk threshold. It is for this reason SSM is not a step-by-step process, but rather a way of thinking. A method of thinking that focuses on organizational improvements over a broke-fix mentality. We always consider changes to the people, process, and tools/technology/things triad. Since we know that our stakeholders will have different perspectives or worldviews, our emphasis should be on collaboration or compromise.

APPRECIATIVE INQUIRY

My personal favorite, appreciative inquiry (AI) is another technique designed to put the power of problem solving in the hands of those who do the work. AI emphasizes what we do well rather than allowing ourselves to dwell on what is wrong. It was developed in the 1980s by David Cooperrider at Case Western Reserve University, based on his 1987 paper (Cooperrider and Srivastva 1987).

AI is the study and ongoing investigation of what organizational systems look like when they are performing to their full potential. It helps to create and sustain optimal corporate systems. As a development methodology, it assumes that inquiry into and dialogue about strengths, successes, values, hopes, and dreams is in itself transformational. The principles of appreciative inquiry are explained in the following subsections.

Constructionist

This theory holds that individual learners construct mental models to understand the world around them. The constructionist principle asks us to envision a positive future. What we believe to be true determines our actions—our perspective and focus projects personal reality. As we develop lasting relationships with our stakeholders, positive thoughts and actions emerge. As we work through the day-to-day tasks, interactions, and discourse, we look for ways to improve our situations rather than dwelling on things that always seem to go wrong. We intend to co-create new ideas, stories, and images that generate new possibilities for action. We can assume, therefore, that an AI constructionist point of view holds that an organization is a human construct, and the reality as we understand it is subjective and created socially through the images and patterns we create through the conversations we have with each other. Constructionists maintain an open mindset. For us, every day is a day of learning and personal and professional growth.

Simultaneity

Simultaneity reminds us that we are storytelling, pattern-seeking social entities. In physics, the term *observer effect* is a phenomenon that states, as an observer, we change the outcome of something through merely the act of observation. In a classic example, we cannot measure the pressure of our automobile tires without changing the pressure itself. Similarly, in my lessons, I often refer to the Hawthorne effect (much like the observer effect) to demonstrate the alteration of a behavior of the stakeholders we are observing due to their awareness of being observed. When you observe someone on-boarding a new customer, for example, their behavior changes because you are there watching. These effect theories apply to the principle of simultaneity. The principle of simultaneity proposes that, as we inquire into human systems, we change them. Change begins the moment we start asking questions.

Anticipatory Principle

This principle posits that the team's collective imagination and discourse about the organization's future are the most valuable resources for generating effective organizational change or improvement ideas. What we do today will guide our future. It is in our nature to look beyond the here and now and plan for the future. AI asks that we plan a picture-perfect future and work toward it, as best we can, rather than starting from a position of compromise and constraints. Future perfect ideas, regardless of their probabilistic implementation odds, can be powerful mobilizing agents. AI uses the original creation of positive imagery on a consolidated basis to refashion anticipatory reality.

Positive Principle

We employ the *positive principle* for collective inquiry and positive change. This principle suggests that we are at our best when the organization shares our values and we believe it is moving in a positive direction. When we feel in sync with the organization, we can think more strategically, absorb data quicker, and make better decisions. Our anxiety decreases, improving our overall health. Sentiments such as hope, excitement, inspiration, camaraderie, and joy increase; and sick days and conflict decrease. This mindset affects projects in countless ways and deliverables tend to complete on time with fewer defects resulting in higher stakeholder satisfaction. Our cognitive flexibility increases, allowing us to solve problems quickly and focus on the things we do well. Overall, we experience strong connections and relationships between people, particularly among groups in conflict.

AI follows an approach known as the 5-D cycle:

1. *Definition*: what is the focus of our investigation?
2. *Discovery*: what is the heart of the matter? An extensive process to understand the inquiry.
3. *Dream*: in the best possible light (blue sky, green field) what *could* the solution be?
4. *Design*: given our current needs, what should the solution be, no more, no less?
5. *Destiny*: what will it be and how can we make our dream come true?[1]

At the center of the AI model is a core team of *dreamers* endlessly following the AI model, making constant gradual improvements (Kessler 2013). Again, this philosophy requires a growth mindset. Figure 9.3 illustrates the AI model.

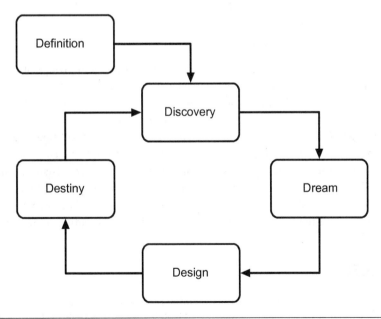

Figure 9.3   Appreciative Inquiry 5-D cycle model

CONSTRUCTIVE CONTROVERSY

We do not usually make decisions or solve problems in a bubble. It is in our nature (some more than others) to involve teammates and other stakeholders, creating a social connection, which makes for a more productive event. As individuals, our line of sight is limited; what may at first appear to be the cause from one point of view is no longer valid when seen from different vantage points. The more complex the situation, the more perspectives we need to examine. I like to refer to confusing, elusive, and complex problems as dodecahedral (a solid having 12 plane faces) because it sells the idea that many organizational issues are indeed dimensional, pentagonal constructs, which require a clear *focus* on the issues at hand, multifaceted *perspectives*, and a sophisticated *depth* of analysis. All of which are determinants of the REPAC Framework.

The objective of constructive controversy is to test opinions by subjecting them to a *clash of ideas*. Each potential cause (or solution), discussed and improved upon by the group, is either proven likely correct or discounted altogether. Concepts evolve through team discussions until a single cause or solution is left. As the survivor, it is likely best suited for its environment. If we and others in our group are confident with our choices, then our position will thrive; if not, the Darwinian effect takes over and our position will *die off* in favor of better ideas. Figure 9.4 diagrams the constructive controversy method. The rules of constructive controversy are:

- Mutual respect for each other and our ideas
- Critique ideas, not the people
- The focus is on sound and logical decisions
- *Winning* an argument is not our purpose
- Practice patience and active listening at all times
- Understand all sides of the issue at hand

Constructive controversy works with individuals, but when performed in groups, it yields its best results. Each group works as a team to make the most persuasive case they can. This process tends to produce better solutions, compared with solving problems using consensus, debate, or individual effort. As we face our assumptions, we are forced to either improve our argument or withdraw it.

Much like the REPAC Framework, the constructive controversy method takes advantage of multidimensional thinking. REPAC creates interdisciplinary discourse through its use of a point of focus, multiple perspectives, and various depths of analysis. Constructive controversy is similar and indeed can be utilized with REPAC because it brings different disciplines together, expressed as teams, converging on the same problem. Multidimensional problem solving is creative and will keep projects fresh and focused. Stagnant approaches repeat themselves throughout the organization, creating ineffective cultural norms.

DECISION TREES

A decision tree is the easiest among the multiple-variable techniques to master. There are many multiple-variable analysis methods; however, the appeal of a decision tree lies in its relative power, ease of use, robustness with a variety of data and levels of measurement, and interpretability. Decision trees help us identify strong relationships between input values and target values in a group of observations that form a

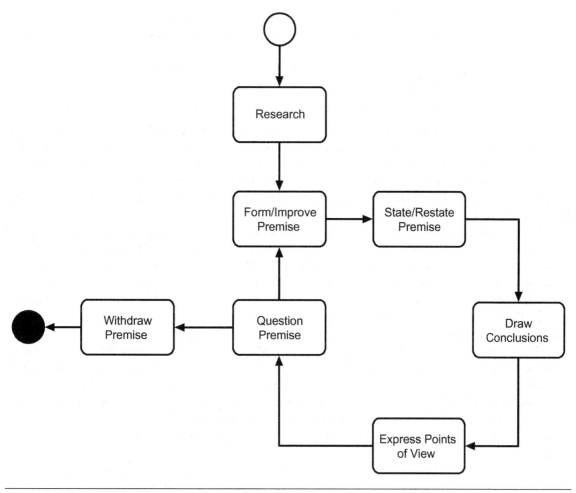

Figure 9.4   The constructive controversy method

dataset. Our goal is to determine clear relationships to a target value. These links group together in a bin, which becomes a branch on the tree. As guardians of requirements performance, quality, and a bulldozer for roadblocks, decision trees are useful and powerful tools.

Both trees and tables are useful when documenting business rules, as each path on a decision tree, bin, leaf-node, or matrix column is a resolved state, respectively. For decision trees, each leaf-node represents a particular choice or element. Squares represent decisions, circles are uncertain outcomes, and triangles denote the end of an outcome path. Downstream branches represent conditions that must be met to satisfy that particular branch. Decision trees assemble in the following manner:

- On the left side of your drawing space, draw a square, representing the decision
- From the initial decision square, draw two or more lines representing the available options (keep the lines apart to accommodate the diagram's growth)

- At the end of the lines, consider how the tree will continue to grow:
  - If the decision path leads to an uncertain outcome, denote it with a circle and write the factor above or inside the circle
  - If the result is another decision to consider, draw another square and write the decision above or inside the square
  - If you have exhausted that particular path, denote it with a triangle

Once you have completed the first set of nodes or bins, continue identifying decision squares and uncertain circles, drawing two or more lines spaced appropriately. As before, these lines represent the possible outcomes of uncertain events or more decisions to be made. Repeat these steps until all the possible outcomes and decisions you can see leading on from the original decision plot. Figure 9.5 is an example of a simple decision tree scheme. Decision trees can become very complicated, especially when we consider probabilities and financial decisions.

After constructing the framework, we must evaluate the tree by measuring the chance events against the outcomes for each decision node. Let's imagine that we want to start a small retail e-business. We have narrowed our choice down to either a website that will sell widgets or a website that will sell sprockets. I am using widgets and sprockets to keep the analogy as generic as possible. Assume, for simplicity, that the widget site has a total earning potential of $100.00 and the sprocket site has an overall return of only $90.00. The choice is clear; we would sell widgets. Business decisions are rarely this simplistic. There is always a chance of failure.

If we develop a website to sell widgets, there will be a 70% chance of success and a 30% chance of failure (assume we conducted research, interviews, workshops, and focus groups to obtain these values). If we succeed, we earn $100.00. If we fail, we will lose $30.00, which would be our start-up costs.

If we develop a website to sell sprockets, our chances of success or failure remain the same at 70% and 30%, and our earnings and losses would be $90.00, and $10.00, respectively.[2]

Now which one do we choose? The answer derives using simple math. We see the equations in Figure 9.6.

As you can see, the expected value (EV) for the widget path is $61.00 and the EV for the sprocket path is $61.20. This difference represents a margin of only twenty cents; seemingly by design! I rigged the numbers to illustrate that the correct path is not always apparent. This result is almost meaningless. Similar to asking if there are penguins south of the South Pole (there is nothing south of the South Pole), so asking whether we should sell widgets or sprockets with this result is a non-question question.

When the results are as close as this, the actual choice almost becomes personal. Regardless, we should never let our feelings into the analysis. For all our noble tactics, we must be nimble. Many of us attach feelings to our beliefs and opinions. We treat them as precious possessions. When contradicted, our instinct is to defend our position emotively rather than consider the opposing arguments. We think changing our mind is a defeat of some kind. Decision trees help remove us from our feelings and allow us to follow physical lines of reason, choices, chance, and probable outcomes.

These results do not indicate that we can expect to earn $61.20 if we sell sprockets, as the name EV intimates. EV refers to the chance of success over several iterations of the same project under the same conditions. Therefore, our average earning, over time, would be about $61.20. If we had historical data, we could perform statistical sampling that would help us understand the EV and distribution of possible

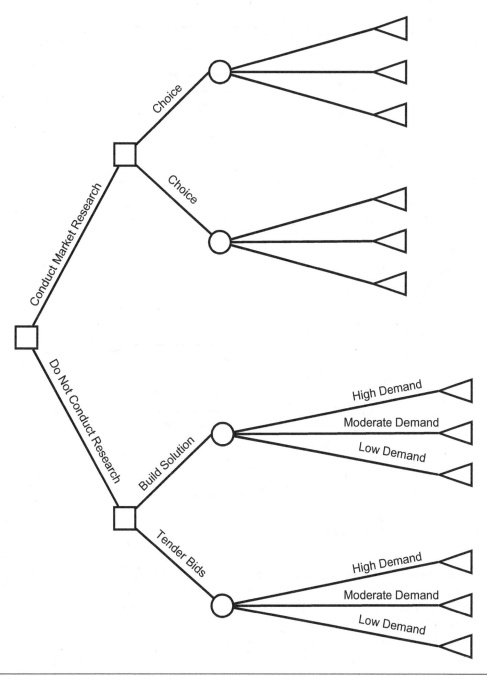

Figure 9.5   Simple decision tree scheme

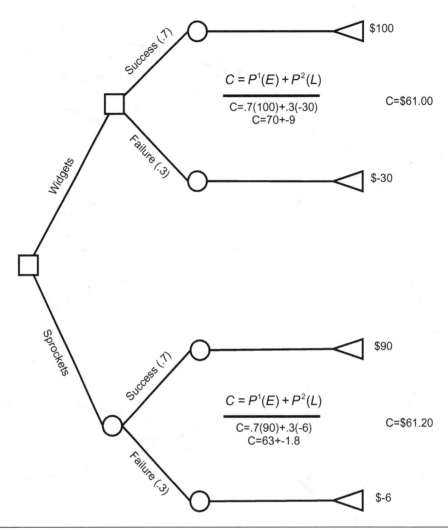

Figure 9.6   Widget/sprocket decision tree example

values above and below the mean, but that is an altogether different tool. The understanding of this concept is essential when using decision trees and communicating their results.

Now, let us try something more complicated. Imagine I want to redesign the way I create, distribute, and manage all of my learning content. I want to make a substantial investment in online education through the purchase of a learning management system (LMS).

I must decide whether to build the LMS solution or send out a formal request for bids. If customer demand is high enough, it may be more profitable to build the solution in-house, rather than having it outsourced. However, due to budget constraints, the build-or-buy decision must be made before the potential market demand is known. Let's assume I am considering a market research analysis at the cost of $10,000 to determine the potential demand from my customer base. I am very anxious to get underway, but unsure if spending $10,000 on market research is justified given the estimated payoffs. As the BA assigned to my project, I develop a multiple variable analysis, also known as a decision tree, to help me understand my options and make a decision. The options presented in this scenario are: (1) conduct a market research analysis and (2) buy or build the LMS solution.

There are several permutations of favorable and unfavorable probabilities and other data-sets that must be reflected in the tree. Rather than writing all of it out in a narrative, I have created two tables that give us all the data we need. The chance events, seen in Table 9.1 (in thousands of dollars), represent the projected outcomes or payoffs for the *do-not-conduct-research* bin. While Table 9.2 shows us the probability data for the other two bins where we do the market study. Once again, we typically obtain this information from the experts at our disposal.

Table 9.1   Build-or-buy decision scenario chance events for *do not* "conduct a market research study"

	Chance Events		
Decisions	**High Demand (30%)**	**Moderate Demand (40%)**	**Low Demand (30%)**
Build	200	60	−30
Buy	140	80	20

Table 9.2   Build-or-buy decision scenario chance events for *doing* "conduct a market research study"

Permutations Legend	
P	Purchase Solution
B	Build Solution
F	Favorable Study Results
U	Unfavorable Study Results
H	High Demand
M	Moderate Demand
L	Low Demand

Permutations		
P(F) = 40%	P(H,F) = 45%	P(H,U) = 20%
P(U) = 60%	P(M,F) = 40%	P(M,U) = 40%
	P(L,F) = 15%	P(L,U) = 40%

Decision trees consist of nodes and branches. A decision node, illustrated by a square, has branches representing alternatives. A chance node, drawn as a circle, has branches that represent states or possible outcomes. Let's recall how to assemble and analyze a decision tree:

- Draw the nodes and branches working from left to right, leaving enough space for calculations and growth

- Assign probabilities to the chance events that were usually determined through conversation with subject matter experts and other project members
- Make sure that each bin's chances add up to 100%
- Assign outcomes at the end of each of the tree limbs—again using best judgment and analogous estimating
- Calculate the values at each node in reverse chronological order (right to left)
- Evaluate the best decision by following the lines of logic

We begin the tree by asking ourselves whether or not we are going to conduct the market analysis. If we conduct the analysis, there is an associated cost of $10,000. Figure 9.7 illustrates this as our first decision node. Let's call it decision node 1. If we conduct the market research, Figure 9.8 shows us that the results will either be favorable or unfavorable. This is our first chance node, which we designate with an *a*. Regardless, we will still have to decide if we are going to build the solution ourselves or tender bids. These are our third and fourth decisions, node 3 and node 4. Each of those paths will end in either a high, moderate, or low customer demand—chance nodes *d* and *e* respectively.

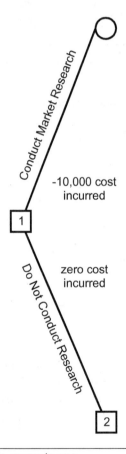

Figure 9.7   Build-or-buy decision scenario example one

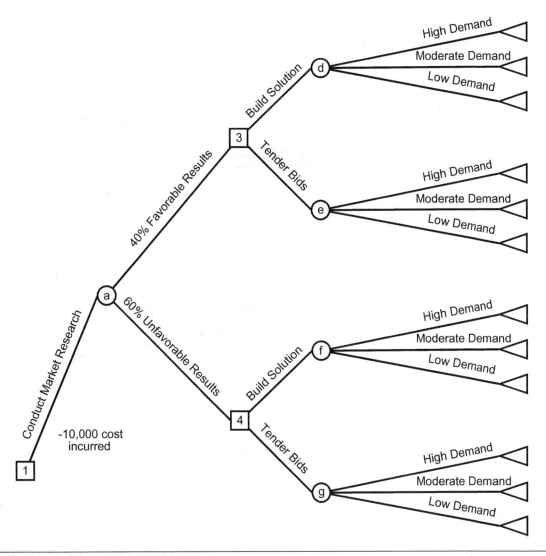

Figure 9.8 Build-or-buy decision scenario example two

As you can see in Figure 9.9, if we decide not to carry out the research, we still have to determine whether to purchase the solution or build it ourselves. This is our second decision node. Following the aforementioned line of logic, each choice has a chance node with three variables: high, moderate, and low customer demand. With the decision tree assembled, we can now begin to input the variables and calculate the values. Remember, the order of operation is top to bottom, right to left. Figure 9.10 gives us a detailed look at the values for the bins related to conducting the market research.

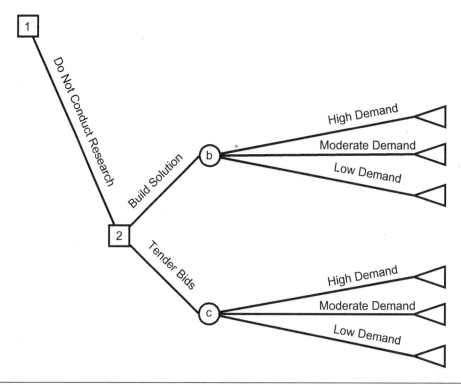

Figure 9.9   Build-or-buy decision scenario example three

Through interviews, analogies, inferences, workshops, chats, and e-mails, we have determined (see Tables 9.1 and 9.2) that the probability of favorable results on the market analysis is 40%—which means there is a 60% chance that the results will be unfavorable. Regardless, we still have to decide whether or not to build the solution or tender bids. If we develop the solution, the chance of high customer demand is 45%, 40% for moderate demand, and 15% for weak demand. Respectively, the payoffs are $200,000, $60,000, and a loss of $30,000 if the customer demand is low. In the event the results are unfavorable, the probabilities, of course, remain the same but the payoffs change to $140,000, $80,000, and $20,000 from high to low demand.[3]

Observe decision scenario example four, each bin on the favorable and unfavorable paths are calculated by multiplying the probabilities into the estimated payoffs and then adding them together. The results for chance nodes *d* and *e* are $109,500 and $98,000. Therefore, for decision node 3, the decision should be to "Build Solution"—of the two, it has the greater value.

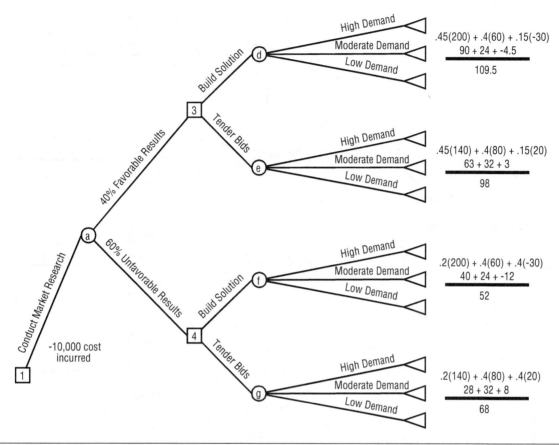

Figure 9.10   Build-or-buy decision scenario example four

Continuing to move from top to bottom, left to right, we observe the unfavorable path's decision node resolves to $68,000; again, it is the larger value between chance nodes *f* and *g*. Alternatively, we may decide to forgo the market research, in which case we simply have to decide whether we should build or buy the solution. Either way, we still have two chance events resulting in a high, moderate, or weak customer demand.

In the final analysis shown in Figure 9.11, we see that the plan to tender bids was approved with the decision to forgo the market analysis for a potential $80,000 outcome. Once again, keep in mind that this report comes with the caveat that the EV refers to several iterations of the same project under the same conditions. Nevertheless, with our goal reached, we gain some confidence and insight into which path may have a better chance of success. That was a lot of analysis; and we still have to take a look at decision tables! I hope you are not feeling too exhausted.

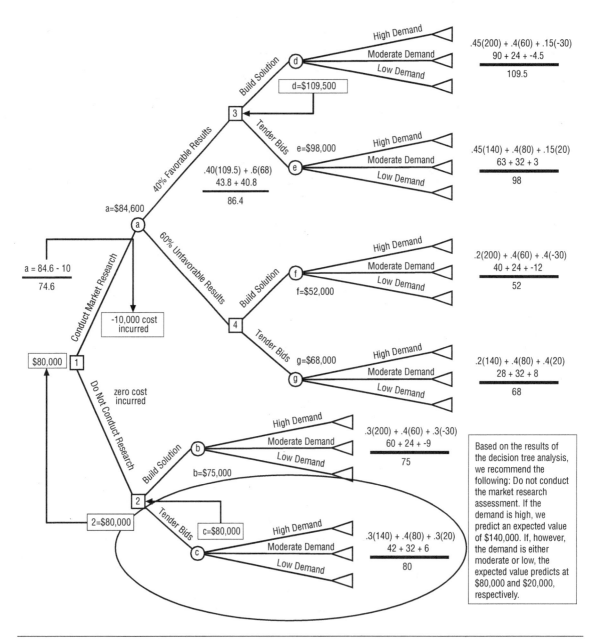

Figure 9.11   TNBA build-or-buy decision scenario example five

DECISION TABLES

Sometimes the only way to deeply involve yourself in a project is to do just that—involve yourself. You must, however, have the right tools to bring to the table and the confidence and leadership to use them. As a thought leader, educator, lecturer, author, and business professional, I want for us the opportunity to feel a part of something. At the risk of being hyperbolic, every project is a chance to showcase your unique skills, and decision trees and tables are an excellent way to impress.

Decision tables allow us to see how something should flow based on which variables are valid and which ones are invalid. Decision tables are easy to construct and they make it possible to detect combinations of conditions that would otherwise go unnoticed. Also, we can clearly identify conditions that do not make sense from a business logic point of view. As a result, requirements present in a compact, cogent, clear, logical, and convincing way.[4] Table 9.3 illustrates the structure of a decision table.

Table 9.3   Decision table structure example

Condition X	T	F
Condition Y	F	T
Actions to Take	A	B

We use decision tables in any analysis workshop where the outcome of an event depends on the combinations of different choices, which is almost all the time. The steps are as follows:

- Arrange a table similar to Table 9.3
- Try to make the condition responses *yes* or *no*
- Determine all possible combinations for each condition by using an exponentiation of the conditions and actions using the equation, where *b* is the base value and *n* is the exponent—example, if there are two states and the initial condition has three possible values (the base) while the second has two (the exponent), nine (3^2) columns are required
- Enter all possible combinations of values in the columns, reducing the number of combinations by half for each new row
- For each unique succession of states, identify the correct solution response
- Clean up the table by placing a "-" into intersections where the rule does not make logical sense, or the evaluation has no business value.

If you have worked out all of the combinations correctly, you will notice that each new row reduces by half and if you divide the table at the midpoint each side is a mirror of the other. Here is a quick example that shows the combinations and condition pattern.

Imagine a table with only two conditions, each resolve to either *yes* or *no* (true/false). We determine the number of combinations by using an exponentiation of the number of condition and action values, which in this case is two. Therefore, two to the power of two (the number of T/F conditions) is four

(2^2 = 4)—thus our decision table will have four columns. Table 9.4 is a simple example of a limited-entry decision table.

Table 9.4   Limited-entry decision table

Test = before the user selects "submit" we want to check if a username and password have been entered.			
Username	F	T	F	T
Password	F	F	T	T
Expected Result	Error: Msg. to user="Please enter a username and password."	Error: Msg. to user="Please enter a password."	Error: Msg. to user="Please enter a username."	Pass: System begin login process.

This example is not intended to promote best practice on requirements writing or decision analysis. In fact, this example is quite the opposite. Were I to pass this to a designer, they would likely want to decrease the number of combinations by half to streamline the code. We can quickly reduce the number of checks by *asking* the system to look for the absence of either the username or password and then return a more general message. Regardless, this example is merely intended to illustrate a simple limited-entry decision table. Now let's take a look at something a little more complicated in Table 9.5, by illustrating the decision table that our designer most likely wants to see.

In this example, we tested two objects—username and password—three different ways: blank, valid, and invalid. Table 9.6 illustrates how the condition pattern is formed using the exponential equation, 3^2 = 9. As you can see, this method of requirements presentation is far cleaner and more efficient than the antiquated *the system shall* writing method. As helpful as this table is, it still needs work. Our next example will focus on refining and cleaning a decision table.

Again, the designers and developers would not code the login exactly the way we see it in Table 9.6, but that does not matter. What is important is that we capture precisely what the table must depict regarding business logic. Notice the messages are deliberately inconsistent. If these requirements were written longhand across a traditional business requirements document, there would be a high probability that the incongruent user messages might make it all the way to development before anyone notices.

The subsequent and ultimately unnecessary change request that is generated is a good example of project waste and low requirements quality. When I consider some of the other diagrams or analysis that might come from this table, I imagine a simple sequence diagram to provide some insight into how the solution exchanges message with the session manager and repository which holds the login credentials. Providing a decision table in this manner facilitates further solution analysis and design with ease.

Let's complicate things even more by testing more conditions and examine how we clean up our decision table by placing a "-" in the intersections where a rule does not make logical sense, or the evaluation of the rule has no business value. Let's imagine that we want to examine whether or not a user is permitted to check out a document from the content management solution. We want to test four conditions:

- Is the user registered within the solution?
- Does the user have access to check out documents?

Table 9.5 Extended-entry decision table example

Test = login rules evaluation.

Conditions										
Username		Blank	Blank	Blank	Invalid	Invalid	Invalid	Valid	Valid	Valid
Password		Blank	Invalid	Valid	Blank	Invalid	Valid	Blank	Invalid	Valid
Actions	Expected Result	Error: Msg: "Please enter your username and password."	Error: Msg: "Please enter a username and a valid password."	Error: Msg: "Please enter a username."	Error: Msg: "Please enter a valid username."	Error: Msg: "Please enter a valid username and password."	Error: Msg: "Please enter a valid username."	Error: Msg: "Please enter a password."	Error: Msg: "Please enter a valid password."	–
	Show User	Login Page								User's Home Page

Table 9.6 Extended-entry decision table condition pattern

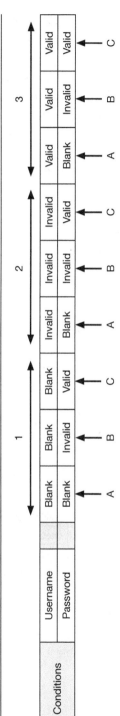

Conditions	Username	Blank	Blank	Blank	Invalid	Invalid	Invalid	Valid	Valid	Valid
	Password	Blank	Invalid	Valid	Blank	Invalid	Valid	Blank	Invalid	Valid
		A	B	C	A	B	C	A	B	C

- Is the user assigned to the project workflow for the document that they are trying to check out?
- Do they already have other objects checked out?[5]

As you can see in Table 9.7, I have labeled each of the conditions' values accordingly—we can use this legend to understand how to clean the table. Remember, we use an exponential equation to determine the number of columns we will need. In this case, we are testing four conditions, two different ways—true or false—therefore the equation is $b^n = 4^2 = 16$. Let's review this chart and identify the means to simplify the amount of logic represented.

Table 9.7   Extended-entry decision table unclean

		1	2	3	4	5	6	7	8	9	10	11	12	13	14	15	16
A	user registered?	F	F	F	F	F	F	F	F	T	T	T	T	T	T	T	T
B	checkout access?	F	F	F	F	T	T	T	T	F	F	F	F	T	T	T	T
C	assigned to project W/F?	F	F	T	T	F	F	T	T	F	F	T	T	F	F	T	T
D	already has a checkout?	F	T	F	T	F	T	F	T	F	T	F	T	F	T	F	T

When we observe columns 1 and 2, we see that they are nearly identical. The only difference is condition D—"Does the user have an active checkout?" Remember, in our scenario, we do not want more than one item checked out at a time, therefore the second rule is redundant. If the user is not registered, has no access, and is not assigned to a project, then they could not possibly have an item checked out. The logic is flawed, thus the rule is moot. Let's apply the same line of reasoning for the rest of the table and remove several of its columns. In each case where the user is not registered, checking the rest of the conditions would be pointless, as Table 9.8 illustrates. Keep in mind, this is not *testing* as an end user or systems tester may think it is; we are testing, or rather verifying and validating, a business rule.

Table 9.8   Extended-entry decision table cleaning

		1	2	3	4	5	6	7	8	9
A	user registered?	F	T	T	T	T	T	T	T	T
B	checkout access?	-	F	F	F	F	T	T	T	T
C	assigned to project W/F?	-	-	F	T	T	F	F	T	T
D	already has a checkout?	-	-	T	F	T	F	T	F	T

After reducing the table from sixteen tests to only nine, we can see that there is even more room for improvement. If the user does not have checkout access, the rest of the rules do not apply; therefore, columns 9–12 in example Table 9.7 can also be removed, as Table 9.9 illustrates.

Table 9.9   Extended-entry decision table cleaned

		1	2	3	4	5
A	user registered?	F	T	T	T	T
B	checkout access?	-	F	T	T	T
C	assigned to project W/F?	-	-	F	T	T
D	already has a checkout?	-	-	-	F	T

X = User permitted to check out project item.   X   Y
Y = User not permitted to check out project item.

Repeat this process until you have removed all redundant logic from your decision table. In the end, we reduced our example table to five columns. As you gain experience, you may not need to start with a table that holds all the possible combinations; but be careful, you might miss something if you do not follow the full line of reasoning using all combinations. One last thing, please do not assume that your system designers will do this for you. They should not have to sift through rows and columns of data to determine what business logic makes sense and what does not.

Understanding the source of our issues and their context becomes important because our invocation of root cause relies on comparing *what happened* to *what could* or *what should* happen. If we get this wrong, we run a high risk of rework, change requests, or missing the stakeholders' needs entirely. We call this modal reasoning. We have explored the REPAC source superset in significant depth. As an educator and behaviorist, there is much more I could share, but I believe I have captured the essential concepts needed to:

- Reason contextually, abstractly, systematically, choreographically, and modally
- Identify and understand stakeholders' professional salience and behavioral characteristics using several techniques and models
- Build an effective requirements team and charter using our stakeholder analysis
- Established a means to get to the root of our stakeholders' issues with a deep understanding of formal logic and causality

As we continue through this book, we will build a REPAC source set that will be used to identify the needs for our case study on which we need to focus, the perspectives we need to take, and the depth of analysis we must explore. Along the way, we will take a look at the methods, tools, and examples that I have been using in my twenty-plus years of project management and business analysis. As we wrap up, we will take all of our mock research, discussions, interviews, observations, workshops, and analysis and use it to create a cogent, clear, logical, and convincing set of stated requirements using the REPAC requirements assembler.

REFERENCES AND ADDITIONAL SUGGESTED READINGS

Argyris, Chris. 1990. *Overcoming Organizational Defenses: Facilitating Organizational Learning.* Pearson.

Bushe, G. R. 2013. "The Appreciative Inquiry Model." *The Encyclopedia of Management Theory.* Sage.

Checkland, Peter and John Poulter. 2007. *Learning for Action: A Short Definitive Account of Soft Systems Methodology, and Its Use for Practitioners, Teachers and Students*. Wiley.

Choice, F., B. C. Fast, and T. E. Time. 2012. "The Appreciative Inquiry Summit." *International Journal*.

Cooperrider, D. L. and S. Srivastva. 1987. *Appreciative Inquiry in Organizational Life*. Retrieved December 3, 2007, from: www.Appreciative-Inquiry.Org.AI-Life.htm.

Cooperrider, D. L. and D. D. Whitney. 2005. *Appreciative Inquiry: A Positive Revolution in Change*.

IIBA. 2015. *A Guide to the Business Analysis Body of Knowledge (Babok® Guide)*. International Institute of Business Analysis.

Johnson, D. W. and R. T. Johnson. 2011. "Constructive Controversy: Energizing Learning." . . . *Research and Practice*.

Kessler, E. H. 2013. "Encyclopedia of Management Theory." *Sage Publications*.

Yaeger, T. F., P. F. Sorensen, and Ulf Bengtsson. 2005. "Assessment of the State of Appreciative Inquiry: Past, Present, and Future." Research in Organizational Change and Development (Research in Organizational Change and Development, Volume 15) Emerald Group Publishing Limited.

ENDNOTES

1. In the initial 5-D model, the fifth stage was called *delivery* but this was changed by Cooperrider to *destiny*. Cooperrider felt that the term *delivery* evoked notions of traditional change management.
2. Note: these numbers are not intended to make business sense, they are arbitrary choices used to illustrate the logic of decision tree analysis.
3. Note: costs associated with the tender process were deliberately omitted since they are part of the procurement department's annual budget.
4. Traditional text-based rule requirements are sometimes presented as quasi-if statements, making it much harder to identify flaws.
5. In our case we only allow one checkout per user at a time. Although this rule, in combination with the others may not be a good requirement, I want to use it here for example purposes.

10

BUILDING THE REPAC SOURCE SET

"I'm selfish, impatient and a little insecure. I make mistakes, I am out of control and at times hard to handle. But if you can't handle me at my worst, then you sure as hell don't deserve me at my best."
—Marilyn Monroe (1926–1962)

A veteran of more than twenty films, from *Love Happy* (1949, United Artists) to *The Misfits* (1961, United Artists), Norma Jeane Mortenson, her birth name, was surely more than her public persona. Discovered in 1944 while working in a factory where she inspected parachutes, Ms. Monroe's stardom rose quickly but, as we know, ended before its time. A fan since childhood, I have referenced the previous quote for years. Our stakeholders may snap at us, bark at us, or even figuratively bite us, but despite how far they may be out of their comfort zone, we must always remember Ms. Monroe's posthumous advice. If we cannot *handle* our stakeholders when they are behaving like *children,* then we certainly do not deserve to work with them when they are at their most productive.

Now that we have covered several causal techniques and many behavioral concepts, we can safely move forward and assemble a Requirements, Elicitation, Planning, Analysis, and Collaboration Framework™ (REPAC®) source set, knowing that we have created a solid foundation on which we can build successful stakeholder engagement. We use the source set as input for elicitation events, planning sessions or collaboration in meetings, interviews, workshops, or anywhere a primitive set of project-related elements may be useful.

BUILDING AND APPLYING A REPAC SOURCE SET

In this chapter, we will build a REPAC source set and apply it to a problem scenario based on our case study. Our ultimate goal is to create requirements at a quantum level connecting the vital elements needed to realize organizational goals and objectives. As we consider the relationships between behavior, action, and response, we begin to identify and associate the characteristics and conditions of the root cause and apply them to elements which drive and constrain the solution and its components.

Much like project management, business analysis, and organizational behavior, many of the techniques I have mentioned were adopted well before this book came along. To my knowledge, however, no one has taken the time to combine all of these ideas into one narrative. So far, we have built a requirements team charter that required us to learn about effective communication, team attitudes, social styles, emotional intelligence and mindfulness, skills assessment, inference, reasoning, critical thinking, influencing, motivation theories, and positive mindsets, among others. Going forward, we examine the process I use when conducting business analysis activities with my team and other stakeholders. I call it the REPAC Framework. Let's quickly review the components of REPAC:

- *The source*: includes all stakeholders and the causal reason for the project, which we express as an opportunity, problem, issue, or some other demand we must address.
- *A need*: expresses as outputs from our source activities. We do not identify requirements with REPAC. Rather, we identify what is needed and then assemble what is *required* to fulfill the need.
- *Focus*: provides a center of interest or activity through which we investigate the cause and identify the current situation, the target state, and a proposal to get there.
- *Perspective*: is an extension of focus, allowing us to narrow our attention to a particular point of view, attitude, or understanding.
- *The depth of analysis*: or depth, will show us how far to take our inquiries, investigations, and analysis. We select a depth once we know what we want to concentrate our efforts on and the perspective that examination will take.
- *Assembly*: is our requirement building factory. Once we identify what is needed to solve the business problems or take advantage of the opportunities, we assemble what we *require* to satisfy those needs, element by element.

To make these tools more effective, we need a set of ideas to get the creative causal juices flowing. This is where the REPAC source subset enters the picture. The members of the source set are as follows:

- *Source members*:
  - Source = $\{c, s, p\}$ where:
  - c refers to the source causality type,
  - s refers to a source subject, and
  - p is the subject perspective.

Each member contains their own elements:

- *Subset elements*:
  - Causality = {linear, sequential, cyclical, spiral, relational, and mutual}
  - Subject perspective = {opportunity, threat}
  - Subject = {acquisition, assets, capitalization, communication, competition, consumer trends, contracts, environmental, expansion, innovation, interruptions, IPOs, legalities, liabilities, market trends, mergers, staffing, skill sets, partnerships, privatization, regulations, resourcing, safety, security, segmentation, social trends, strategy suppliers, supply chain, shared values, vendors, etc.}

Each subset of elements comes with a set of general rules:

- *Subset rules*

  1. When selecting a source causality, only one selection is permitted. Causation types are disjoint or mutually exclusive, meaning a cause-and-effect relationship cannot be cyclical and mutual at the same time.
  2. When selecting a source subject, the order does not matter, and repetition is not allowed. It would not make sense to build a REPAC source set with two or more of the same elements. It is expected that you want to discuss many subjects; in this case, each subject is its own set. This keeps conversations, meetings, and agendas clean and on-point. Every attempt has been made to add as many subjects as needed for most projects. However, you may add subjects to the subset as the need arises.
  3. When selecting source perspective, the order does not matter, and repetition is not allowed. Subjects are perceived as opportunities, threats, or both. In this event, we would discuss threats and opportunities separately.

Remember, small changes can happen in isolation, at any time, which may cause unforeseen issues to the project at a later date. The effects they cause can diminish or amplify through other things that are going on—a causal chain of events. When thinking about impacts, the context we are operating in must be considered while also giving thought to how people might react to the changes—will they work with it or against it? The following section is an example of a workshop agenda that could be put together using our source set as a guide.

WORKSHOP MEETING REQUEST

1. *Subject*: initial discussions for problem definition—recursively examining opportunities and threats as we cycle through each of the objectives outlined here.
2. *Introduction*: welcome to our first official workshop for the learning management system project for The New Business Analyst (TNBA), Ltd. If you are receiving this meeting request, it is because your attendance and full participation are required for the workshop's success. If you are unable to attend, please refer to the requirements team charter we ratified last week, which is *located here* on the project's intranet site, for instructions on how to proceed.
3. *Workshop goal*: by the time this workshop is complete, the project team will discover a partial set of mutual causes that are affecting TNBA and its various internal and external stakeholders with respect to its current learning system's end-to-end workflows and processes. Each objective that follows is an agenda item (these are our source set members), for which we build timed activities such as open discussions, causal analysis, decision trees, or brainstorms.
4. *Objective One*: for our first objective we create a concept diagram intended to define the problem space (we will develop this target further, as the REPAC Framework continues to unfold). Further information will follow on how to build a useful concept diagram.

5. *Objective Two*: using the concept diagram that we created for our initial target, our second objective is a series of brainstorming tasks, lasting no more than fifteen minutes each, for the following topics:

     With the conceptual diagram in hand, we conduct a context level end-to-end supply/value chain (as you can see, this is one source-set subject) analysis using a Six Sigma suppliers, inputs, process, outputs, and customers (SIPOC) tool. This technique helps illustrate how our industry *works* as a general best practice (this involves pattern-based thinking, which we discuss as part of REPAC's depth of analysis).

     The facilitating business analyst, using the concept diagram as a conversation signpost, will conduct a brainstorming session on general communication issues related to the problem space (another source set subject).

     With the results of the Six Sigma SIPOC diagram, we will have a 20-minute discussion on the interruptions (another source set subject) experienced through the value-chain; after which we will brainstorm operational options for improvement.

     Last, we close our workshop with any liabilities concerning the previous exercises. Further information will follow on how to work together as a requirements team to complete each of these tasks.

As you can see, each exercise inexorably led to the next, culminating into a cohesive workshop. Notice the source set subjects were not combined, but rather bulleted as separate activities, tasks, deliverables, objectives or different points of conversation. Also, recursively we explore opportunities and threats separately, again, so we can keep conversations clean and focused. This approach is a recipe, of sorts. A straightforward and powerful tool to help you arrange your thoughts, plan meetings, conduct analysis sessions, and so on.

The REPAC Framework's source superset serves as a means to begin on solid ground—an entire foundation for all project work. As the old cliché reads, "you cannot build a good home without a solid foundation." I do not know about you, but I do not want my house to start sinking two-thirds of the way through its construction because we could not bother to find out with whom we are working, why we are working with them, what their real causes or issues are, and how we intend to build a successful, lasting relationship.

I am sure you have noticed that our meeting request is incomplete—we have not finished our exploration of the REPAC Framework. As we continue to explore REPAC, we will expand on this example until we have a sufficiently complete workshop agenda.

SECTION 3:
The REPAC Superset

11

CHOOSING A POINT OF FOCUS

Almost everyone I work with or teach agrees with the need for organizations to be more nimble. However, when you ask stakeholders to break free of some of their artifacts, permissions, sign-offs, gates, and the like, eyes shift, their hands go up in some celestial bench press, as they express, awkwardly, that there is no way to make those kinds of changes. Suddenly we all become victims of our own devices.

Our understanding of a *requirement* is one such example. We are comfortable talking about value but what is it exactly? We will get more into that later; for now, let's declare quite plainly that purpose and value are not the same things. Use, or the reason for existing, is an objective to be reached—a target, an aim, or a goal. Why are we doing what we are doing? What is our purpose? *Value* is the quality or qualities that render something desirable. Value may be intrinsic or extrinsic. Value may possess great utility to minister to my wants or needs and yet have little or no *exchangeable value*; it is of importance to me, and only me. For projects to be successful, their solutions must create both *value* and *purpose* for whom they exist.

The traditional notion of a requirement as a proper noun representing declarative statements that must elicit from our stakeholders has been with us for a very long time and cannot be pruned easily. Stakeholders do not have requirements; they have needs—project or solution needs. This reasoning refers to all stakeholders and the organization itself—even you. Our fundamental task is to determine those needs and identify what we *require* of the project and the solution and all of its components[1] to satisfy those needs. Therefore, we conclude that it is the solution itself that holds the requirements and that *which is required* is fulfilled by performing work—project work. This idea coincides with the agile mindset.

The Requirements, Elicitation, Planning, Analysis, and Collaboration Framework™ (REPAC®) focus, which is part of the larger REPAC collaboration superset (focus, perspective depth), contains several elements, any one of which we select for needs elicitation, project planning, solution analysis, or general stakeholder discussions. At the highest level, we focus on elements inside or outside of the organization, as Figure 11.1 illustrates.

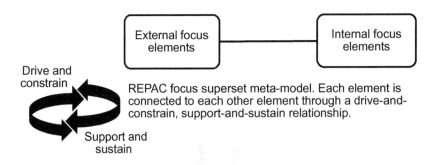

Figure 11.1   REPAC focus collaboration superset meta-model (© The New BA, Ltd.)

As you can see, the drive-and-constrain, support-and-sustain paradigm persists. The entire REPAC analysis framework employs a model known as a mesh network, which is a topology in which each node relays data to each other node. A peer-to-peer network is a simple example of a mesh. All nodes must cooperate in the distribution of data or, in our case, business analysis and project management work. For REPAC, all I have done is to replace traditional data nodes with organizational concepts and group those concepts into sets, subsets, and supersets.

Within each of the subsets, we see elements such as suppliers, vendors, ecologies, and geopolitical and other social issues consistent with common organizational discourse.

EXTERNAL FOCUS ELEMENTS

These external elements are forces that are expressed within the organization, causing it to evolve as the environment changes. These entities have a drive-and-constrain effect on each other and the organization, where change is the driving force and each element interacts with each other element.

Observe in Figure 11.1 that the relationship is bidirectional. Indeed, the organization can have far-reaching effects by driving the external environment to change. Companies such as Intel, Microsoft, and Apple come to mind. Apple, for example, pushed the smartphone ecosystem by challenging many of the mobile industry's established business models, taking a lot of the power away from phone companies. Providers were subsequently forced to support Apple's strategic plans if they wanted to sustain themselves through continued relations. Apple's business model changed the mobile communications industry forever.

One half of the goal of the REPAC focus superset is to create a common framework for combining the external macro-cultural, socioeconomic, geopolitical, ecological, supply chain, and other dimensions of organizational ecosystems into precise elicitation, planning, analysis, and collaboration sets. The organizations we work for are multi-stratum hierarchical systems influencing and influenced by and modifying and modified by the external environment through overall societal goals; hence the drive-and-constrain, support-and-sustain bidirectional paradigm. Figure 11.2 illustrates the REPAC focus superset of external elements, with each element bidirectionally interacting with each other element.

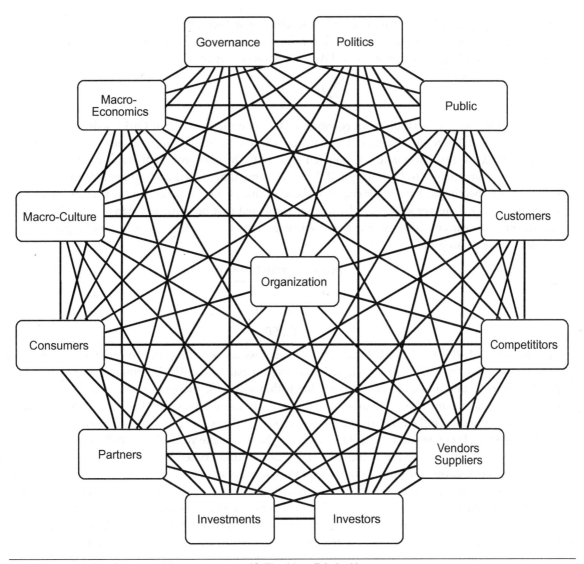

Figure 11.2 REPAC external focus superset (© The New BA, Ltd.)

Various combinations create topics of interest. Where the elements converge, we find meaning. Mathematical induction forms the structure of the model itself. The REPAC external focus elements interact with each other in a three-dimensional space creating a geodesic of 78 (including the organization itself) bidirectional, drive-and-constrain, support-and-sustain relationships. We see this shape form consistently throughout the entire model. Because of these multiple exchanges, we expect that the system external to the organization, as a whole, is not entirely knowable or controllable; however, it is somewhat predictable, because we are predictable.[2] A project is not a collection of stakeholders—*a project is stakeholders*. The cloud of what is not known will always grow faster than the sphere of what is known. Equation 11.1 gives us the proof for building any piece of the REPAC collaboration superset.[3]

$$\sum_{r=1}^{n} R = n(n-1) / 2 \qquad \text{[Eq. 11.1]}$$

This equation is just a variation of an equation by German mathematician Carl Friedrich Gauss. The formula is an original proof for the sum of n consecutive integers, known simply as $(n(n+1))/2$. Famously, Gauss developed this proof when he was only ten years old! The story goes that one day while in school, Carl's teacher, in an attempt to keep his pupils busy for some time, asked each student to sum the numbers 1 to 100. Expecting to have a relaxing day ahead of him, Gauss approached his teacher after just a few minutes with his answer of 5,050. The teacher suspected that he somehow had cheated, but Gauss had discovered a means of side-stepping the problem; and the rest, as they say, is history.[4] Equation 11.2 illustrates the Gaussian proof.

$$n = \frac{n(n+1)}{2} = \frac{100(100+1)}{2} \qquad \text{[Eq. 11.2]}$$
$$n = (50)(101)$$
$$n = 5,050$$

In Equation 11.1, R is the REPAC Framework element we are selecting, and the notation n denotes a pattern series or sequence of the items selected. Building any part of the REPAC Framework collaboration superset requires a determination of the *nth* value within a specific group of numbered elements. This equation tells us how many choices we have for our set. In the numbered series *3, 6, 9, 12, 15*, for example, 12 is the fourth number in the range or the *nth* value. Nine is the *n−1th* number, and fifteen is the *n+1th* number, and so on. Imagine you have n elements with which to make your REPAC collaboration set. You select *n−1* values to determine the number of viable causal links. When we multiply n by n we double count, so we need to divide the product by 2 to get the correct result of set elements.[5]

We use this logic in our everyday lives without realizing it. Imagine yourself trapped at the airport, and you must determine how many direct flights there are between where you are and where you want to go. You may also consider how many direct connections you need to make between eight computers in your home.[6] Like all other REPAC elements, the internal focus components group in the same manner.

INTERNAL FOCUS ELEMENTS

The other half of the REPAC focal purpose is to help us understand the elements within the organization that are important when it comes to helping stakeholders identify their needs and determine what is required to satisfy those needs. The views of the internal system, characterizing different levels, must be mutually compatible—meaning that each layer of the business must agree to share stories, plans, analysis, methods, processes, and the like in the same way—a lexicon, of sorts.

Data and information, in all its derivations, must be able to flow unimpeded throughout all parts of the REPAC system framework. This reality imposes requirements for timely resolutions to all project-related issues; thus reinforcing the need for the model. Although the model does not depend on a specific approach such as predictive or adaptive, it becomes evident that agile teams are better equipped to take advantage of REPAC's full potential. The stakeholder or stakeholders for each variable in the framework must commit themselves to the system, wholly. If we meet these demands, the construction of a robust multi-stratum model of interacting human, process, and technological ecosystems can be carried out and validated with relative ease.

As you might expect, some of the elements that are external to the organization repeat themselves when we look internally. Figures 11.3 through 11.6 demonstrate our interior view of the REPAC focus superset. Remember, REPAC is a way to organize our thoughts, plans, workshops, meetings, and by extension, the things that are required to meet the needs of our stakeholders at various levels of applicability. REPAC focus separates the collaborations and conversations that are worth having from those that are not useful. This approach helps us identify needs and assemble the required solution components we may have neglected otherwise.

With such a substantial number of ways in which these elements may interact with an organization at any one given moment, it is a wonder that some teams ever accomplish anything! Honestly, when visualizing the complex web of intercommunications, synergies, and interplays between the objects of this model, my heart goes out to economists and other financial leaders who try to make sense out of any of it. Remember, the drive-and-constrain, support-and-sustain bidirectional relationship is persistent for each line in these models.

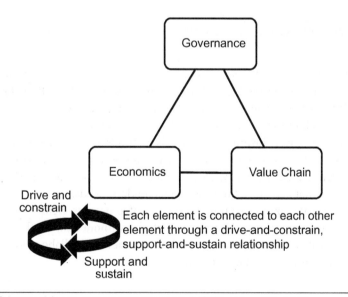

Figure 11.3   REPAC internal focus superset meta-model (© The New BA, Ltd.)

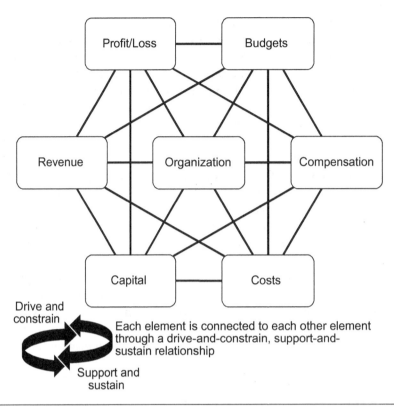

Figure 11.4   REPAC internal focus superset economics subset (© The New BA, Ltd.)

Did I get them all? Perhaps not, but it is a good start. Together, there are 12 external (from Figure 11.2) and 58 internal elements (from Figures 11.4–11.6), which gives us 2,415 ((70(70−1))/2 = 2,415) possible agenda items, workshops, interview objectives, or planning initiatives.[7] When we consider the numerous individual topics within each of the focal elements, the sum of combinations could easily number in the millions or conceivably, figuratively infinite. Indeed, this methodology expresses a useful framework with which to form meaningful discovery workshops, plans, analysis sessions, and collaborative interactions with stakeholders to identify, clarify, verify, and validate needs, which assemble into an unambiguous quantized expounding of what is required to satisfy stakeholders' needs.

As we have learned, human communication is a complicated process. Before having any conversation, we must acquire context and perspective. As previously stated, without context, there is no understanding. In the next chapter, we will continue building a REPAC Framework collaboration superset through an examination of perspective and a revisit of context.

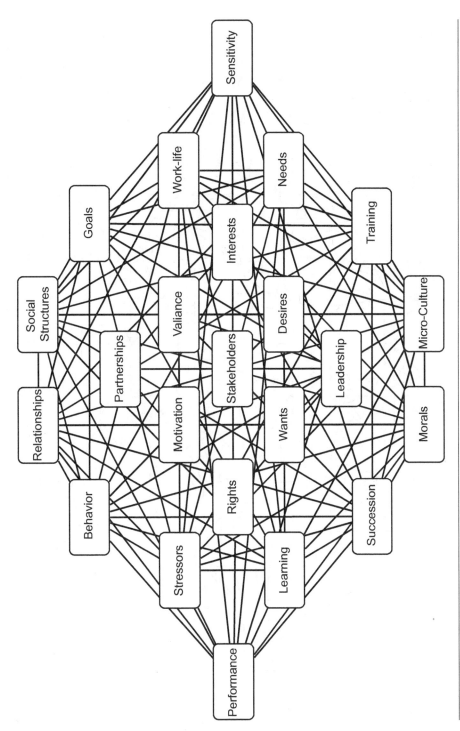

Figure 11.5   REPAC internal focus superset value-chain subset (© The New BA, Ltd.)

Figure 11.6   REPAC internal focus superset governance subset (© The New BA, Ltd.)

ENDNOTES

1. Remember, solution components include things such as subsystems, processes, policies, rules, help guides, documents, procedures, etc.
2. The same applies for all internal elements. With so many random moving parts, it is almost impossible to *know* the system with any great degree of accuracy. Predictions, however, are possible with enough reliable historical data, with which we may create informative models.
3. We apply this equation to all REPAC sets throughout the framework.
4. Gauss has made many immeasurable contributions to mathematics, including Gaussian distributions that bear his name and are used in statistics. These curves are otherwise known as normal distributions or bell curves.
5. In this context, A is to B as B is to A. Discussions about economics and culture are the same as those regarding culture and economics.
6. We would apply the Gaussian proof for these examples, but the general principle still applies.
7. The math of the model follows a mesh algorithm of $(n(n-1))/2$ where n is the number of elements in the model.

12

PUTTING FOCUS INTO PERSPECTIVE

Perspective is highly subjective. To improve communication and overall understanding, we must do all we can to help our stakeholders perceive clear, accurate points of view so they can draw useful and unbiased conclusions. Aiding our teams in understanding a particular attitude toward or way of regarding something about our projects requires patience and foreknowledge. An accurate perception of the relative importance of something can only come from context, reasoning, inference, and many of the other subjects discussed in this book.

We previously explored contextual reasoning. We must now put it to use by determining what our contextual frame of reference is or improving upon it when the option presents itself. In many cases, context is what it is. There are times, however, when we can set up a more conducive contextual frame of reference for our stakeholders. For example, when we have the opportunity to improve the circumstances of a meeting, interview, or workshop, we should. Other contextual frameworks such as historical, cultural, behavioral, relational, linguistic, and modal may also improve with proper learning and awareness by all collaborative parties.

Whether we are looking at inbound or outbound logistics, motivation, or succession, the Requirements, Elicitation, Planning, Analysis, and Collaboration Framework™ (REPAC®) perspective is a way to perceive focus; therefore, each of its elements must apply to all focus entities. Figures 12.1 through 12.10 describe the REPAC perspective superset. As you can see, the drive-and-constrain, support-and-sustain relationships that formed the geodesies we observed as part of the REPAC focus also apply to perspective—each element connects to each other element, throughout.

Many of the elements in these diagrams are self-evident; however, there are a few expressions worth noting. For example, the procedural and material frameworks are perhaps the most nested and complex sets within the REPAC model. Together these elements manifest as behaviors, characteristics, specifications, instructions, and work—which form the basis of our quantized requirement.

The procedural perspective subset contains the term *objects*, a multi-definition element that we also find in Figure 12.9. Semantically, the *object* possesses two senses—a physical sense and a systematic one.

Objects

Physically, an object is a material thing that is perceptible by our faculties. Objects may also be people or things to which we direct a specified action or feeling; for example, behavioral science and the first principles of quantum mechanics are the objects of my intellectual affection. In solutions design, however, and particularly in object-oriented analysis and design, an *object* takes on a different meaning.

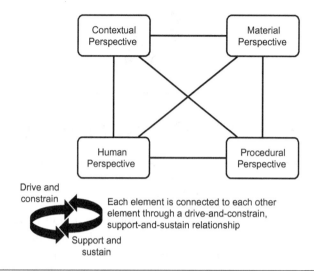

Figure 12.1 REPAC perspective on focus superset meta-model (© The New BA, Ltd.)

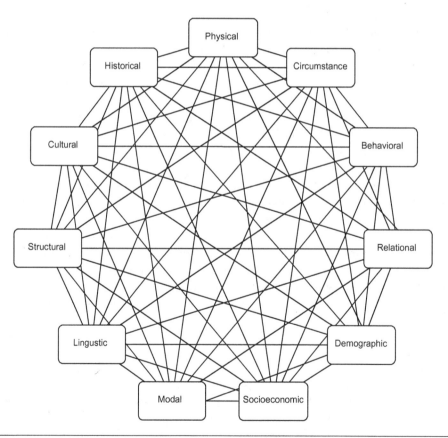

Figure 12.2 REPAC perspective on focus superset—contextual subset (© The New BA, Ltd.)

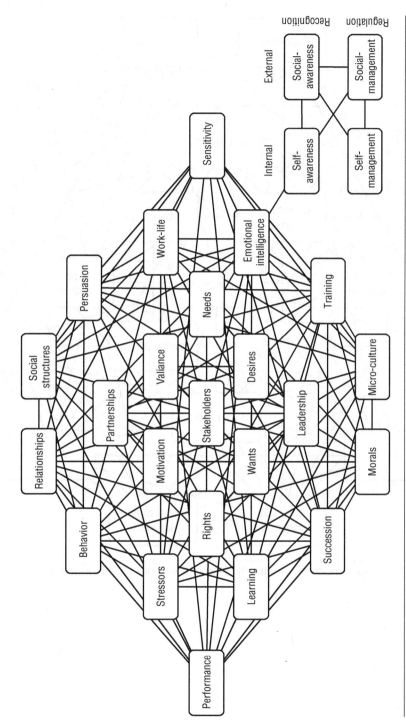

Figure 12.3   REPAC perspective on focus superset—human subset (© The New BA, Ltd.)

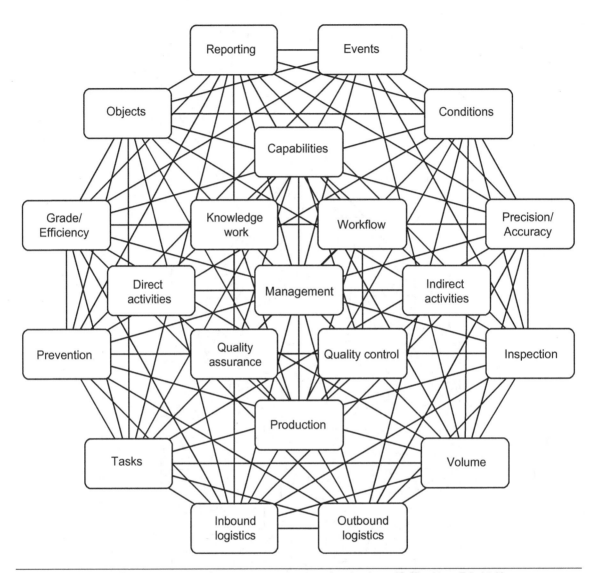

Figure 12.4 REPAC perspective on focus superset—procedural subset (© The New BA, Ltd.)

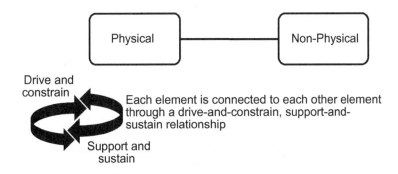

Figure 12.5   REPAC perspective on focus superset—material subset meta-model (© The New BA, Ltd.)

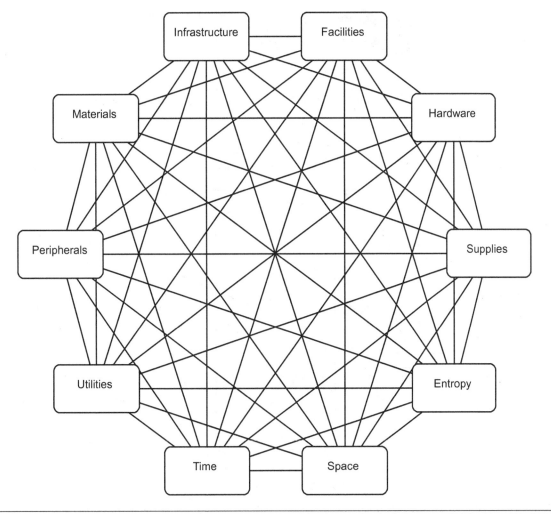

Figure 12.6   REPAC perspective on focus superset—material subset, physical elements (© The New BA, Ltd.)

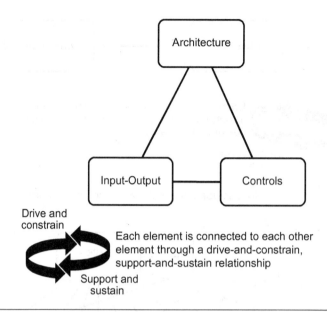

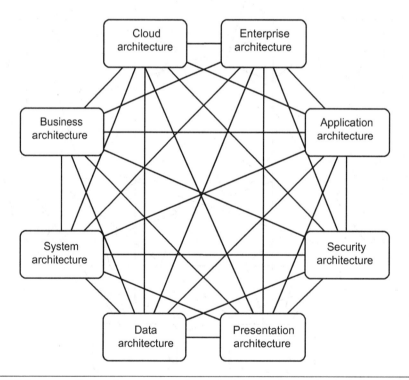

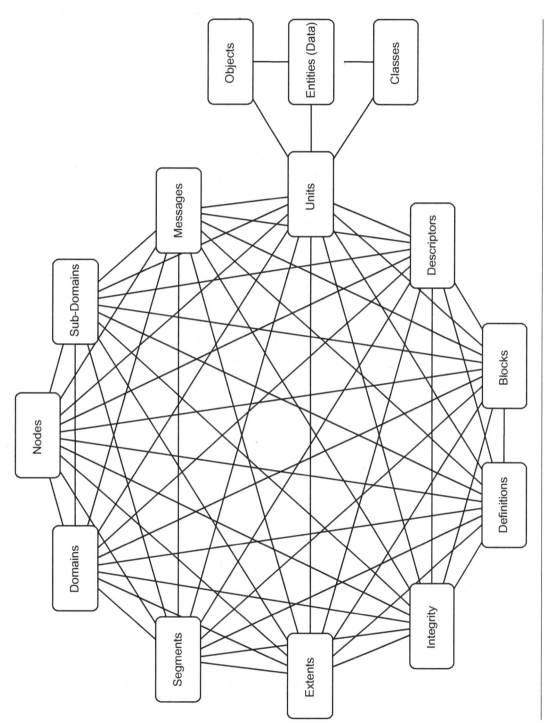

Figure 12.9 REPAC perspective on focus superset—material subset, nonphysical elements, and input-output (© The New BA, Ltd.)

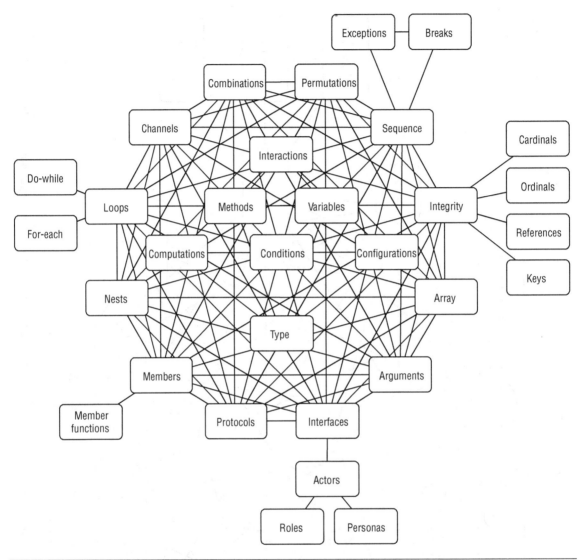

Figure 12.10   REPAC perspective on focus superset—material subset, nonphysical elements, and controls (© The New BA, Ltd.)

Object-oriented design is a development approach that designs and implements solutions as a collection of interacting *state-full* objects with detailed structure and behavior. There have been many academic attempts to define what an object-oriented paradigm is or should be, and I do not want to belabor the point, so I will defer to an author and colleague who has had a significant influence on my development as a business analyst (BA) over the years: Howard Podeswa.[1]

In his book, *The Business Analyst's Handbook*, Howard describes an object as an instance of a class, and a class is a template for creating an object. Howard provides an example from the class *customer*. In this example, *Jane Dell Rey* would be the object, a programmatic reflection of the real Jane. Howard goes on to suggest that BAs are accountable for defining business objects, which are used to capture business activities and things the organization needs to track correctly, such as an invoice (Podeswa 2008).

Business objects are instances of entity classes, which hold semantic significance and usually tie to business logic. Objects are encapsulated and create, read, update, delete data or conduct operations; moreover, objects perform their functions by sending synchronous and asynchronous messages to other objects. The only way to access the data within the object is through its encapsulated operations.

An object is an object; be it programmatic or physical. Each has intrinsic value, carries data, transfers messages, and performs functions; however, how we approach conversations about them are different enough to justify describing the element as both material-physical and material-logical; hence the need for my REPAC ontology.

ACCURACY AND PRECISION OF PERSPECTIVE

I have never found accuracy and precision to be intuitive words. Accuracy is a measure of how close something is to the actual, preferred, or *true value*; while precision is how close the measured values are to each other—how clustered they are. When we consider the quality of our estimates, requirements, or any other quantitative activity, is it our goal to be both accurate and precise? Which is better, given the option?

Accuracy aims for the bullseye, and precision asks us to be consistent with each measure. We should remember, however, that hitting the same value every time is not necessarily accurate. Measuring something over and over and getting the same result each time does not mean the result is precise—there may be bias. Bias is a systematic or built-in error that invalidates all measurements by a certain amount. Our degree of accuracy depends on the instruments, such as the types of mathematics applied. As a general rule, the term *degree of accuracy* is usually half a unit on each side of the unit of measure.

DIRECT VERSUS INDIRECT PERSPECTIVE OF DELIVERABLES AND ACTIVITIES

Direct activities contain an intrinsic value. Anyone who performs an immediate action can see the result of value as a real tangible thing. Retail sales are probably the best example of this phenomenon. Suppose I work at the Gap and I sell a pair of jeans to a customer who was *eyeing* them for a few weeks. She tries them on, they fit, and we complete the sale. We all receive value. I feel good for helping the customer acquire something she desired; she feels satisfied because the coveted object is hers, and most notably, the store received compensation for the transaction. Included are any sub-activities or tasks directly related, such as sending out marketing flyers advertising the jeans or even greeting the customer with a friendly smile when she entered the store. Direct value is easy to see and measure.

Value-added indirect or support activities are a little harder to measure. Looking back at the Gap example, my manager is providing support to me and the rest of the sales staff by scheduling our hours, keeping an accurate record of our sales and commissions, marking items for sale, deciding which items to place at the point-of-purchase, and other general management activities. Without the duties performed by the manager, the sales team would not be able to provide direct value to the store, at least not effectively or efficiently. Our challenge is determining the value, as a percentage, the manager brings to the overall sales cycle. This idea connects closely to our stakeholder analysis regarding understanding which stakeholders create direct or indirect value for the project and its outcomes.

A PERSPECTIVE OF KNOWLEDGE VERSUS TASK-ORIENTED WORK

We, and for the most part, our stakeholders, are knowledge workers. As a knowledge worker, you follow best practices, *not* business processes (laws and guidelines notwithstanding). Your central capital is knowledge, its acquisition, and its useful dissemination. When stakeholders keep information close to the vest, they are doing so because they see it as security; it is their intellectual capital and measure of personal and professional value. Anyone who gets paid to *think for a living* is considered a knowledge worker. This assertion is not to say that task-oriented workers have less societal, economic, or organizational value; in fact, we often observe quite the opposite. Where would we be if all of the so-called *low-level* sanitation workers suddenly disappeared? Our civilization would collapse in a matter of days. Although some may consider task-oriented workers to be less necessary, I prefer to find their value as foundational. Knowledge- and task-related work create an inseparable symbiotic relationship, entirely dependent upon each other. Therefore, we require honest and informed perspectives from all of our stakeholders.

Our last step in determining our stakeholders' needs is establishing the depth of our perspective. Will our analysis and subsequent quantized requirements assembly be a *deep dive*; should we risk jumping into that rabbit hole or do we want to keep the discussion *high-level*? What is a high-level discussion? How deep is deep? I don't know about you, but I am tired of hearing "just get me the high-level requirements." It is time to quantify these terms, and in our next chapter, we will do just that; with our depth of analysis of focus and perspective.

REFERENCE

Podeswa, Howard. 2008. *The Business Analyst's Handbook*. Cengage Learning PTR.

ENDNOTE

1. Howard Podeswa is the co-founder of Noble Inc. (a business analysis training and project consulting company) and the author of several books including *UML for the Business Analyst*. Howard is also an internationally known Toronto-based artist.

13

DEPTH OF ANALYSIS OF FOCUS AND PERSPECTIVE

How do we begin to understand fully the focus and perspective of our stakeholder discussions so that we can determine their needs? We start by understanding the very nature of our analysis. I define the Requirements, Elicitation, Planning, Analysis, and Collaboration Framework™ (REPAC®) depth of analysis using the following elements:

- Paradigms
- Classifications
- Forms
- Types
- Aspects
- Functions
- Expanse

Figure 13.1 illustrates the REPAC depth of analysis subset. I will briefly introduce each set and then provide details over the next several chapters.

PARADIGMS

We are at the point where we need to begin to "talk the talk" as it were. Our style of analysis should mimic, as closely as possible, the design and development style of our purposed solution and its components. Remember, we still employ a systems mindset; however, now we must adapt our reasoning and approximate how the system and all of its parts will function.

CLASSIFICATIONS

As a species, we love to group, organize, clarify, categorize, and classify things. After all, we are pattern-seeking, storytelling, social creatures. Classification schemes date as far back as our earliest known writings—Sumerian archaic and Egyptian hieroglyphs. Any organized language would require a method

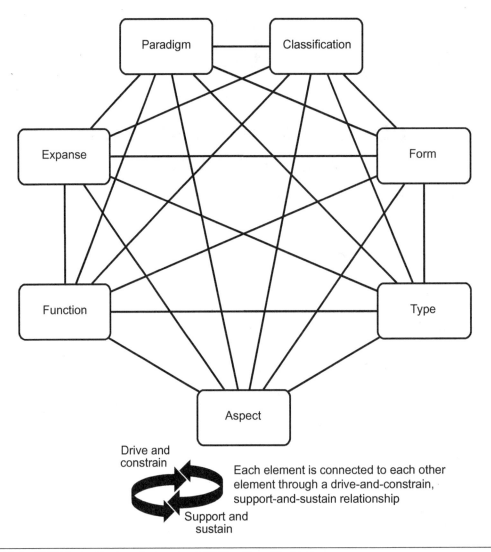

Figure 13.1   REPAC depth of analysis subset (© The New BA, Ltd.)

to group ideas into meaningful stories. Classifying things helps our brains compartmentalize and segment concepts into coherent thoughts through which we have meaningful conversations.

FORMS

Our analysis manifests itself as elements of behavior or structure. The way a business system (and all of its components) functions is mostly event-driven. Systems operate through the use of rules. Rules and other elements join to form a whole, which we regard as structure.

TYPES

Our analysis of a system is either qualitative or quantitative, that is, we are looking at the standards by which the system measures, or more important, the language, documents, and diagrams used to describe the system. Our quantitative analysis focuses on measuring the mechanisms and causes of the system; as well as predicting future needs.

ASPECTS

The aspect through which we examine the system (or any of its components) is logical or physical or both. Logically considering the characteristics of a solution requires a look at the solution in and of itself, outside of its physical implications. We ask ourselves, "Will this logically function independently of the solution?" Our physical examination completes once we make our choice and have *plugged in* all the parts that eventually make up the solution. Our third aspect of the analysis is a little murky.

FUNCTIONS

All systems have at least one function, that is, the named operation or operations that give the system purpose and value. Functions operate in many ways. Some are hierarchical, and others rely on interdependence. In any event, all systems must reach a state of relative stability with its environment.

EXPANSE

The expanse of a system relates to its logical and physical footprint. Questions such as, "How large is it?" "How long does it take?" "Is it dynamic or static?" and "How much does it decay, over time?" are all related to our analysis of the expanse of a system.

As you can see, this model provides some insight into how we join these concepts to create unique ways of looking at the problem space and building quantum requirements with great clarity. In the chapter that follows, we will take a closer look at the paradigms of analysis.

This book has free material available for download from the
Web Added Value™ resource center at *www.jrosspub.com*

14

PARADIGMS OF ANALYSIS

The Requirements, Elicitation, Planning, Analysis, and Collaboration Framework™ (REPAC®) recognizes the following analysis paradigms:

- Imperative
- Declarative
- Object-oriented
- Event
- Logic
- Symbolic

An analysis should follow the methodologies and principles of design and implementation of modern solution development. Rather than focusing on a specific programming language, an analysis should have the ability to use inferences and propositions shared by large classes of solution options. Figure 14.1 illustrates the REPAC depth of analysis paradigm set.

IMPERATIVE PARADIGM

With any imperative-based language, we *tell* the compiler—the program that converts the business analyst's (BA's) instructions into machine code—what we want to happen, step-by-step. This process is the key distinction of this paradigm. Not unlike the imperative[1] mood of linguistics, imperative solution development focuses on changing the state of a system. Imperative languages *run commands* for the system to perform. Also known as procedural programming, this paradigm allows analyzation of knowledge that exercises in the performance of some task carried out by the stakeholders.

Procedural programming breaks down programming tasks into collections of variables, data structures, and subroutines. The opposite of this is object-oriented programming, which we discuss shortly. Object orientation breaks down a programming task into objects that expose behavior (methods) and data (members or attributes) using interfaces.

The methods and techniques that we follow are often institutionalized; that is, they weave into structured and often highly formalized processes, templates, timelines, and expectations. Without proper

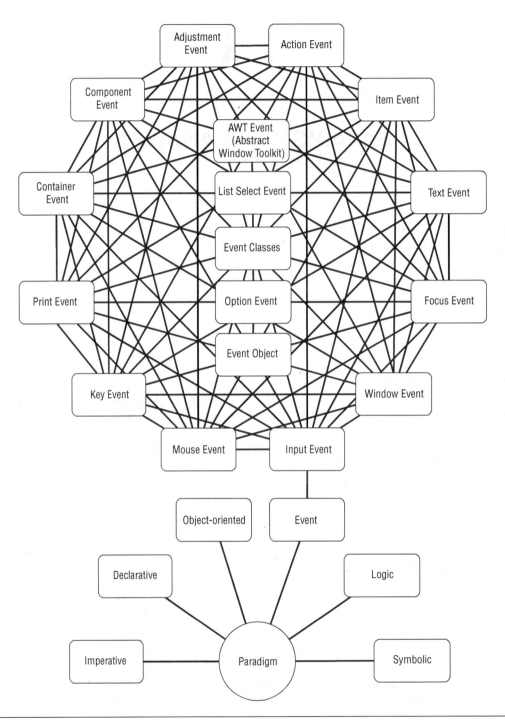

Figure 14.1   REPAC depth of analysis paradigms of analysis set (© The New BA, Ltd.)

attention, the requirements serve little value when they are rushed to design, only to return for more clarity. Requirements are at the heart of every project and BA's job—they are the currency on which we trade.

Many of the requirements we elicit and analyze are on legacy, procedural-based systems. Outdated applications are often referred to pejoratively, even though many of them still support mission-critical business processes. Regardless, BAs spend a great deal of their time handling change requests related to old solutions. Remember, requirements are a direct reflection of what we require of the solution by the stakeholders. Further, projects do not *have* stakeholders; projects *are* stakeholders.

In a structured or procedural analysis, we draw parallels to archaeology—the scientific study of material remains such as fossils and relics—in that it is important to investigate out-of-date entities to determine what has or does not have value for the transformation to the new solution. Despite urgencies to recreate all of the old processes within the new aggregate, it is imperative we follow due process and ensure that only activities that add value transfer into the proposed solution.

Once we complete our analysis, the transitive integration of the old into the new should proceed more smoothly. Before legacy requirements excavation begins, however, the BA must familiarize themselves with the systems at hand. Prudence suggests a *just enough just-in-time* (JIT) approach—learn what you need to learn, at the time it must be discovered. Borrowed from the manufacturing world, JIT is a concept that developed in Japan in the 1960s and '70s, most notably at Toyota Corporation. JIT's goal reduces the time it takes to manufacture something by creating a lean production environment—I added the *just enough* portion. For our purposes, we want to make use of a concept within JIT that concerns itself with inventory. Here, inventory is synonymous with elements such as procedures, rules, policies, tasks, exceptions, workflows, and the like.

Legacy systems tend to be quite complicated and after years of changes, resemble something similar to a bowl of knotted spaghetti. Navigating out-of-date systems necessitates the need to break the spaghetti into small chunks; hence, a JIT approach to research and analysis. We do not excavate what we need until it is wanted. There is little point in spending weeks of effort learning about business processes that we will not take action on for several weeks or perhaps even months.

Many legacy systems are procedural or imperative, built on languages such as assembly, Pascal, basic, COBOL, C, Fortran, PHP, and even Java Scripting. These languages use procedural calls—known as routines, subroutines, or functions—to carry out computational steps. Because procedural languages allow for multiple cycles to be *called* anytime during the program's runtime, great care must be taken to understand which procedures or functions are in use at any one given time. Similar to a relay race, routines and subroutines stop, start, overlap, and then start again. Excavating these procedures requires accurate structured analysis and design technique tools (SADT) such as:

- Context diagrams
- Interface diagrams
- IDEF0 models
- Process flow diagrams
- Data-flow diagrams
- Decision trees and tables
- Entity relationship diagrams

- Create, read, update, and delete (CRUD) tables
- Data dictionaries

Data dictionaries are often an essential artifact in a structured analysis, but they can offer some disadvantages for analytical purposes. Data dictionaries often reveal the core skeleton or the actual fabric of the information technology system. Data dictionaries answer the question: how is the machine *thinking*? However, since data dictionaries are by definition generated from the database and data tables, they are more implementation oriented than requirements oriented.

The SADT approach takes advantage of a standard known as Integrated Computer Aided Manufacturing Definition for Function Modeling—commonly known as IDEF (Ross et al. 1980). Within the IDEF family of models, the diagram designated zero (IDEF0) offers us precise means to excavate the rules, routines, subroutines, and steps from procedural-based systems and organizations.

In archaeology, researchers *sweep away* the dirt and dust to reveal the bones of an ancient beast. For us, the *bones* are the detailed business logic that other teams buried or codified within the solution or one of its components. How far a BA *digs* depends on his or her scope of work, experience, and the deliverables expected. Celebrated computer scientist Niklaus Wirth purposed a top-down method for understanding the various levels of procedural abstraction using a technique known as *stepwise refinement*. According to Wirth, this style of analysis terminates when we reach the programming language. This macroscopic statement of a general function to a microscopic set of precise procedures is best described using Wirth's own words (Wirth 1971):

> "In each step (of refinement), one or several instructions of the given program are decomposed into more detailed instructions. This successive decomposition or refinement of specifications terminates when all instructions are expressed in terms of any underlying computer programming language.... As tasks are refined, so the data may have to be refined, decomposed, or structured, and it is natural to refine the program and the data specifications in parallel. Every refinement step implies some design decisions. It is important that ... the programmer business analyst be aware of the underlying criteria (for design decisions) and the existence of alternative solutions...."

Stepwise refinement is commonly known as top-down design and is widely accepted in problem solving, project management, systems analysis, testing, and other domains closely related to business analysis. The process of breaking big ideas into little ones closely resembles how our brains evolved.

Applying these techniques allows us to quickly de-scope redundant, non-value-add processes. Structured analysis tools describe a system as a set of hierarchical functions. Process and data are kept separate using procedure models and data/entity models. As functions get called, they are tracked using stack machines, a set of processors designed to keep order among multiple processes, data calls, and retrievals. How we diagram the legacy system depends on the programming paradigm used.

DECLARATIVE PARADIGM

In this paradigm, we use declarations rather than imperative statements. Declarative development expresses the logic of the solution without describing its control flow. The developer *tells* the compiler what he or she *wants*, not necessarily how to get it. We *declare* our desired results, not the steps to get it. Statements, conversely, are single units of instructions containing expressions that follow a given sequence. Below is a comparison between imperative and declarative development:

Imperative
"List<int> results = new List<int>();
For each (var num in collection)
{ if (num % 2 != 0) results.Add(num); }"

Declarative
"var results = collection where(num => num % 2 != 0);"

These are both straightforward examples, but they express the differences well. The first example asks the program to (1) create a number set, (2) cycle through each number in the set, and (3) check each number, and if it is odd, add it to the results. The later declarative example accomplishes the same goal by asking the program to pass anything that is numerically odd without having to cycle through the set, one inter-ference at a time. Developers seldom use one style over another. Coders choose one method over another because it best represents the issues at hand or because it is the *code base* that the system is already using. This statement reinforces the necessity to capture stakeholder needs and convey solution imperatives with a methodology that the designers and developers will understand, minimizing the chances of code-based errors stemming from poorly articulated *requirements*.

Functional programming is a specific subset of declarative programming that treats computations as the evaluation of mathematical functions and avoids changing the state of the program itself. With origins in lambda calculus, functional programming expresses algorithms based on function abstraction and ap-plication using variable binding and substitution. Fixed as declarative expressions, the algorithms for each function create issues if the function changes during development. This risk creates problems for projects where the requirements are not well understood, frequently changing, or poorly derived.

In functional programming, the output of a function depends on the arguments passed to the function. Therefore, analyzing solutions using this paradigm requires understanding the arguments themselves. Any visual tool, such as activity diagrams, that help display these algorithms will help developers under-stand which declarative expressions must be used to build each function.

Understanding how the functions and arguments construct also aids our developers with the eventu-ality of programming *side effects*, which are changes to the state of the system or a variable, unanticipated reads, writes of data, or any other unwanted modification outside the scope of the function itself. One of the most powerful tools a BA brings to the table is the ability to ask questions like *why?* and *what if?*

OBJECT-ORIENTED PARADIGM

The *requirement*—born in the crucible of elicitation, analysis, and specifications writing—is at the heart of any successful business solution. A common way to capture this information is through the use of use cases. Use cases are at the heart of object-oriented analysis and design (OOAD); they drive all efforts such as planning, business rules identification, and data needs.

OOAD focuses on an abstraction known as an *object*, which is its core unit. The next level of abstrac-tion is a class, which serves as a *blueprint* for an object. A class is just a special kind of object which carries the instructions for making objects—not unlike the deoxyribonucleic acid (commonly known as DNA) of a cell, a molecule that carries the instructions for life. Classes and objects encapsulate;[2] that is, they hold their instructions or methods and data within themselves—again like a cell or an atom. If you see some similarities between OOAD and REPAC, it is intentional. Objects can inherit instructions from other objects, and they may also take on the traits of other objects, polymorphically.[3,4]

I am a fan of the process of considering something independently of its associations, attributes, or concrete accompaniments. An abstraction quarantines function from implementation. Through abstraction, we reason concepts without knowledge of application; and execution without knowledge of use.

If you would like to learn more about OOAD, please visit the Object Management Group's website (omg.org), which details the Unified Modeling Language (UML) and how to apply it to business analysis and software design. When I use this approach, which is often, this is the process I follow:

- *Descriptive modeling*: We use basic shapes to develop a business-oriented view of a process or problem domain without necessarily describing all objects, exceptions, relationships, and errors in detail. Descriptive modeling gives us the euphemistic five-thousand-foot look of the problem or opportunity. Describing real-world events and the relationships between the business factors responsible for driving and constraining them helps avoid digging too deeply, too soon.
- *Analytical modeling*: Next we use an extended palette of shapes to show more detail of events and exception handling, necessary to create detailed imperatives for identifying what we require for implementation. Analytical models are closed-form solution diagrams illustrating how business logic functions within a solution, independent of any notion of physical implementation. Also used in mathematics, analytical modeling allows us to design what-if, sensitivity, and optimization analyses without compromising the current or proposed solution or any of its components.
- *Executable modeling*: These are the details in our devil. This method is the art of something I call *adequate approximation*. No models or experiments are entirely accurate. We figure out what level of accuracy we need of a prototype to answer a question satisfactorily, for now, and then continue to build the model or design an experiment allowing us to fully understand the current level of precision required before proceeding to the next layer of analysis or prototype. Usually, we capture models and review them as conceptual diagrams with supporting text. Instead of symbolic pictures, however, an executable model is a working prototype. Exploring the prototype allows us to agree with the model, settling on a solution approach. Participation in this process does not require technical training in modeling, such as UML. This technique aligns well with the agile mindset as it focuses on user functions. Prototypes are deep or shallow, evolutionary or throwaway. Preliminary versions may focus on one function or many. Prototypes can use code or wireframing, and rapid prototyping software is designed to approximate a user's experience.

EVENT-DRIVEN PARADIGM

The event-driven paradigm is orthogonal[5] to other programming paradigms. It is possible to implement event-driven programming in languages that do not support it directly; this is often the case. Developers combine object-oriented ideas with those that are event-driven. We can also develop an event-driven solution without it being object-oriented or imperial. It is for this reason that I include event classes using the mesh equation, where every class is connected to every other class, as seen in Figure 14.1. In these situations, you may have events processed by simple procedural event handlers or more elaborate systems in which events, message queues, and other aspects of the system represent as objects. Hence the orthogonality lays between an event-driven solution and other aspects of programming.

Unlike imperative or declarative systems that operate by stating requests and waiting for responses, event-driven solutions process events as they occur. This method allows the system to observe, react dynamically, and issue responses relevant to the current situation. Considering that patterns connect the events that take place in any system, the event-driven analysis offers a unique opportunity to work closely with the business users and solution developers.

Event-driven analysis and its corresponding programming languages focus on events that include user inputs through a graphical user interface (GUI), networking requests from websites, or other online properties. Actions such as mouse clicks, sorting data, keyboard presses, messages from other programs, moving and resizing windows, and other various object manipulations justify using programmatic concepts known as events.

Before the widespread use of GUI, computer solutions would typically *wait* for the user to input a procedural command. As GUIs became more complicated than the green screen command line solutions of the past, developers had to determine what actions a user might do with the GUI and the many ways they may do it. Commands on the keyboard or clicks on the screen were now considerations. Data entry also became more complicated with the advent of multiple points of entry or channels.

For users working in a web-based environment, this technique offers us advantages including the ability to communicate to the designers and developers which pages should be returned based on the user's events. This process allows for dynamic page creation with tools like JavaScript. As we move away from the programming language aspect, it can be beneficial to think of the event-driven technique as a system design paradigm rather than a programming paradigm. Over the years I have come to understand that regardless of how the rest of the solution or any of its components construct, the event-driven aspects dominate.

The event-based analysis focuses on the simple question, "What do you do—show me?" Similar to use cases or some process mapping techniques, we write simple sentences such as "User selects print"; "User sorts data results from oldest to newest"; or "System X sends an asymmetric message to pass variable Y to process A." With these statements, designers and developers know what work they must perform to implement the stakeholders' needs. They know *what is required*!

LOGIC PARADIGM

Sentences, written in the logical form that is formal logic, use the logic programming paradigm. We read these statements declaratively as reasoned implications. Formal logic follows specific rules and symbols such as a logical consequence. Symbolized by a double arrow pointing to the right, it denotes an *if/then* statement; for example, $A \Rightarrow B$ (if A is true then B is also true). The use of mathematical logic to develop solutions is also a feature of the lambda calculus, although we consider it its paradigm. I have never spent time with anyone who has used this method to develop programs, but the use of logic as a means to determine the imperatives required to satisfy a need is beneficial. If logic is free of contradiction, it is a simple matter to define the work necessary to bring purpose and value to the stakeholders.

SYMBOLIC PARADIGM

Symbolic programming allows the solution to manipulate itself as if it were plain data. Sometimes referred to as *learning programs*, symbolic solutions nest small units of logic to create complex functions and complex processes. The engineering, mining, farming, scientific, and gaming communities are among some of the industries that develop applications such as artificial intelligence, expert systems, natural language processing, and open world games.

Any technique that uses abstracts such as X and Y over integers is said to be symbolic. The symbol carries inherent properties that we or the system itself manipulate based on business logic.

CONCLUSION

Regardless of the paradigm applied, we always layer our analysis at distinct levels of abstraction; from general context/concept to detailed procedures. As a general approach, I use the following method:

- *Assemble and research source data*: any good analysis needs data. Start with sourcing all information you can find about the problem area. Think of data as the raw material and the value you get from it as information—what you learn is knowledge. Remember, JEJIT; only learn what you have to, when you must.
- *Establish correlations*: remember, *correlation does not always imply causation*! Look for patterns that are verifiable and repeatable. How strong is the relationship?
- *Establish causality*: determine the causal relationship and its temporal identity. Are things happening in close succession or spaced out by department and time?
- *Determine the issues to address*: once you have established correlations and causality, you will know what must be addressed and resolved. This strategy involves selecting items from the REPAC source set for needs identification and further analysis.

In the next chapter, we continue to understand our depth of analysis by examining the classifications of different systems.

REFERENCES

Ross, D. T., J. W. Brackett, R. R. Bravoco, and K. E. Schoman, Jr. 1980. "Architects Manual, Icam Definition Method Idef0." *Computer Aided Manufacturing International.*

Wirth, Niklaus. 1971. "Program Development by Stepwise Refinement." *Communications of the ACM* 14, no. 4, pp. 221–27.

ENDNOTES

1. This is why I use the word *imperative* for understanding what we require to satisfy stakeholders' needs. Regardless of what programming language developers use, we need to pass step-by-step instructions encapsulated as a quantized requirement or imperative in order to ensure the quality of our work.

2. Encapsulation is a design concept that *wraps* data (variables) and the code acting on the data (methods) together as a single unit.

3. *For the lay business user*: We combine the words *form* and *morph* to describe how business objects can do the same thing in different ways, achieving the same outcome. This technique allows analysts, designers, and developers to assign a different meaning or usage to something in different contexts (this is another example of the importance of contextual perspective).

4. *For the technophile*: Static or compile-time polymorphism and dynamic or run-time polymorphism describe operations and functions which are built or run off templates (static parametric polymorphism) that apply to more than one type of argument. Polymorphism applies different meaning (semantics, implementation) to the same symbol (message, operation) in various contexts. Using the operator "+" as the example in the expression "sum = a + b;" produces a polymorphic operation which uses different types of integers, strings, or vectors, for example. Specific static context—types of operands "x" and "y"—will determine at compile time which implementation of "+" applies.

5. In computer science, something is said to be orthogonal if it is isolated or partitioned from something else, but not necessarily independent. Object-oriented and event-driven programming are orthogonal because we can isolate objects from each other while still taking advantage of what each offers the solution or any of its components.

15

CLASSIFYING SYSTEMS

"Trying to understand the way nature works involves a most terrible test of human reasoning
ability. It involves subtle trickery, beautiful tightropes of logic on which one has to
walk in order not to make a mistake in predicting what will happen."
—Richard Feynman

Feynman's work was integral in the formulation of quantum mechanics, one of the inspirations for this book. Earlier, I wrote that I firmly believe we are, by profession, business-systems analysts. In that same chapter, we took a quick look at what defines a system. Systems are self-governing in fulfilling their purpose and are made up of discrete entities/objects, processes, activities, and tasks, among other things.

Recall that in Chapter 9, we took a look at the soft systems methodology (SSM) as a means to identify causality. Peter Checkland, in his development of SSM, divided systems into five classes: natural, human, designed-physical, designed-abstract, and transcendental systems (Checkland and Scholes 1999).

Checkland's book on systems thinking—a book every analyst should read—documents the fundamental basis of SSM. Figure 15.1 provides a typological example of how three of his systems interact (I removed the triangle enclosing the terms from the original for easier reading) (Checkland 1999).

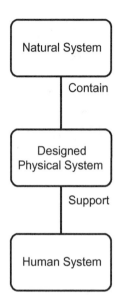

Figure 15.1   Checkland's SSM system interaction example

NATURAL SYSTEMS

Bio-ecosystems, climate systems, planetary systems, and the like fall under the classification of natural systems—essentially, any biological or other naturally occurring system based upon physical, morphological, or anatomical properties and relationships.[1] We are natural systems, but because we interact with computers and organizations, we also live in another classification—a human system.

HUMAN SYSTEMS

Human systems or human activity systems, as the model conceived initially, would naturally include socio-technical systems. The classic people, process, and tools/technology (PPT) triad is an example of a simple view of a human system. Considering purpose, procedures, interactions, integrations, and the emergence of concepts such as quality, value, and teamwork are salient markers of understanding the systems with which we interact daily, it makes sense to spend a little time on this classification.

British historian Ian Morris (1960), Willard Professor of Classics at Stanford University, describes social [systems] development as:

> *"The bundle of technological, substance, organizational, and cultural accomplishments through which people feed, clothe, house, and reproduce themselves, explain the world around them, resolve disputes within their communities, extend their power at the expense of other communities, and defend themselves against others' attempts to extend power." (Morris 2011)*

This analogy directly relates to how an organization, which is also a social system, functions—to know one is to understand the other. Quantitative studies of our projects and their expected performance will only get us so far. We must also look to qualitative assessments of success. This notion maps directly to the Project Management Institute's idea of stakeholder satisfaction as the primer for project success. A business analyst could measure, and measure all day, but if the stakeholders don't *feel* satisfied after having been given their fill at the project banquet, what is there to do?

Quantitatively, it is easy to see who has the most or who is the fastest. Perhaps the more critical question is: *what is the best way to identify who has the happiest customers and the best and most satisfied workforce?* Moreover, which of our clients are with us because of *why* we do what we do, not *what* we do? These are the hard questions that project professionals must pursue. Measuring something does not necessarily make everything more objective. Others will always argue the results or the interpretation of the results or perhaps the method that was used to collect the data. Measuring offers the results as more explicit, that is stating our conclusions clearly and in detail and leaving less room for confusion. An analyst must take in all the data he or she can find, qualitative and quantitative.

These arguments are indispensable when we compare how we have managed projects over the decades. The traditional waterfall approach matches well with the classic locked-in idea of western dominance, while the more recent accidental theory seems to agree with the need to become and remain agile in the approach to a project and organizational management. There can be no doubt that social changes directly affect our organizations, projects, and us, in a perpetual drive-and-constrain, support-and-sustain partnership. I don't imagine a swinging pendulum of change shifting to and fro, but instead a circle with no end, no beginning, and no distinct point of origin.

Figure 15.2[2] is an example of how we may view a human. This diagram depicts parts of the system that, like many other Requirements, Elicitation, Planning, Analysis, and Collaboration Framework (REPAC®)

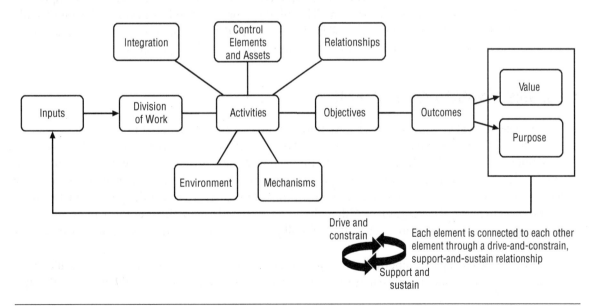

Figure 15.2 Human/socio-activity/technical system example (© The New BA, Ltd.)

models, connect through a drive-and-constrain, support-and-sustain relationship. Mechanisms, such as people, machines, tools, technology, and the like are the elements performing the activities. The activities of the system are carried out by behaviors; this creates the system's structure. The system's structure is purposed, designed, and managed by the mechanisms of the system. This thought confirms and establishes relationships that must be cultivated and sustained. These relationships, in turn, are governed by rules, habits, and rituals experienced within a system we have designed and of which we are a part.

DESIGNED PHYSICAL SYSTEMS

According to general systems science principles, "there is constant interplay between theories and practice, with theory informing practice and outcomes from practice informing theory" (Bourque and Fairley 2014). Collectively, the system serves a purpose and creates value for the entity, as a whole. The system must also serve a purpose and create value for its collective members and must set out to create an equal balance with its external environment. Designing a system, therefore, is not just identifying what is required for the *machines to work*; our analysis must go deeper.

Checkland defines a physical system as something purposefully designed and subject to the constraints imposed by physical laws. These limitations form the basis of the specifications that we build into a system to account for estimations of how the arrangement will behave in real-world scenarios; for example, the stresses on an automobile braking system at given speeds.

Systems become more abstract as they interact with each other. *A Guide to The Software Engineering Body of Knowledge* (*SWEBoK®*), *Version 3.0*, further classifies designed physical systems as *enterprise, product, service*, and *system of systems capability*[3] (Bourque and Fairley 2014). All of these systems fit within a business architecture. This theory is exemplified in Figure 15.3, which depicts a comprehensive, transparent view of a business ecosystem. This model is part of The Business Architecture Guild's *A Guide to the Business Architecture Body of Knowledge®* (*BIZBOK® Guide*), *Version 5.5*. John Zachman,[4] TOGAF®,[5] and others have similar depictions of business architecture design theory and practice.

DESIGNED ABSTRACT SYSTEMS

Taking a closer look at Checkland's model, we note that no one system can exist in and of itself; they all seem to align with the commonly known PPT triad. We channel most of our energy into abstract systems. Abstractions seem to embed themselves at the interaction points and incorporate elements in and of themselves. Designed abstract systems do not contain physical artifacts. They are developed to serve some illustrative purpose such as a mathematical model, a logical process, or system design. Abstract systems are not subject to physical laws, as such. Although there are no underlying theories that can be devised to support the construction of an abstract method; for all practical purposes, we consider all constraints for real-world testing.

Projects, for the most part, embody abstract systems. Diagrams, models, processes, policies, rules, procedures, software, and code are constructs that are not subject to physical laws.[6] Thinking back to the PPT

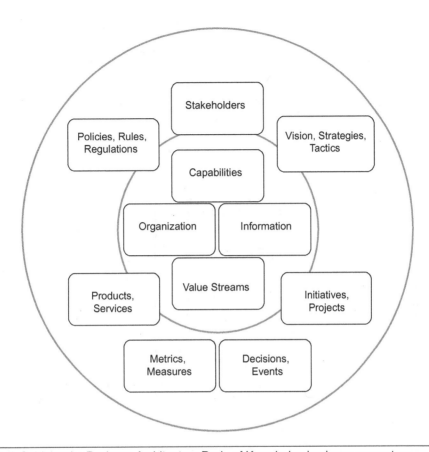

Figure 15.3   A Guide to the Business Architecture Body of Knowledge business ecosystem

triad, human, physical, and abstract systems are combined, thus creating software, processes, and artifacts such as reports and other metrics—all (hopefully) aligned to some organizational goal.

TRANSCENDENTAL SYSTEMS

Checkland considers transcendental systems beyond our ability to measure and understand. This view is best described in Figure 15.4 using systems scientist and interdisciplinary philosopher Kenneth Boulding's hierarchy of system complexity, which is considered a compliment to theoretician Ludwig von Bertalanffy's general systems theory (Boulding 1985). Boulding defined transcendental systems as: "the ultimates and absolutes and the inescapable unknowables that also exhibit systematic structure and relationship" (Boulding 1985). Checkland refers to these five systems as constituting a *system map of the universe* (Checkland 1981).

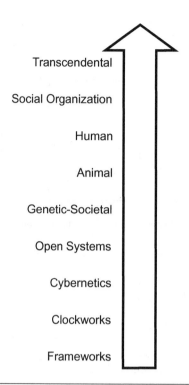

Transcendental

Social Organization

Human

Animal

Genetic-Societal

Open Systems

Cybernetics

Clockworks

Frameworks

Figure 15.4   Boulding's hierarchy of system complexity (from Skyttner, 1996)

With an understanding of how systems classify, we can now begin to explore forms and types.

REFERENCES

Boulding, Kenneth E. 1985. *The World as a Total System*. SAGE Publications, Inc.

Bourque, P. and R. E. Fairley, eds. 2014. Guide to the Software Engineering Body of Knowledge, Version 3.0, IEEE Computer Society, www.swebok.org.

Checkland, Peter. 1981. *Systems Thinking, Systems Practice*. Wiley.

———. 1999. *Systems Thinking, Systems Practice. Includes a 30-Year Retrospective*. Wiley.

Checkland, Peter and Jim Scholes. 1999. *Soft Systems Methodology in Action*. Wiley.

Morris, Ian. 2011. *Why the West Rules—for Now. The Patterns of History and What They Reveal About the Future*. Picador.

ENDNOTES

1. Some argue that we can only call something a natural system if there is no human intervention. With this assertion, therefore, there are few truly natural systems left.
2. I hope this diagram gives you a hint of where we will find that which is required to satisfy the needs of our stakeholders.
3. The SEBoK is another book I encourage you to read. You can purchase it in paperback or download the PDF from: http.//sebokwiki.org.
4. Zachman International—Enterprise Architecture Framework. The Zachman Framework is an enterprise concept and is a fundamental structure for enterprise architecture that provides a formal and structured way of viewing and defining an enterprise (Wikipedia).
5. The Open Group Architecture Framework (TOGAF) is a framework for enterprise architecture that provides an approach for designing, planning, implementing, and governing an enterprise information technology architecture (Wikipedia).
6. They follow their own rules, but those rules are also abstract.

16

FORMS AND TYPES OF ANALYSIS

---

*"The human brain is a complex organ with the wonderful power of enabling man
to find reasons for continuing to believe whatever it is that he wants to believe."*
—Voltaire

We are so often fooled by other people and even ourselves that we *need* the tools of critical thought and careful analysis to protect ourselves from our own biases, blunders, and even delusions. Understanding how we analyze keeps our thoughts reasonable.

FORMS OF ANALYSIS

Our form of analysis will be either the examination of an object that does something or the arrangement of and relations between the parts or elements that make up the object that we are analyzing. Figure 16.1

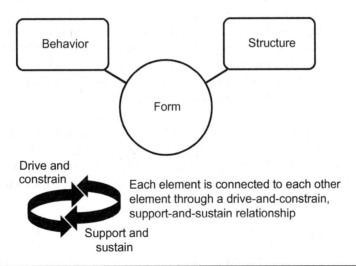

Figure 16.1 REPAC depth of analysis form of analysis set (© The New BA, Ltd.)

illustrates the Requirements, Elicitation, Planning, Analysis, and Collaboration Framework™ (REPAC®) depth of analysis form set.

Behavior

A behavior is something that defines a range of actions in combination with itself and its environment. It is the response of a system (including organisms) to various stimuli or inputs, whether internal or external, conscious or subconscious, overt or covert, and voluntary or involuntary. Quite simply, we are examining what the solution is doing at a point in time or over a period of time.

Structure

The concept of structure is fundamental. All things, from the atom to the tallest building, have structure. Structure pertains to intangible things too, such as culture and even working relationships. A structure is an assemblage of physical entities or concepts in spacetime that is intended to form a system capable of supporting the intrinsic or extrinsic value of the structure itself. Structures may be permanent or temporary. Regardless, anything that has structure possesses patterns with interdependencies between its constituent elements. The arrangement of and relations between the parts or components of something complex has the quality of being organized.

TYPES OF ANALYSIS

Sometimes people go from (a) an abject statement of ignorance to (d) an abject statement of certainty without ever crossing through (b) and (c). This misapprehension is an argument from ignorance and people do it all the time because we live in a business culture where the answers need to be known up front—there is no time for research and analysis. When the reliance on information is informal and based principally on hearsay, things become distorted (remember the telephone game from kindergarten). In colocated teams, this is not an issue. However, many stakeholders spread across buildings, cities, cultures, and countries. Integration between audio and visual information in, say, a video conference may cause this illusion to occur. Thus, it is vital to follow up on all conversations with clear, formal written communication, even in an agile environment. This example is just one problem emblematic of a grimmer situation—our inability to communicate effectively, consistently, and honestly.

The perception attributed to an event at a point in time depends on what we think may happen next, weighed against things that have already occurred in the past. So, we give our best guess, and that guess is very subjective. The philosophical challenge of a mind getting to know itself creates delusive memories (some based in fallacy) that must confirm with qualitative and quantitative data. Figure 16.2 illustrates the REPAC depth of analysis *type* set.

Qualitative Analysis

Unlike quantitative analysis, a qualitative study does not involve the collection of data. Qualitative elicitation focuses on gathering information from the stakeholder's point of view. Once acquired, the data

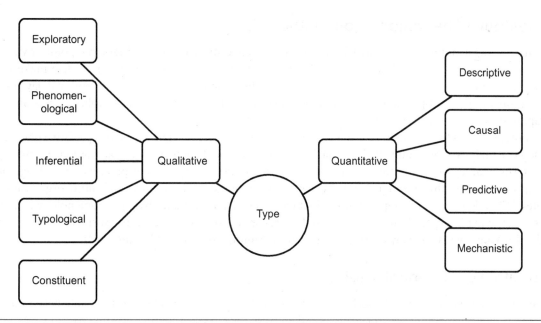

Figure 16.2   REPAC depth of analysis type of analysis set (© The New BA, Ltd.)

is quantized and analyzed, interpretatively. Qualitatively, the goal focuses on patterns, the hypothesis is broad and concerned with the picture as a whole, and the research is exploratory.

As with most elicitation and analysis efforts, we usually rely on techniques such as interviews, passive observations, interface studies, and the review of organizational artifacts. The intent is to qualitatively assess cause (before quantitative verification and validation) and how the stakeholders conduct their business. Next, look for patterns within the business ecosystem that apply to our stakeholder's unique situation. Once identified, the patterns create instances specific to a stakeholder's needs. The REPAC Framework takes advantage of exploratory, phenomenological, inferential, typological, and constituent analyses to assess the qualitative nature of the system under study.

Qualitative Exploratory Analysis

An exploratory analysis concerns itself with identifying previously unknown relationships between phenomena. Many of the qualitative analyses presented center on formal written communication. Remember, the solution options rely on the clear and concise use of language.

Exploratory models are useful for discovering new interactions between the people, processes, tools, technology, or things under our microscope. This approach helps define situations, targets, and proposals early in the solutions management life cycle. We cannot expect definitive data, however, which means we should not apply this technique to generalizing or predicting future events. Correlation does not imply causation!

Qualitative Phenomenological Analysis

A qualitative phenomenological analysis is an interpretative study from an idiographic point of view, as opposed to a nomothetic analysis. We intend to discover how stakeholders in a given context make sense of their organizational environment; in particular how they respond to regular and exceptional day-to-day operational duties and processes. A nomothetic analysis seeks to identify rules to follow, while an idiographic study concerns itself with specific events distinct from business rules.

I borrowed this technique from the world of psychology where it is known as interpretative phenomenological analysis. Commonly, this approach applies to personal context—trauma, relationship management, social acceptance, and the like. The combination of psychological, interpretative, and ideographic components makes this technique a reliable tool to begin our analysis of causes and future organizational states. When looking at phenomena as distinct elements in and of themselves, phenomenology is in use. When applying interpretation to events based on research and experience, it is considered hermeneutically thinking (Lyons and Coyle 2016; McLeod 2011; Smith, Flowers, and Larkin 2009).

Qualitative Inferential Analysis

Inferential analysis asks us to logically test our ideas about the organization's future state based on scenarios, user stories, and other process assets taken from the current situation or some part of it. We want small samples or slices of the current state. We see this same approach applied to user stories and other tools such as use cases under the section *fit criteria*, *acceptance test*, or some similar expression. In project management, managers ask for timelines analogous to previous experiences. This tactic is an example of an inferential application of thought—drawing from memories to derive an approximate mean or mode. As is already known, projects are randomly determined or have a random probability distribution analyzed statistically but not predicted precisely.

Qualitative Typological Analysis

Typologies are formed through categorization, not by hierarchical arrangement. The categories, domains, or concepts in a typological model are related to one another, not subsidiary. There are no generalization-specialization relationships within a typological diagram. Applied as a business analysis tool, typological investigations create business models. These models may be very meta, in that they describe broad organizational concepts; or discrete, as in the structure of a division, department, or business process. I often build typological models to emphasize the core logic that an organization realizes to create purpose and customer value.

Michael Porter, the creator of Porter's Five Forces, is an American academic known for his prolific theories on economics and social causes. He describes the emphasis in business models on generating revenues as being "a far cry from creating economic value" (Porter 2001). In contrast, business author Joan Magretta argues that business models tell stories and are essential for understanding scope, among other concepts. Organizations that equate revenue and profit as value are short-sighted. An organization's quest for profit relates to a purpose (although not a good one); however, value belongs to the customer. Organizational models describe how all the pieces relate to each other and fit together. Business models have the added insight of being comparable across industries—hence their usefulness for establishing design patterns (Magretta 2002; Magretta 2011).

Because developing an initial model of the problem space is crucial to project success, I will take time to describe how to create one. My approach uses many of the critical thinking techniques already discussed. Business models (or business domain models, as I prefer to call them) help us understand the boundaries of the problem space, how a process performs, and how to realize customer value and organizational purpose.

There is no *correct* way to distinguish different types of business models nor is there the *right* type to use over another; however, some typologies are indeed more useful than others. In developing the REPAC ontological framework, I tried to imagine the most appropriate entities for planning, eliciting, analyzing, and collaborating all things related to what we require to meet stakeholder expectations; and then used a simple algorithm to connect each element. Recall, REPAC describes and integrates the relations between the data, concepts, and categories of project management and business-*systems* analysis, meshed together through many levels of applicability.

Using the concept's *purpose* and *value* as driving forces, any typological model we create must be intuitive and sensible. Grouping purpose and value-based ideas is a useful way to identify gaps, overlaps, and redundancies within the problem space. Identifying similarities and differences between activities based on value is in line with structural business modeling. Our designs must also be comprehensive in that they sufficiently describe and classify concepts across the entire organization at each level of applicability—a unified taxonomy.

A typological analysis must refrain from subjective interpretation and judgment. This constraint forces the establishment of precise rules, classification schemes, methodical frameworks, and nomenclature, which apply to all areas of the organization, not just the problem space under analysis. Ideally, different analysts can use the same framework with the same outcome.

The upside to this exercise is that once complete as an archetype, the model should remain the same over an extended period. The downside is that these models are abstract, complicated to make, and go through several revisions before we reach an acceptable level of understanding. Therefore, I only conduct a qualitative typological analysis when the problem carries enough value, return on investment, risk, organizational maturity, architectural significance, change, or other driving elements which warrant the effort. If the culture will not use or support the models as reference material for subsequent activities, deliverables, phases, projects, and other initiatives, then the exercise is moot.

Let us consider a simple typological example. Let's ask ourselves what a *business does* at the highest order of abstraction. Remember, our model is not primitive; that is, it will not discuss specifics. This example characterizes specific stakeholders' needs, which informs what we require to satisfy their needs.

Consider an organization and its central purpose, which, for the sake of argument, is the creation of revenue and the capability to maintain profitability. This definition also applies to *nonprofit* organizations if we define *profit* as a positive net financial gain. Logically, we assume that profit must supersede value. Without a positive net return, the organization cannot offer value—whatever it defines as its value-add statement. Is this a valid assumption? To understand the difference between an organization's value and its desire to generate profit, I refer you back to Simon Sinek's movement-starting book *Start with Why*.

"There is a big difference between repeat business and loyalty. Repeat business is when people do business with "you" multiple times. Loyalty is when people are willing to turn down a better product or a better price to continue doing business with you. Loyal customers don't often even bother to research the competition or entertain other options. Loyalty is not easily won." (Sinek 2011)

Regardless of what kind of organization you work for, there are only four things you can do: make things, intermediate or broker things, distribute, or manage. The things we make, broker, or distribute are called assets. There are only two rights assigned to an asset; we may use them or own them. When we sell to a buyer the right to *use* an asset, the owner retains ownership and control over its use. Once we sell the widget, warranties notwithstanding, the owner assumes legal custody and has the right to do with it whatever he or she wants (within the boundaries of the law).

Figures 16.3 and 16.4 illustrate diagrams we use to brainstorm conceptual applications of the taxonomy scheme provided in Table 16.1. Having selected the focus and perspective of these taxonomical depths, we then ask any number of specific inquiries. Questions such as:

- What is the widget's purpose?
- What is its customer value-adds?
- Who is making the required widget?
- What widgets is our supplier responsible for creating?
- How will our supplier make the widgets?
- How many objects of a permit should we allow?
- Under what conditions will we revoke the right to object permission?

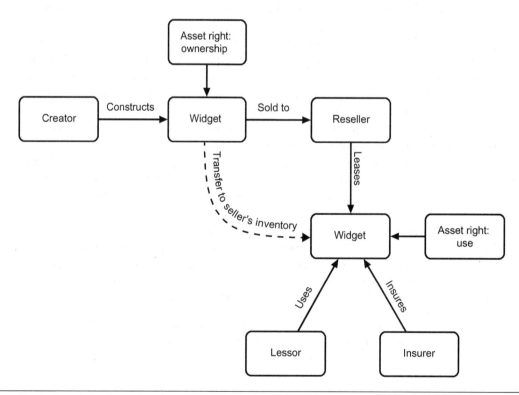

Figure 16.3   Simple business typology diagram one (© The New BA, Ltd.)

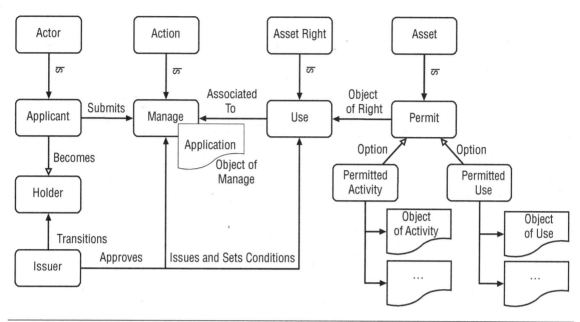

Figure 16.4 Simple business typology diagram two (© The New BA, Ltd.)

Table 16.1 Simple business typology scheme

Actions	Construct, Broker, Distribute, and Manage
Assets	Physical, Financial, Intangible, Human
Asset Rights	Own, Use, Match
Actors	Creator, Trader, Seller, Reseller, Manager, Lender, Matcher, Insurer, Lessor, Publisher, Attractor, Contractor, etc. . . .

Together these concepts shape the constituents. In a syntactic analysis, a constituent is a word or a group of words that function as a single unit within a hierarchical structure. The structure forms generalized and specialized relationships between the objects under consideration.

Qualitative Constituent Analysis

The disorders of the language used to express that which is required by stakeholders compel us to take the documents we write and the scenarios we attempt to understand far more seriously than studies currently reflect. I used several references in my research and development of my approach to qualitative analysis (Bloomfield 1933; Akmajian and Heny 1975; Chomsky and Ronat 1998). As we examine the language of our stakeholders' needs, pay particular attention to the following types of constituents:

- *Hierarchical structure*: the organization of language
- *Ambiguity*: elements open to more than one interpretation
- *Markers*: the indication of position and placement

- *Discontinuous*: gaps and intervals of communication

A sentence is not just a string of arranged elements (which hopefully convey meaning and context); it is a layered construct, not unlike the business solutions with which we work daily. Each *node* inexorably leads to the next node. This notion is especially important to structure clear declarative statements directing project teams toward concise and unambiguous efforts. Figure 16.5 illustrates the basic structure of English. Following the figure, I have outlined a few reminders of common structures that are fundamental to linguistics, as related to the structure of formally documenting our stakeholder's needs.

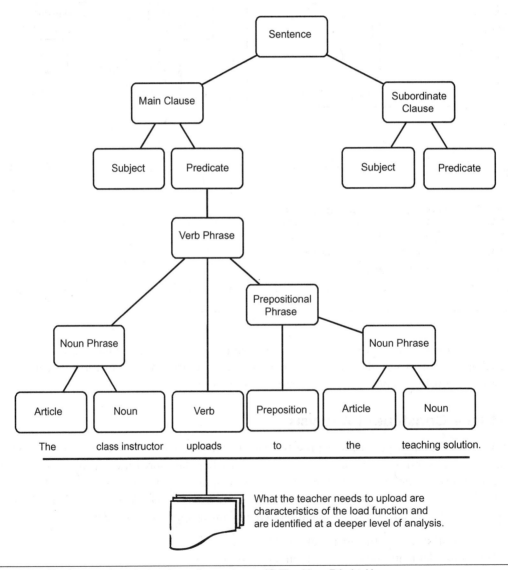

Figure 16.5.   Basic constituent structure of a sentence (© The New BA, Ltd.)

A Sentence

When I am teaching, I sometimes find myself at a loss for words—or trip over my words as my thinking moves ahead to the next instructional idea. When this happens, I quip, "Don't you hate it when bad things happen to good sentences?" as a means to refocus myself. My self-mockery is meant to provide levity while I collect my thoughts. Think of your own experience if this has happened to you. Too many *hmms*, *uums*, and *I mean* while you fumble around for your words could cost you trust and credibility or even a potential job or project assignment. When it comes to structuring essential elements into cogent statements designed to motivate action, *incorrect sentences* spell rework, change requests, defects, or even disaster for projects. Everything we communicate begins with a sentence. Project professionals must train themselves to speak as the sharpshooter with his bullet, not the hunter with his shotgun shell. The pellets of the shell spread out creating complex sentences with too many subordinate clauses making the statement too challenging to read and break down into original methodical statements of what is required of the solution to satisfy stakeholders' needs. Here is a simple example:

> "Janice needs a dashboard."
> "The dashboard needs to identify any customer's purchase history."
> "The customer's purchase history is a list of classes taken at The New Business Analyst, Inc."
> "The dashboard will display all customer profile data . . ." and so on . . .

This statement shows what Janice needs; there is no dispute. It is plain and straightforward. What is required to build a *solution* for her needs, however, is something entirely different. These are elementary statements describing from the stakeholder's perspective what she is asking for in order to perform her work. The statement does not mention what we require to solve and satisfy her needs, however. These stakeholder requirements are simple subject, verb, and object statements, conveying simple needs. It is for this reason I refrain from using the word *requirement* at this point. Linguistically, the sentence speaks of nothing required. It only describes what is necessary, which is how the sentence is precisely designed to read.

A sentence is simply a set of words that is complete in itself. As an author, I afford myself some flexibility. This book, for example, is a crafted mixture of technical, creative, academic, and business styles. A well-crafted sentence contains one subject and one predicate contained within one main clause and, if needed, one subordinate clause. All of our statements must be declarative and direct someone to take action. As a successful writer of imperatives, your sentences should not exceed one subordinate clause.

A Clause

I approach requirements the same way a linguist studies language, which makes sense because I am using words, along with diagrams, tables, and some equations, to convey imperatives. If a sentence is a quantized collection of data used to satisfy a need and build a *requirement*, then a clause is its principal component. A clause consists of subjects and predicates. There are many types of clauses such as dependent and independent, subordinate conjunctions, relative and nonessential relative, finite, and adverbial, among several others.

The primary clause is a stand-alone unit while subordinate clauses, usually introduced by conjunctions, make parts of and are reliant upon the main clause. Subordinate clauses help establish context, giving the sentence meaning. In an example, we might write that Janice needs the dashboard to *refresh* when the sales process completes. The word *when* provides the temporal reference for satisfying the need. The *need* directly expresses through the sentence's subjects, nouns, verbs, and predicates. Again, drawing a connection between a *requirement* and a sentence, these make up the indivisible quanta (and near quanta, in the case of a predicate) of what we require.

The Subject and Predicate

I will skip most of the guts or word classes of a sentence such as subjective, objective, possessive, and reflexive pronouns, determiners, exclamations, prepositions, and conjunctions, as I hope they are self-evident. I will also skip noun and verb describing adjectives and adverbs because they affect statements of what we require and must specify as separate units. However, the subject of the sentence is imperative since it declares what we must construct, design, process, solve, or resolve to satisfy our stakeholders' needs. Subjects link to noun phrases functioning as the primary component of the clause. The subject is the thing on which the provision premises. We describe this as the structure of predication.

A Noun Phrase

A noun phrase is a syntactic unit. It contains one noun and any words clustered around it; giving it meaning. A noun phrase functions as one of the main components of a clause. It is an element about which the rest of the clause predicates. We see noun phrases in work breakdown structures, representing deliverables, sub-deliverables, and work-packages. *Server Racks* exemplifies a work-package in which all the tasks for installing the racks are contained.

A Verbal Phrase

Functioning as auxiliaries, modifiers, and complements, verbal phrases are also syntactic units serving the same function as noun phrases except the verb offers us insight into our stakeholders' needs. A use case, for example, may read as *Schedule Summary Report*. This verb-phrase tells us the object under development and the behavior of the object. Do we know the requirements or what is required, however—not even close?

A Phrase

Phrases contain more than one word but lack a subject-predicate relationship. Phrases begin with a headword, a single word that is more important than others. This strategy helps readers identify the intent of the required statement. Remember to separate specifiers, premodifiers, modifiers, and complements of the headword. Phrases should not contain restrictors, predeterminers, determiners, ordinals, quantifiers, adverbs, adjectives, classifiers, or any other elements that may imply complexity. Looking back at Figure 16.5, the user's need is very plainly stated using proper cadence:

- *Article*: the
- *Noun*: class instructor
- *Verb*: uploads
- *Preposition*: to
- *Article*: the
- *Noun*: teaching solution

If we continue the sentence with "so that she can . . ." we would have a simple user story. Without adding value and purpose, we have still managed to capture the *who, what, where,* and *how.* We did not add any "the system shall" nonsense, and we have conveyed the exact information. Again, this is still limited to the stakeholder's point of view. This simple sentence is their depth of perspective—their *need.* We need to dig deeper into quantitative analysis if we want to identify what is required to satisfy the need.

When I conduct a qualitative constituent, I determine the most efficient way to communicate what the solution must *do* and *be* for the stakeholders. I apply this technique to solution design by analyzing the constituents of stakeholder issues and scenarios to determine causes and purpose. This approach helps me eliminate their problems and formulate organizational value.

The quality of the reports, documents, and diagrams directly affects the quality of the solution and all of its components. This fact is why we need to qualitatively understand what we read and write by using some of the tools I have described.

QUANTITATIVE ANALYSIS

The manipulation of quantified data has become a fact of modern existence. Why then should any quantifiable method be used to analyze the needs of stakeholders? Results are often corollary, a proposition that follows something that is commonly known. Poor requirements management will result in higher project costs, change requests, defects, and lower quality, among others.

Why take the time to measure just how many defects there are or how many requirements were sent back for further analysis? What is the purpose of these numbers? Is it necessary to know how many calls per hour the call center can process? The answer to that is *yes* if the goal is to improve it. We may write the same statement about the quality of our requirements management process. If we attempt to change something, we need to know if we have succeeded. The only way to see if we have accomplished that which we set out to achieve is to measure.

Everything we measure is part of a system. In physics, a physical system is a portion of the physical universe chosen for analysis. Everything outside the system is known as the environment. We ignore the environment, except for its effects on the system. Our language is a system, I am a system, you are a system, and your stakeholders are systems. The solution—and all of its components—is a system. Our organizations are systems, and when we all interact, our collective systems can be analyzed, measured, and predicted (to some degree). All of the focus and perspective models you have seen so far visualize the connectivity of these systems.

Quantitative Descriptive Analysis

The most popular tool for quantitative descriptive analysis is an entity relationship diagram. We have already seen an inkling of this method in Figure 16.4. We maximize our utility as analysts by continuing to layer our models and diagrams, successively providing more context. Figure 16.1 illustrates another example of a typology diagram, while Figure 16.2 evolves the design into a sample of a quantitative description of entity relationships.

Recognize that the only difference is the addition of some, but not all, of the entity attributes. Why bother with both of these approaches? That may not be necessary; it depends entirely on the situation. If we do not know the characteristics during the initial scoping phase, a typological representation will aid stakeholders as they help deepen the analysis.

Quantitative Causal Analysis

Identifying causes and exploring alternatives forces an examination of reasons that we can resolve—as opposed to merely treating symptoms, which seldom affects a lasting cure. Frequently the source of bitter debate, a causal analysis is often seen as a non-value-add exercise. Sometimes the signs are considered to be the cause. Quantitative causal analysis requires us to explain why things are the way they are and what specific changes will improve the stakeholders' situation.

Quantitative Predictive Analysis

A predictive analysis uses methods that are designed to identify the probability of something happening based on numerical data. We may still use historical testimony, but this is often seen as anecdotal, subjective, and repetitive, regardless of our experience, and therefore, qualitative. Accurate prediction depends heavily on measuring the right variables as well as having ample sample data from which to draw. The further out we try to predict, the less accurate our predictions will be.

Quantitative Mechanistic Analysis

The systems we study are animate; that is, they are dynamic. Changing one variable could have far-reaching effects downstream. Because of this, I do not believe we can conduct an accurate quantitative analysis of organizational solutions. We must accept a certain amount of variance and subjectivity. Quantitative mechanistic studies require the most effort and examination while they are in motion. This technique is not a slice-in-time analysis but a slice of time. We want to understand changes in variables that lead to changes in other variables for individual objects, which lead to other changes, and so on. Business systems, including people, process, and technology, are incredibly complex. Everything leads to every other thing. Precise measures require deterministic equations usually reserved for engineering science. In manufacturing, it is relatively easy to see how one variable changes another; this is not so in business process analysis. Sometimes, the solution specifications are imposed by stakeholders, leaving conversations about cause, understanding, and ambiguity to be more or less moot. This kind of cultural situation often leads to equivocation and goalpost shifting.

However, in a more mature environment, when genuinely trying to identify a cause and improve the complex interactions between people, process, and human-activity systems, it becomes tough to reach agreement on what is required to satisfy stakeholders' needs and achieve the goals of our initiative. Subjectivity must give way to an attempt to determine the *hard facts*. Different stakeholders will see different things differently—thank you Captain Obvious!

Stakeholders' needs seldom change. Instead, it is what we require that is often the subject of a request to change something because we fail to understand or document needs adequately. Thus, the specifications are often ambiguous and unstable. It is for this reason that the REPAC Framework exists.

Unlike physical systems that are constrained by physical laws, there is no agreement on how our actions can affect the quantitative outcomes of a software-based solution. We lack a completely objective means to establish entirely unambiguous success criteria for our solutions and to then measure these solutions against the criteria. Our best quantitative analysis will always contain a certain amount of subjectivity.

There are many reasons for this lack of communication, most of which stem from the ways we behave within the human, business, and technological ecosystems. The REPAC Framework joins different organizational layers, allowing for a smooth line of collaboration across strata. Categorically, the REPAC external focal elements, along with the intricate drive-constrain, support-sustain relationships, illuminate the many ways these components act upon an organization.

We see how these diagrams begin to stick together to create an architectural ontological model of the organization. When it comes time to identify causality and determine new solutions, these models serve as an advantageous starting point.

REFERENCES

Akmajian, Adrian and Frank Heny. 1975. *Introduction to the Principles of Transformational Syntax*. MIT Press.

Bloomfield, Leonard. 1933. *Language*. H. Holt and Company.

Chomsky, Noam and Mitsou Ronat. 1998. *On Language: Chomsky's Classic Works Language and Responsibility and Reflections on Language in One Volume*. New Press.

Lyons, Evanthia and Adrian Coyle. 2016. *Analysing Qualitative Data in Psychology*. SAGE Publications Ltd.

Magretta, Joan. 2002. "Why Business Models Matter."

———. 2011. *Understanding Michael Porter: The Essential Guide to Competition and Strategy*. Harvard Business Review Press.

McLeod, John. 2011. *Qualitative Research in Counselling and Psychotherapy*. SAGE Publications.

Porter, Michael. 2001. "Strategy and the Internet." *Harvard Business Review* 79, no. 3, pp. 63–78.

Sinek, Simon. 2011. *Start With Why: How Great Leaders Inspire Everyone to Take Action*. Portfolio.

Smith, Jonathan A, Paul Flowers, and Michael Larkin. 2009. *Interpretative Phenomenological Analysis: Theory, Method and Research*. SAGE Publications Ltd.

Turing, Alan Mathison. 1937. "On Computable Numbers, With an Application to the Entscheidungsproblem." *Proceedings of the London Mathematical Society* 2, no. 1, pp. 230–65.

17

ASPECTS AND FUNCTIONS OF ANALYSIS

"I beg this committee to recognize that knowledge is not simply another commodity. On the contrary; knowledge is never used up, it increases by diffusion, and grows by dispersion. Knowledge and information cannot be quantitatively assessed as a percentage of the G.N.P. Any willful cut in our resources of knowledge is an act of self-destruction."
—Daniel J. Boorstin

While serving as the Librarian of Congress, American historian Daniel J. Boorstin in the previous quote urged the House Appropriations subcommittee to restore money cut from the library's budget. Short-sighted organizations that do not value a learning mindset seem quick to cut training when their profits become a little thin.

ASPECTS

Change is troublesome for all of us, but cutting learning really can be a path to self-destruction. Sometimes I wonder if we see the *numbers* and react too quickly. I do not believe enough of our stakeholders educate themselves as to how to understand and interpret quantitative information. It is ironic since much of our analysis depends on reasonable choices. This activity is a cornerstone to business literacy. As we read in Chapter 16, much of our analysis will be either qualitative or quantitative. The aspects of those studies will either be logical, physical, or phase space, as we see in Figure 17.1.

Logical

The term logic has many meanings, depending on its usage. Philosophy teaches us that logic is a formal discipline where one reasons a solution using the rules of logical thinking. Logic may be formal, informal, symbolic, or even mathematical. Arguably, this notion underpins everything in our civilization. Logic is the basis for systems such as biology, physics, mathematics, computer science, engineering, economics, civics, philosophy, psychology, other sciences (the scientific method), and law. Despite its widespread applications, logical thinking remains a mystery for many. As project professionals, we cannot afford to deny ourselves the power of logic, reason, and critical thinking.

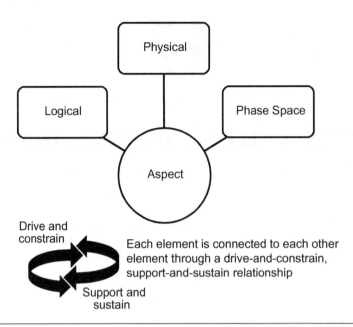

Figure 17.1. Depth of analysis aspects of analysis set (© The New BA, Ltd.)

But knowing how to read propositional logic is not necessary. What matters is applying rigor to our thoughts. We start with the basic premises, usually denoted as P. This notation is our first *if-then* conditional claim. If P is true, then so is Q—simple enough. This forward chaining is easy when we only have two conditions to evaluate. However, business elements often interact in complex and unpredictable ways. What if I add X as a new variable? Is X a subset of P? If this claim is true, then $X \rightarrow P$. The danger comes when our logic is flawed, the premises are incorrect, or we abuse the rules of argumentation. As you engage your stakeholders (including developers, designers, and other team members) in logical discussions about issues and possible solutions, always remember to avoid these fallacies:

- If you make a claim, then the burden of proof is on you. Reversal of burden of the evidence is a cardinal sin of logical discourse.
- Never attack the other person, only the argument.
- As an extension, do not allow yourself to become emotionally intertwined with your premise. It is important to be passionate but always strike a balance between the argument and how you *feel* about the subject.
- Never impose a non sequitur or hasty generalization, assuming if X is true for A and X is true for B; therefore, X is true for C, D, and so on. This misjudgment also includes a faulty generalization. In the absence of sufficient evidence, drawing conclusions based on induction is gratuitous.
- Never allow yourself to cherry pick, which is to pick and choose which data you will share, avoiding facts that may harm your argument; or present an argument, which seems rigorous, but fails to address the issue.

- Do not create a false dilemma, dichotomy, division, or contrast between two things represented as being opposed or entirely different. This type of thinking is jointly exhaustive, mutually exclusive, or neither and is also known as *either-or thinking*. Stakeholders will sometimes conclude that there are no alternatives, the alternatives overlap, one alternative is wrong therefore the other must be true, or neither option is correct.
- Do not beg the question by presuming your premise is correct or claim that a chain of events will take place and end in some dire consequence if you do not have enough evidence to make such a claim.
- Never assume a false cause or dichotomy by believing something is true just because it came first. Two events that seem related in time may not be related at all.
- Avoid the Dunning-Kruger effect. Do not allow yourself to argue from ignorance just because you lack the data (get your data straight before you engage). Bravely excuse yourself from the discussion, gather your research, and re-engage. Remember, own your data and hold your argument.
- Avoid measurement fallacies. The proliferation of metrics through *big data* for strategic or organizational authority may create an *information tsunami* and cause false analogies or unsound comparisons between data points.

Regardless of which analysis approach we take, we must always look for ideas that will solve a problem and for proof that those ideas have a reasonable chance of passing logical tests. In project management and business-systems analysis, design, and development, we are still using the basic rules of formal logical discourse, except our ideas and tests must be independent of the actual physical solution. We must be able to imperially say that "regardless of how we decide to proceed and regardless of the choices made, this logical analysis must hold for the physical solution."

The key takeaway with this aspect of the analysis is that our thoughts are independent of any solution. We *must* be sure that the *logic* of the proposition will resolve the cause before we make any attempt to develop and implement.

Physical

The physical analysis is quantitative and determines the properties of the solution and all of its components. Physical analyses are intended to measure the transformations or evolutions of the states (the observables) of the system (and its various components). Also, this type of analysis provides insight into exactly where things will go, what solutions we intend to use, and how it will all fit together on our machines with our process and people at this and other moments in time. Like a logical analysis, a physical analysis will help you to understand the actual solutions that you have chosen intuitively.

Phase Space

Again, I have co-opted a specific term used in mathematics and physics. In these disciplines, a phase space represents all possible states of a system with each possible state corresponding to a unique point in the phase space. Naturally, this definition does not apply to a business system, but the idea does. People, process, policy, and technology interact in strange and often unpredictable ways. Organizational systems can be very complex, large, and have many possible states. I only apply this level of analysis in situations where the solution can take on many states at a given moment and it is necessary to understand the complex interactions between these simultaneous circumstances.

Our exploration of the aspects of our analysis was brief but significant in that we need to know how the system will logically behave independent of an actual solution and how that solution will physically transition and evolve.

FUNCTIONS

As a species, we depend on each other for emotional survival. Numerous studies have shown that humans raised in or that experience prolonged exposure to isolation often suffer from mental disabilities. While not as extreme, a project team suffers when it is not colocated. Today's global economy prohibits this in many instances; however, as a project professional, I go to enormous lengths to help my stakeholders feel as though they are all together (think back to the team charter). I often encourage people to leave the voice and video connections open while they work. Just knowing someone is there to help, should you need it, goes a long way in maintaining morale.

In analyzing organizational systems for functions such as dependence or interdependence we are not always looking for computer systems. Remember, we must always examine the relationships between the people, processes, tools, and technology they use. Figure 17.2 illustrates each of the Requirements, Elicitation, Planning, Analysis, and Collaboration Framework™ (REPAC®) depth of analysis functions outlined in the following paragraphs.

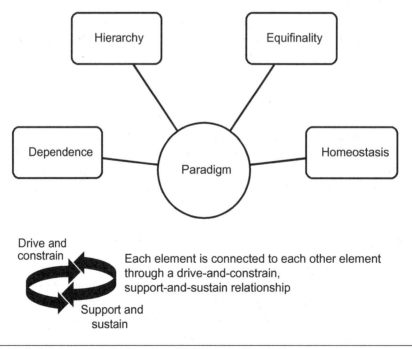

Figure 17.2 REPAC depth of analysis functions (© The New BA, Ltd.)

Dependence and Hierarchy

Dependence or interdependence is merely the relationships required by each of the systems we analyze. Again, it is important to remember that we must also focus on the relationship between different teams and departments. Many systems depend on a hierarchical command and control system which is a form of scrutiny in which a set of elements arrange themselves in a hierarchical tree. Some examples include safety and emergency management systems, legal systems, manufacturing, file systems, procedural systems, and most functional organizations such as government agencies.

Equifinality and Homeostasis

Under the rules of general systems theory, equifinality is the expected result of an open system. There are often many paths or channels through which the end value may conclude, but there can be only one equifinal result. In practice, we use the principle of equifinality in every area of management: project management, change management, industry, safety, and many others. In almost every analysis, it is good practice to imagine the result before you determine the path or paths. Typically, the more intellectual the work is, the more essential it is to ensure that the equifinal principles are in place.

Related to equifinality is homeostasis, which is the tendency toward a relatively stable equilibrium between interdependent elements. Fundamental goals in business-systems analysis include a balance between what goes in and what comes out (such as waste) and a balance with the system's external environment. Homeostasis comes from the Greek words for "same" and "steady" and means any process that living things use to maintain the relatively stable conditions that are necessary for survival. Although this definition pertains to living organisms, we can extend it to our business systems—even the ones that are not *alive*. They too must *survive*—that is, persist with utility, purpose, and value; and we must ensure their survival.

Next, we will examine the expanse of analysis—in particular, the issues we face with time and entropy.

18

EXPANSE OF ANALYSIS AND EVIDENCE-BASED REQUIREMENTS MANAGEMENT

Time is one of the most magnificent abstracts of our era. As much as we depend on it for our projects and our very lives, we do not understand what it is. Time estimates tend to fall under a psychological phenomenon known as the mere-exposure effect. This irrational and subjective circumstance is a preference for people or things merely because they are familiar. With no basis in logic, we often feel like we *know* the answer because the circumstance is, in some way, comfortable. The reasons for and causes of project issues and problems, even when related to time, are not fundamental; they are emergent—they emerge from other causes and reasons. Figure 18.1 illustrates the model for the depth of analysis expanse of analysis set.

Of course, we do not want to follow this path back to the moment just before the *Big Bang* some 14 billion years ago (BYA). I doubt our stakeholders would accept our explanation: "Well, stakeholder Bob, the solution is defective because of a causal chain of events that started out in a very particular arrangement around 14 BYA and have followed the laws of physics up to this point; thus, there is no other arrangement

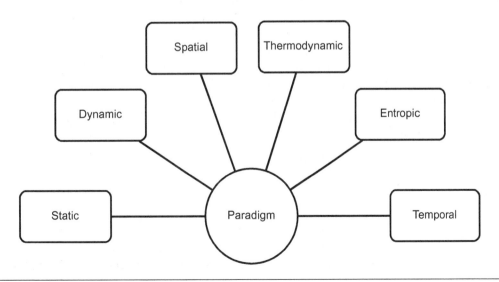

Figure 18.1 Depth of analysis expanse of analysis set (© The New BA, Ltd.)

in which the solution could be." So how far back do we go? How do we avoid paralysis by analysis? We bring our stakeholders along for the ride, stopping to reevaluate each time we learn something new— remember, just enough, just-in-time (JEJIT). In this chapter, I will discuss some fallacies about time and how we can manage it better through a theory I call stochastic project entropy.[1] But first, let's explore the first four expanses.

STATIC AND DYNAMIC

Although this is an exhaustive subject, in our context this is just systems at rest (static) or systems in motion (dynamic), or analyzing a point in time (time-slice) or a period. Our goal is the examination of an effect that is immediate and understood in and of itself without consideration of long-term responses. A common mistake in static systems analysis is the extrapolation of immediate events over the expected long-term results.

Dynamic systems analysis is far more complicated. Dynamic systems theory deals with long-term behavior. Usually involving differential calculus, even simple nonlinear dynamical systems often exhibit seemingly random behavior.

SPATIAL AND THERMODYNAMIC

We consider spatial analysis in two ways—the first is geographical and the second is more related to reasoning. Traditional spatial analysis seeks to understand and explain patterns of behavior in terms of mathematics and geometry. However, using tools such as a spatial map provides geospatial data that we can use to understand how our systems are physically set up and to determine whether its footprint best utilizes our resources. A simplified approach known as nearest neighbor analysis examines points between elements and compares the results to expected values. Imagine using spatial analysis to set up a team for a long project.

Spatial reasoning is a skill that is employed when wanting to understand objects in three dimensions and draw conclusions based on the data we gathered. For example, imagine setting up an office space or rearranging a living room. Strong spatial reasoning allows us to imagine the placement of objects without having to place them physically. As mentioned, there may be much need for this type of analysis in a typical business routine; however, I would be remiss if I left the Requirements, Elicitation, Planning, Analysis, and Collaboration Framework™ (REPAC®) estimation technique incomplete. Expanses that have far-reaching consequences to our projects, and indeed our daily lives, are entropy (uncertainty) and time itself.

ENTROPIC

Let's keep our discussion within a Newtonian frame of reference. In the worlds of quantum mechanics and relativity, things are strange almost beyond comprehension. I will not pretend to be an expert on entropy and time, but I will share my thoughts and ideas on the subject and how I believe it relates to probability, requirements, and project management. There are two ideological camps for the study of probability. In the first camp, we have the traditionalists or *frequentists*, as they are known.

Frequentists contend that probability is nothing more than *how many times would something happen given an infinite number of chances*. Just like the coin flip or dice example, we observe how many times heads or tails would come up or how often we would roll a certain number given infinite tries. The second camp, the Bayesians, of which I am proud to call myself a member, defend that probabilities are expressions of our states of belief in cases of ignorance or uncertainty. Bayesians reason that the coin and die have a 50% chance of either outcome because we have zero incentive to favor one over the other. However, if you were to *load* either the die or the coin, we would have to accept this new information—this is the essence of Bayesian ideology. Consider our projects; we would never observe infinite iterations of the same project. In the same vein, we may consider the time in which it takes to complete a task or handle an issue as Bayesian due to the subjectivity of our estimates.

Our perception of time depends on how much attention we pay to it, how we are moving through space at any given moment, and how we arrange our memories. As patterns in our brains evolve through the observation of countless interactions in the world around us, we perceive individual moments or slices of time, but what is it that we are sensing? Dr. Sean Carroll, physicist, California Institute of Technology, said it best when he referred to time in the following way, "We live in a world of stuff, and that stuff always changes position. Time is just the label we use to count and describe all those changes."

Entropy, broadly, is the degree of disorder or uncertainty in a system. Low entropy can be thought of as *order*, while high entropy is *disorder* (the term disorder, while not wholly accurate, serves our purposes). When a system reaches its maximum entropy, it achieves equilibrium with its environment. Put another way; entropy is a measure of useful energy or capacity to do work that is unavailable to a system. High entropy would designate less energy while low entropy would imply that a more significant potential for action is available to the system (Pincus 1991). This example is as close as we want for our purposes.[2]

Work is a property we use to measure the amount of force or effort used to displace a deliverable, activity, or task; that is, moving the project towards its intended objective. If we did not move the job in some way, then work was not performed regardless of force or effort applied. If you spend three hours going through your e-mails, but you made no progress (displacement) on your project deliverables in any way, then you didn't get any project work done. "Yes, but I am writing and answering e-mails that pertain to my project," you say. Sure, but if those e-mails do not manage to resolve anything, then we cannot attribute work to your efforts. Imagine trying to push a transport truck. You can huff and puff all you'd like, but I doubt you will have any effect. Therefore, we consider physical work as the amount of stuff that has or might occur. Thus, energy is the capacity to do work. For us, earned value is the best measure of the displacement of the force applied to an activity or task. I consider earned value a vital tool for understanding how much *credit* or displacement I *earn* for applying force (energy or effort) to deliverables. This measure helps us know if our efforts are well employed or if we are spinning our wheels.

Earned value is a point in time analysis. In addition to assessing time loss or cost overruns, earned value analysis (EVA) determines if a project is providing value (I use purpose, saving value for my customer) for money. EVA uses three basic concepts: (1) how much work do we plan to complete? (2) how much work did we complete? and (3) how much did it cost to complete the work? By integrating three measurements into numerous equations, we provide consistent, numerical indicators with which we evaluate and compare projects. As we complete our work, we earn credit—this is a measure of the displacement. I use EVA to help my teams understand the relationship between the force, energy, or effort applied to an activity vs. its evolution, which we measure as work. So, let's slice up that truck into tiny pieces and maximize its displacement!

When I reflect on a project and the time it takes to complete the work, I think about entropy. I use the term *stochastic project entropy* to describe the amount of energy (the capacity to do work) that is no longer available to the project and its subsystems and to reflect the probabilistic nature of project and requirements management. If we allow our minds to be system oriented—that is, see the universe and everything in it as one system within another, and another, and another, and so on, all the way down the quantum realm—we begin to see our projects in the same way. Consider causation, the agency that connects one thing to another, and another, and another.

An organization as a whole, represents a system, while the projects, people, and other resources represent all of the subsystems within. Imagine a deflated balloon; the deflated balloon mirrors a plan that has little form. Its entropy is high and disordered; it has low energy. As we give it goals, objectives, scope, resources, and the like, we give it form and order; the project begins to take shape and its entropy decreases, allowing for more potential energy. The project's entropy increases once more as work completes—energy transforms into the organization's purpose and value for the customer. If we have a lasting relationship with our customer, then the system remains closed; they return to us with funds (energy) to complete more work. This process describes stochastic project entropy. The trick is to minimize entropy by striking a balance between what we require of the solution, and its threats, issues, assumptions, constraints, and the resources at our disposal.

Utilizing our resources, spending our time, and translating ideas, designs, requirements, and specifications into real solutions deflates our project balloon, returning the energy as purpose and value back to the more extensive system—the organization and customer. Sadly, I have never had a leak-free balloon. Sometimes, despite our best efforts, we unknowingly put the holes in balloons; and sometimes the leaks are there all along.

Any efforts to poach talent and energy (the capacity for work) from another project or operational task disrupts its entropy, which in turn, disturbs another, and another, and another, and so on, down the line, like a set of dominoes. This circumstance increases cost, decreases solution value and purpose, and compromises quality. Projects are part of the physical world and thus are subject to the same physical laws as everything else. Meanwhile, leadership scratches its heads, wonders why the project missed its mark, and demands to know how we spent all the money. When we take from another project, we must give back what we stole. To coin a popular idiom, we cannot take from the Church of Peter to pay the Church of Paul.

TEMPORAL

Time is the ultimate frenemy (friend-enemy); it is the companion through life that stalks us in the night. We live in the eternal present or now-slice. We can remember the past but not the future. Punctuated by ever-increasing deadlines, time seems to pursue us even while we break for coffee. Instead of continually needling someone about a due date, let us take the time to understand time a little better.

> *"Urgency engulfs the manager; yet the most urgent task is not always the most important."*
> —Alec Mackenzie, The Time Trap

Many business analysts (BAs), project managers (PMs) and other project team members such as subject matter experts, customers, users, and other stakeholders work in functionally organized environments.

Functional hierarchies bring project team members together from other areas within the organization. This paradigm causes many issues such as competing for resources, self-interested management behavior, poor coordination between projects, over-commitment of resources, and a fundamental disregard for best-practice project planning techniques.

In the case of opportunistic management behavior, many functional organizations allocate resources based on project priority. In such instances, there is an incentive for project sponsors and senior managers to keep priorities high by any means possible. On the other hand, those who already have resources assigned to their projects would want to protect them from poaching. As we may expect, this poor time-management behavior leads to an adverse effect on project accounting practices. Organizations often account for costs based on hours spent by team members on projects.

In contrast, the time devoted to internal activities, such as meetings, are viewed as non-project expenses. In these situations, there is a built-in incentive for management to keep as many people as possible working on projects. A side-effect of this is the lack of availability of resources for new projects. Moreover, we never identify real project costs such as tracking meetings and time spent on e-mails or other communication as legitimate project expenses. Adding to this predicament, we see project resources tied to the operational duties that they were initially hired to perform. The final blow comes when we lock in project timelines, presuming that we have an idea of how long a piece of work will take.

Our ability to understand time is limited. When we plan requirements activities and other deliverables, we possess only a modest understanding of the randomness of future developments, the entropy of these events, and the interdependence and relationships these circumstances have on other incidents. This fallacy drives us to take on much more then we should—forcing multitasking; a woefully unhealthy behavior.

How often have you heard people brag about what great multitaskers they are? Perhaps you've made the same boast yourself. You might even have heard that members of Generation Y are natural multitaskers, having lived their whole lives constantly switching their attention from texting to *Facebooking* to watching TV—all supposedly without missing a beat. We even see training classes designed to teach managers how best to multitask their staff; the implication being that asking someone to focus on a single task through to completion has now become ridiculously old fashioned for, if not downright heretical to, the new world order. Don't believe it! Your brain did not develop this cognitive function.

Imagine dutifully writing a solution requirements specification document, carrying on an in-person conversation with a tester about which tests must be completed before the end of the week, all while messaging a stakeholder about some missed requirements when suddenly, the phone rings—it's the project manager. Seems like just another day at the office—right? What if I were to tell you that your brain cannot multitask? You may think that you can carry on a conversation while texting or some other task that requires you to juggle multiple things at once, but you cannot—go on, try it!

As I write this, my wife and I are both sitting in my den; she on her laptop and me on my Mac. As a lark, I asked her to talk to me about her day, while continuing to type. She managed to get a sentence out, which, as it happened, wound up in her report. We tried again, and almost immediately she froze, unsure how to proceed. Why did this happen? What happened to her mind?

As it happens, our brains did not evolve to process multiple cognitively taxing tasks at one time. We can handle a few things when the cognitive load is light, but even then, quality suffers. As expected, this behavior wastes time and drains project entropy. With a basic understanding of entropy and the arrow of time, it becomes apparent that the most significant waste produced by a project subsystem is not time itself—rather our misunderstanding and abuse of time.

Estimating time in projects is typically done using a single point estimate derived from experience and a best guess. As I mentioned in the introduction, many organizations are a functional chain of command and control. The structure is hierarchical in nature, wherein people group according to their area of specialization, titles, departments, knowledge domains, and other means. This all-too-familiar arrangement demands that stakeholders and project staff take on multiple roles and multitask deliverables as they stretch themselves over many projects at once. Paradoxically, this is not something our brains can do (Meyer et al. 1997). Multitasking is a misnomer; the term task-switching more accurately describes this phenomenon.

People who consider themselves multitaskers would be more precise to mention their ability to switch from task to task. Those who make this boast, however, may be fooling themselves. Except for walking and talking (something our brains have built extensive patterns for), task switching uses up an enormous amount of cognitive energy and involves no fewer than four major areas of our brain (Meyer et al. 1997). The switch itself may seem quick—hence, the illusion—but the ability to become productive at the task especially when picking it up from a previous state can be very time consuming, emotionally draining, and cognitively expensive.

The importance of task dominance and the cognitive load imposed in the workplace for multitasking cannot be understated. The evidence is clear: we require cultural change. As knowledge workers, we must push back and educate our leaders about the dangers, not just to ourselves but to project entropy and its stochastic nature. The waste and imbalance created by these dangerous work habits will not end until we change the way we plan, track, estimate, and work.

Despite these findings, we juggle multiple assignments, estimate when they will complete, and attempt to maintain timelines that have little chance of success in the first place. To visualize this, let's assume a scenario: a PM assigns a significant package of work to a BA. The package is on the critical path and is due by the end of the day. The BA already has two previously assigned tasks that are also due by the end of the working day. To deliver on time, the BA must manage her other responsibilities against this critical assignment. Table 18.1 and Figures 18.2 through 18.4 provide some insight into how time slips away from the BA, or any of us for that matter, over the course of a day. Project entropy on this timeline was not consistent and did not achieve equilibrium with its environment.

When we examine the approximation of a standard distribution curve, we see that the analyst's productivity skews to the left (Figure 18.4). Also, the amount of energy that went into the deliverables was inconsistent with what came out. Since the energy must conserve somehow, what happened? Where did the time go? The most reasonable inference is that the cognitive load required to manage the multiple deliverables was too much for the analyst.

Although the BA had the perception that she completely moved from one task to another, her reality is more indicative of Figure 18.3. Here we see the cognitive load for each task overlap. These illustrations provide insight into how time slowly slips away from us over the course of a day. Overall, the analyst was only productive for about 71% of the day (see Table 18.1). This phenomenon is known as the fifteen-fifteen effect, which states that a person is only useful for about 70% of the day. Fifteen percent of the day is typically taken up by non-project-related distractions while the other fifteen percent attributes to personal

Table 18.1   Time slippage over a day

Time	Task	Minutes Elapsed	Minutes Worked	Minutes Not Worked	Productivity	Minutes Remaining	Percent Remaining
9:00:00 AM - 9:45	Main	45	30	15	67%	180	86%
10:00:00 AM - 10:15	Task 1	15	10	5	67%	50	83%
10:30:00 AM - 10:45				Morning Break			
11:00:00 AM - 11:30	Task 1	30	27	3	90%	23	38%
11:45:00 AM - 12:00	Task 3	15	7	8	47%	23	77%
12:15:00 PM - 1:00				Lunch Break			
1:15:00 PM - 1:45	Task 3	30	23	7	77%	0	0%
2:00:00 PM - 2:45	Main	45	35	10	78%	145	69%
3:00:00 PM - 3:15	Main	15	10	5	67%	135	64%
3:30:00 PM - 5:00	Main	90	75	15	83%	60	29%
5:15:00 PM - 6:00	Task 1	45	23	22	51%	0	0%
6:15:00 PM - 7:45	Main	90	60	30	67%	0	0%

Total Work Minutes	Actual Work Minutes	Total Minutes Tasked	Total Minutes Not Tasked	Total Minutes Worked	Total Minutes Not Worked	Average Downtime	Average Productivity
480	390	330	60	132	48	12	71%

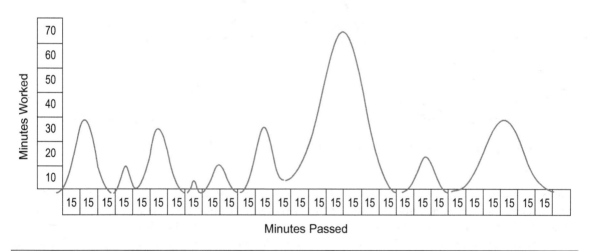

Figure 18.2   Time slippage over a day distribution curves

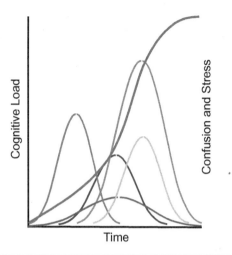

Figure 18.3   Overlapping tasks, cognitive load and stress

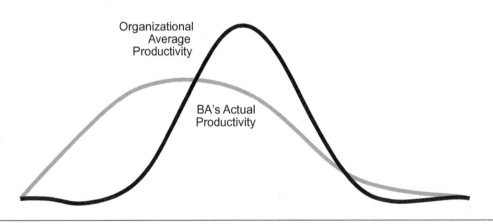

Figure 18.4   Normal productivity distribution versus actual

things such as getting coffee, personal calls, bio-breaks, web surfing, and personal e-mails. Compound this by several days or weeks, and we can see why deliverables are often late. We cannot imagine (with any accuracy) the length of time something will take; we cannot juggle multiple deliverables.

For many years, science has known that we can only do one thing at a time. More specifically, we can attend to only one cognitive task at a time. We can process one and only one significantly cognitive activity at a time—we can either talk or read, but not both at the same time. People lose time when they have to change from one task to another and a significant amount of time when switching between increasingly sophisticated tasks. Time costs were also more significant as the participants turned to relatively unfamiliar tasks.

"Although switch costs may be relatively small, sometimes just a few tenths of a second per switch, they can add up to significant amounts when people repeatedly switch back and forth between tasks. Thus, multitasking may seem efficient on the surface but may take more time to the end and involve more error." (American Psychological Association, 2006)

Meyer (1998) states that even small "mental blocks created by shifting between tasks can cost as much as 40 percent of someone's productive time." In another study from the University of California Irvine, researchers shadowed workers on the job, investigating their productivity. The leader of the study, Gloria Mark, revealed the following:

"You have to shift your thinking entirely, it takes you a while to get into it, and it takes you a while to get back and remember where you were. We found about 82 percent of all interrupted work is resumed on the same day. But here's the bad news—it takes an average of 23 minutes and 15 seconds to get back to the task." (American Psychological Association, 2006)

It is necessary to pull ourselves away from work now and then. Breaks are one thing, but distractions are another. Breaks are focused and deliberate. Distractions, on the other hand, catch us off guard and derail our energy. It seems unlikely, at least in the short term, that we will be able to refocus company culture to accept the virtues of more efficient work habits. If this behavior is inevitable and predictably unpredictable, what can we do about it? Any answer will always begin with organizational culture.

If our stakeholders were at our disposal 100 percent of the time, always completed activities on target, and worked a full eight-hour day without distraction or a loss of productivity, estimating time would be a mere 1:1 ratio rather than what we see in Equation 18.1.[3]

$$d \equiv e \qquad \text{[Eq. 18.1]}$$

In this example, duration (d), the terminal calendar period it takes from the time the work begins to the moment it completes, and effort (e), the actual amount of work required to accomplish the task (usually measured in hours), are not equivalent. Naturally, the duration can never equal effort. This truth presents us with another fallacy. Stakeholders are seldom at our full disposal, no one can work all the time, and there are always other duties to perform.

Planning project timelines are not absolute. Estimates based on probabilities must always come with a margin of error. Our project leaders sometimes forget this very basic idea. It is not reasonable to assert *the project will complete on January 1st*. Though, it is sensible to prognosticate that: *Project X has an 87% probability of delivering on January 1st within a margin of 5 business days based on the uncertainties analyzed in this report. These risks may change daily. As they deviate from predetermined tolerances, updates will post on the project's internal wiki in a section marked "Status and Projections."*

Figure 18.5 illustrates an approximation of best practice order of magnitude concerning project time. We may also use a graph like this for other project measurables such as requirements defects, solution defects, or change requests. Theoretically, risk decreases as we learn more about the project. Best practices suggest that we refine our estimates each time we learn something new. This model is known as the cone

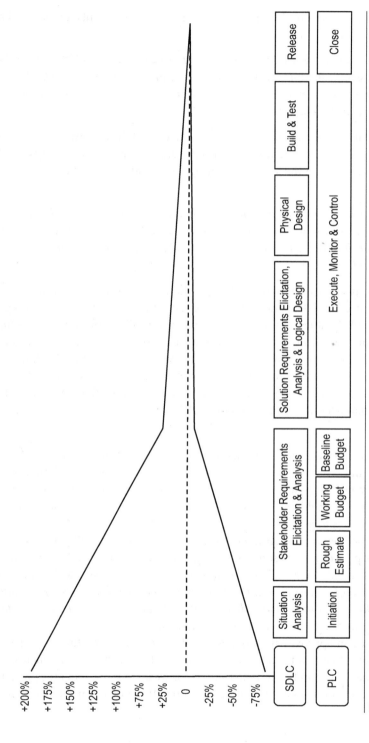

Figure 18.5   Approximation of cone of uncertainty (© The New BA, Ltd.)

Table 18.2   Margin of error estimates

Phase	Low Range (≈)	High Range (≈)
Situation Analysis	-75% to -50%	+200% to +150%
Stakeholder Requirements	-50% to -25%	+150% to +25%
Solution Requirements	-20% to -15%	+25% to +15%
Physical Design	-15% to -10%	+15 to +10%
Build and Test	-10% to -5%	+10% to +5%
Release	-5% to 1%	+5% to +1%

of uncertainty. In project management and software development, the cone of uncertainty describes a theory that states that project risk decreases with time. The argument goes on to assert that change also lessens its impact on risk management and decision making (Antunes and Gonzalez 2015). Table 18.2 is an approximation of the REPAC estimation technique assessment of appropriate orders of magnitude.

We have already seen that estimating time in projects is typically done using a single point estimate derived from experience and best guess. At best, a single point estimate gives us a 50 percent probability of success. We can increase those odds a few percentages by accounting for both the availability of a resource and their average productivity, which we have learned through studies is about 70 percent.

Classic time estimation on projects, done using two simple techniques, yields a broad range of results. The first method, as seen in Equation 18.2[4], assumes that the person giving the estimate can account for the variables needed to provide a thoughtful assessment.

$$d = e \qquad \text{[Eq. 18.2]}$$

Regrettably, this approach has a low success rate and is ironically used in most cases, even when the project timelines carry substantial risk. It is not reasonable to expect the project members and stakeholders to assess the inconsistency of their work forecasts. We must account for our loss factors, which are expressed as $D = E/LF$, where LF is a correction factor. As a species, we have no intuitive sense of the variation of an uncertain quantity of time. Especially when the endpoints of the time curve move in relation to other deliverables' time curves. The second classic technique accounts for stakeholder availability, but still only offers a single point estimate of work time.

In this example, the duration (d) is equal to the amount of effort required to accomplish the task, divided by the availability (a) that the stakeholder has to work on the task (a is our first correction factor). We cannot assume that our resource will work on the deliverable 100 percent of the time. Ideally, resources should dedicate themselves to a task 100 percent of the time that they are working on that task, but this is seldom the case. Culturally, project team members and stakeholders alike are expected to be able to multitask. Rather than trying to change this behavior, it is far simpler to account for it mathematically and report this justification to project team members. Equation 18.3 is a single point estimate with availability as a variable.

$$d = \frac{e}{a} = \frac{10}{50\%} = 20h$$ [Eq. 18.3]

This equation is telling, in that the projected 10 hours of work has doubled because the resource is only available to work on it for half of their time. Availability for most projects is not constant and tends to change frequently due to work habits such as multitasking. Each time we switch from one deliverable to another, time is required to bring ourselves back to the productive state we were in previously.

Due to the degree of randomness in the project from plan to release, we must treat time as a stochastic resource. In Equation 18.4 and Equation 18.5, (d) represents duration, (e) represents the amount of effort needed to complete the task, (a) represents the resource's availability, and (pr) represents the average productivity of an average knowledge worker. What we are saying here is that duration is effort over all loss factors ($D = E/LF$).

$$d = \frac{e}{a} / pr$$ [Eq. 18.4]

$$d = \frac{10h}{50\%} / 70\% = \frac{20h}{0.7} = \lceil 29 \rceil$$ [Eq. 18.5]

Equation 18.5, rounded with ceiling brackets, is easy to calculate. This technique is helpful when the hours given come with high confidence and the work is relatively routine. When the number of hours cannot be guaranteed, however, we need to be comfortable saying, "I don't know" or "I'm not sure when it will be complete." We have already seen how difficult it is for most people to articulate with any predictability the accuracy of their timelines. Multitasking or task switching is rampant in our fast-paced culture. Since this work ethic is not likely to change—we must acquire historical data and use probabilistic mathematics.

Program Evaluation Review Technique (PERT)

Recommended by the Project Management Institute and first developed by the United States Department of Defense in the 1960s, the *program evaluation review technique* was designed to help the United States government manage numerous contractors on its Polaris weapons program (Malcolm et al. 1959). Originally it was designed to help engineers assess the variances of their duration forecasts.

In Equation 18.6 and Equation 18.7, (μ) represents the PERT mean. The mean is calculated using a pessimistic (p), an optimistic (o), and a most likely (ml) estimate. The formula is divided by six to account for the weighting of the most probable estimate by four (there are six values in the equation). To establish the standard deviation (σ), we use the square root of the two extreme values.[5]

$$\mu = \frac{p + (4ml) + o}{6}$$ [Eq. 18.6]

$$\sigma = \sqrt{\left(\frac{p-o}{6}\right)^2}$$ [Eq. 18.7]

$$\mu = \frac{72 + (4 \times 43) + 15}{6} = 43h$$

$$\sigma = \sqrt{3.08} = 1.75$$

The standard deviation is a measure of the instability of the estimate itself. It is not statistical inference. The larger the deviation, the less confidence we have in the numbers provided. A small standard deviation denotes some confidence in a project estimate. The implication is that the optimistic and pessimistic values are closer together.

PMs use PERT and the simplified standard deviation calculation as a means to easily and quickly identify the work that needs completing, who can do it, and a reasonably objective assessment of how long that work might take. The variance helps PMs to determine how well thought out the estimates are. The higher the variance, the more likely it is that the PM might ask us for more refined estimates.

PERT was designed to make the curve fit the circumstances. It was designed to meet the moment, not all moments. Known as curve-fitting, this can be a beneficial way to predict future events if the underlying statistical processes stay the same. Since all projects are different and all projects change from one day to the next, they fall victim to stochastic or random variables.

PERT is not a statistical measure—it is an estimation planning tool. We improve this estimation by adding our resource's availability and productivity. Equation 18.8 is an example of this technique.[6] In this instance, we replace a single-point estimate (e) with the PERT formula. Equation 18.8 is about as complicated as any project manager would choose; however, there are many more equations which help us improve our estimates and offer us accurate statistical measures in a stochastic environment. These equations are too complex to review in this chapter. If you would like to learn more about measuring details such as Bayesian reasoning, random sampling, and how to track requirements error rates, please read my paper available on my website: http://www.silverbirchlearning.com/articles.

$$d = \frac{e(PERT)}{a} \, / \, pr \qquad \text{[Eq. 18.8]}$$

$$d = \frac{e = \left[\dfrac{(p + (4ml) + o)}{6} \right]}{a} \, / \, pr$$

We have completed our analysis of analysis. Understanding how things work is at the core of what we do.

REFERENCES

American Psychological Association. 2006. *Multitasking: Switching Costs*. URL: http://www.apa.org/research/action/multitask.aspx.

Antunes, Ricardo and Vicente Gonzalez. 2015. "A Production Model for Construction: A Theoretical Framework." *Buildings* 5, no. 1, pp. 209–28.

Malcolm, Donald G., John H. Roseboom, Charles E. Clark, and Willard Fazar. 1959. "Application of a Technique for Research and Development Program Evaluation." *Operations research* 7, no. 5, pp. 646–69.

Meyer, D. E., J. E. Evans, E. J. Lauber, L. Gmeindl, J. Rubinstein, L. Junck, and R. A. Koeppe. 1998. "The Role of Dorsolateral Prefrontal Cortex for Executive Cognitive Processes in Task Switching." Poster presented at the annual meeting of the Cognitive Neuroscience Society, San Francisco, CA.

Meyer, D. E., J. E. Evans, E. J. Lauber, J. Rubinstein, L. Gmeindi, L. Junck, and R. A. Koeppe. 1997. "Activation of Brain Mechanisms for Executive Mental Processes in Cognitive Task Switching." Poster presented at the fourth annual meeting of the Cognitive Neuroscience Society.

Pincus, Steven M. 1991. "Approximate Entropy as a Measure of System Complexity." *Proceedings of the National Academy of Sciences* 88, no. 6, pp. 297–301.

ENDNOTES

1. I understand that entropy is not a measure of randomness or disorder; these are just suitable metaphors. Entropy helps describe why physical processes go in one direction, but not the other; for that reason, it is a suitable concept for our description of the arrow of time as it relates to projects and requirements management.

2. I am not the first to use this analogy. Others have linked computer code to entropy. The more the code modifies the higher its entropy and the less energy or usefulness it has within a system.

3. Effort (e) here is the independent variable while duration (d) is the dependent variable. In much simpler terms, d is dependent on e. This dependence, however, does not connote the direct equivalence between d and e because several other variables may help account for the relationship between d and e.

4. In this equation, $d = e$ offers a much more simplistic understanding of the dependence between duration and effort. It is important, however, not to misconstrue this relationship as *equality* between the two variables.

5. The mean (μ) is the expected value of the duration *guesstimates* from stakeholders on when certain tasks are expected to be completed. A combination of p, o, and 4 values of ml provides six values, which when divided by six, provides the expected value of the duration (minimum time needed to complete a project). The standard deviation σ denotes the dispersion (spread) of the *guesstimate* values about the mean.

6. Here, e is characterized with the PERT mean formula. Effort (e) is now less of an abstract and more of a quantifiable variable.

SECTION 4:
Finding the Need

19

THE REPAC COLLABORATION SUPERSET

"A paycheck is a sufficient impetus to motivate some employees to do the minimum amount to get by, and for others, the challenge of getting ahead in the organization provides a satisfactory focus for a while. But these incentives alone are rarely strong enough to inspire workers to give their best to their work. For this a vision is needed, an overarching goal that gives meaning to the job, so that an individual can forget himself in the task and experience flow without doubts or regrets. The most important component of such a vision is an ingredient we call soul."
—Mihály Csíkszentmihályi

Mihály Csíkszentmihályi is a Hungarian psychologist who focuses primarily on creativity and the *zone* or *flow*; that mental state where we completely immerse ourselves in whatever we are doing. Biologically, the *zone* is a place that is full of endorphins and other peptides that are reaching out to our opiate receptors, causing an analgesic effect that says, "It's fun here, this work is excellent!"

Naturally, we feel energized, focused, complete, committed, and happy. Wouldn't it be great to feel that every day? What is the immaterial, essence, embodiment, or soul of your work? Do you know? For me, it is seeing a person understand or *get it*; you know, that *aha* moment when all of the little pieces come together, and they become a little bit different because of what they now know and what they can do. Find your impetus, and you will spend the rest of your life *in the zone*.

If work is an activity involving mental or physical effort that is done to achieve value, a purpose, or result, or the energy transferred to a system by force acting at a distance (remember, work is force x displacement), then the impetus is the force through which a system moves. Thinking back to the beginning of this book, the impetus—or that which got the ball rolling, as it were—was the cause. We examined the cause as the type of causality, the subject and perspective of a cause. Examples include:

- *Causality*: linear, sequential, cyclical, etc.
- *Subject*: acquisition, assets, interruptions, partnerships, regulations, resourcing, safety, shared values, vendors, etc.
- *Subject perspective*: opportunity or threat

You may recall that there are a few rules for causal analysis. When selecting a source causality, only one selection is permitted. Causation types are disjoint or mutually exclusive, meaning a cause-and-effect relationship cannot be cyclical and mutual at the same time. When selecting a source subject, the order does not matter, and repetition is not allowed. It would not make sense to build a Requirements, Elicitation, Planning, Analysis, and Collaboration Framework™ (REPAC®) source set with two or more of the same elements. It may seem necessary to discuss many subjects, but in this case, each is its own set. We perceive subjects as opportunities, threats, or both, simultaneously.

The second force of source is the stakeholders themselves. Recognizing that stakeholders are emotional beings just like the rest of us, it is fundamental that we understand them as professionals and people. We must not judge them as a group on a single curve. Generalized ranking systems of production incorrectly evaluate performance; make people feel like bees in a hive; and breed fear, insecurity, and dissatisfaction. Generic bonus systems that are designed to treat everyone equally offer the same thinking to top performers. Lazy succession policies only avoid the hard and necessary work of evaluating each objectively, based on his or her merits.

From the impetus of causality and stakeholder, we identify goals from which we create a series of interrogatives that become imperatives such as objectives, needs, and deliverables. Figure 19.1 illustrates how we move from impetus to interrogatives to purpose and value (more on this later).

Goals are qualitative statements of our project's destination, aim, or the desired result. Goals drive and constrain imperatives and imperatives support and sustain goals. The organization owns the project's goals (from which objectives derive); although they may pertain to a service, division, line of business, department, or team. Common goals include statements such as encouraging sustainable smart organizational and personal growth, shifting toward an agile culture mindset, building a business analysis center of excellence, improving corporate citizenship, or helping customers embrace *why we do what we do*, not just *what we do*. Remember, repeat customers come back out of convenience, among other things, but loyal customers are worth their weight in Francium (worth approximately $1 billion per gram) because they believe in your vision and usually stay with you even when prices increase.

For the case study, the end game is a complete redesign of the way The New Business Analyst, Inc. (TNBA) creates, distributes, and manages all of its content—including its proprietary learning material. There are many stakeholders to consider for this project. Keeping things simple, we have been following a particular cohort known as millennials.

TNBA wants to determine which consumer segments will adapt to a customer relationship management and online study solution that it is considering. Using the information given in Figure 19.2 as a guide, we concentrate on a dialogue about the cultural norms of a particular market segment—for example, Generation Y—and their financial behaviors. On what do they like to spend their money—how

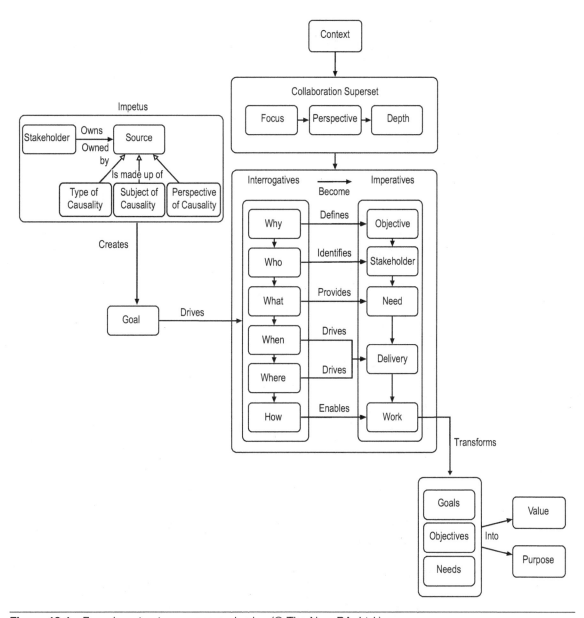

Figure 19.1   From impetus to purpose and value (© The New BA, Ltd.)

much goes to education? It is also relevant to consider how this particular customer demographic might interact with the proposed solution, given certain technological or regulatory constraints. This process will help with developing external user personas and fictional user types, which help us understand what we require of the solution to satisfy their particular needs. Figure 19.2 contains the REPAC collaboration superset members.

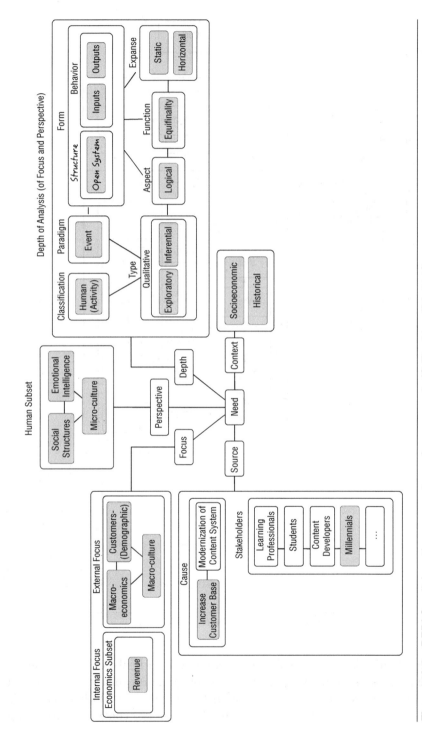

Figure 19.2　REPAC collaboration superset members example (© The New BA, Ltd.)

EXAMPLE SUPERSET PACKAGE MEMBERS

- *Stakeholder*: user, millennial, male and female, average online and mobile experience
- *Context*: socioeconomic, historical
- *Cause*: a desire to increase TNBA customer base
- *External focus*: macro-economic, customer demographic, and macro-culture elements
- *Internal focus*: economics subset / revenue element
- *Perspective / human subset*: social structures, emotional intelligence, and micro-culture elements
- *Paradigm*: event element
- *Classification*: human—activity element
- *Type / qualitative*: exploratory and inferential elements
- *Form / structure*: open system
- *Behavior*: input and output elements
- *Aspect*: logical element
- *Function*: equifinal element
- *Expanse*: static and horizontal elements

Personas are the lifelike, fictional characters that reflect stakeholders' needs. We create personas across many business sectors such as government, consumer goods, finance, technology, advertising, retail, and many others. It's such a critical step in our needs assessment because it allows a deep understanding of what our customers require of us.

To build and maintain successful solutions, we must know a lot about our users, such as their likes, dislikes, spending habits, social behaviors, fundamental needs, desires, and opinions. Creating user personas is one of the most significant ways to build vibrant and meaningful cases for usage, epics, themes, stories, scenarios, and imperatives. We cannot effectively identify what we require of the solution until we have a rich backlog of user personas.

Millennials, born between 1979 and 1994, account for about 27% of the U.S. population as of 2019. This group enjoys juggling many responsibilities at once. They are tech-savvy and very connected through social media. Millennials tend to seek instant gratification and recognition, they strive for a flexible work-life balance, and are career-focused. However, because they require instant gratification, they are not willing to put in the hours to slowly and carefully build their brand. From this, we might assume that as a group they desire education on an on-demand basis. Further, we could suppose their need is small, topic-based seminars, no more than one hour in length.

SOURCE AND CONTEXT SUBSETS

Understanding context is essential because our invocation of causality relies on comparing what we need, what happened to what we might need, or what could have happened in a different hypothetical set of circumstances. It is not possible to fully understand our stakeholders or goals without understanding the context in which we wish to help or satisfy—without context; there is no meaning.

Focus Subset

Millennials tend to have unhealthy relationships with money—the 'Ys' want it, and they want it now! With a sense of entitlement and a shortfall of disposable income, some millennials live beyond their means. As a technology-empowered group, millennials seek out their desires and then try to figure out how to pay for them. As a behavior, we can use this to our advantage. Offering fast prerecorded access to education, we can help millennials get the jobs they want and the promotions they need to pay for the things they desire.

Millennials often feel they will not be able to acquire their material desires. Paying off student loan debt has become increasingly difficult for many who are struggling with unemployment and low-paying jobs. The Great Recession of 2008 left over 15% of millennials in their early twenties out of work, many of whom are still struggling as of 2019. These issues have far-reaching effects on their life goals and retirement plans.

Perspective Subset

A recent (2016) survey from the American Institute of Certified Public Accountants reported that over 75% of millennials in the United States desire the same clothes, cars, and gadgets as their friends. Without the money to pay for these things, many live off of their credit cards, borrow from their parents, and live in debt or collections. One of the more disturbing findings reports that seven out of 10 members of this group define financial stability as the ability to cover their minimum monthly responsibilities. With this information, we can target millennials with a clear marketing plan to help them acquire the education they need to meet their fiduciary obligations and build the skills that today's employers demand. However, that is just the beginning.

Emotional intelligence, our capacity to be aware of, control, and express emotions, and to manage interpersonal relationships judiciously and empathetically, transcends socioeconomic and cultural boundaries. Millennials are fortunate in that they have access to a wealth of data via the internet. They are aware of a need to increase their ability to relate to others and may seek online courses that promise instruction pre- and post-evaluation in this area.

The traditional perspective on managing people has been mainly analytical and rational, forgoing our emotions. I sometimes wonder if millennials, like today's parents, are desperately trying to avoid the pitfalls of their parents yet wind up rehashing the old behaviors they swore they would never repeat when they got to be in charge. Employee motivation goes beyond the usual monetary reward systems for a multigenerational workforce. Today's human capital requires intellectual and emotional engagement; it is imperative to engage minds and captivate hearts. We achieve this state through social and emotional intelligence. This pursuit requires training for both workers—in this case, the millennials—and their employee counterparts (Njoroge and Yazdanifard 2014).

Depth of Analysis

For Bayesians (like me), probabilities are expressions of our states of belief in cases of ignorance or uncertainty. When new data presents itself, we must reevaluate our beliefs against this new evidence. Non-Bayesian logic does not take into account new data, which keeps its thinking rudimentary.

For many, pathos is an important tool of persuasion in arguments and analysis. Pathos is a method of convincing people through an emotional response. For those who rely on reason, a pathos-fueled argument can be challenging. The REPAC depth of analysis of focus and perspective is intended to temper our emotional tendencies by showing which analytical tools are useful in which situations. Combining sound reason and pathos with the particular spirit ethos makes for a better winning position.

Paradigm

Processes are the driving force in business. An understanding of process execution has a proven return on investment. The event-driven analysis is orthogonal to other paradigms; meaning we can comfortably use this device even if the developers select a different programming standard. Event-driven computer systems react dynamically to user actions. My favorite tool for understanding the events that trigger responses such as messages, flow, exceptions, and even executables is Business Process Modeling Notation (BPMN).

BPMN, developed by the Business Process Management Initiative, circa 2005, has become a standard for modeling how business *really* functions. An advantage of BPMN over simple diagramming tools is its notational elements, which follow specific diagramming rules. Also, execution semantics offer developers a chance to decompose models down to the programming level. BPMN is comprised of the following element categories and decomposes into three modeling levels.

Element Categories

- *Flow objects*: events, activities, and gateways
- *Connecting objects*: sequence flows, message flows, and associations
- *Swim-lanes*: pools and lanes
- *Artifacts*: data objects, groups, and annotations

LEVELS

Descriptive Modeling

- Basic shapes develop a business-oriented view of a process without describing exceptions and errors

Analytical Modeling

- An extended palette of shapes shows more detail of events and exception handling, necessary to verify and validate stakeholders' needs

Executable Modeling

- Full executable process implementation identifying the precise functions necessary to satisfy our stakeholders' needs and realize the solution and all of its human and machine process components

There isn't anything I could write about BPMN that would add to the already extensive knowledge base. If you would like to learn more, please see the following materials: *The Object Management Group® Standards Consortium.* http://www.omg.org.

CLASSIFICATION

You may recall from Chapter 15 that human activity systems include socio-technical systems—the classic people, process, tools/technology triad. The purpose is to understand how millennials would interact with the procedures and interactions that will emerge from the quality and value that the selected solution will provide.

Type

It is necessary to conduct a qualitative analysis that is both exploratory and inferential. We already know that a qualitative assessment is a conclusion reached from evidence and reasoning; however, because our focus is qualitative, quantity is not the focus—for example, how many millennials will be attracted. Earlier we took a look at some inferential reasoning techniques such as contextual, modal, abstract, systematic, and choreographic thinking. For this REPAC collaboration superset, we may use any number of these skills to learn more about our target stakeholder.

Because qualitative elicitation focuses on gathering personal information from our stakeholders' point of view, we must rely on our communication skills—something we have talked about extensively in this book. Communication is not about broadcasting your message to others; it is about reaching an understanding with your communication partner. As we communicate through our analysis efforts, we must remember to speak the same *language* as our partners. I do not mean English or some other traditional notion of language; I am referring to something more abstract. For example, I think in pictures and metaphors. We may all *see* the problem differently, which causes it to hold a different meaning for each of us.

Form

The initial analysis is an open system. Open systems interact externally within its system boundary. When exploring how millennials may interact regarding the inputs and outputs of our solution, it may be necessary to venture outside of this system of analysis and explore their interactions with employers or even their parents. We intend to examine what the solution must do for the stakeholders whom we are investigating.

Aspect

We are now ready to consider the physical attributes of the solution or any of its components. A logical analysis requires putting forward a series of *if/then* dependent claims that must be true regardless of which solution the stakeholders choose. It is similar to saying, "Despite this or in spite of that, it must perform in this manner, regardless."

Function

Equifinality is always something on which we should keep our analytical eye. Having the same end or result to where the project started is the very minimum we should expect from any solution. Similar to a doctor, we should never make things worse. General systems theory reveals that equifinality is the expected result of an open system. Remember, our ideal is a closed system; however, this will never be the case. Equifinality is the analysis term we use to define our better state.

Expanse

The expanse of the analysis, for now, will not be a *deep dive*. I like to call this my *rake approach*. Imagine grabbing a spade and digging yourself a narrow six-foot hole deep into your front yard or better yet, your neighbor's garden. The hole is just big enough for you. You know all there is to know about that hole, but you know nothing about the rest of the yard. Since the hole is too narrow, none of your neighbors can crawl into your hole to see how cool it is. This analogy is a deep dive, analytically speaking.

Now imagine that you wish to shave off six feet from your front yard. This approach may seem like more work, nevertheless it is not. As you pull back each layer, you and the whole neighborhood—your stakeholders—know everything you need to know about that layer. If you are lucky enough to have a good team, then some of those neighbors will help you pull back your layers of analysis. This tactic is the essence of a static horizontal approach. It is also a principle of any adaptive or agile approach—just enough, just in time. Take a look at Figure 19.3. From the skateboard to the car, each layer of analysis, design, and eventual development creates purpose and value. In contrast, we can clearly observe that the assembly approach visible at the top of the diagram, indicative of a predictive method, forces deep dives to learn all there is for each stage in the predictive delivery (waterfall) process.

Predictive Analysis, Design, and Development (Control and Assembly)

Adaptive Analysis, Design, and Development (Evolutionary and Emergent)

Figure 19.3   Different ways to think about analysis (© The New BA, Ltd.)

Now that we have some examples of how we may approach our analysis, it is time to define some needs so we can identify what we require to satisfy our stakeholders.

REFERENCE

Njoroge, Caroline Ngonyo and Rashad Yazdanifard. 2014. "The Impact of Social and Emotional Intelligence on Employee Motivation in a Multigenerational Workplace." *International Journal of Information, Business and Management* 6, no. 4, p. 163.

20

THE SOCIAL SCIENCE OF
IDENTIFYING A NEED

*"Truly listening is hearing the needs of the customer, understanding those needs,
and making sure the company recognizes the opportunities they present."*
—Frank Eliason, Global Director of Client Experience Team at Citi

Eliason—referred to as "the most famous customer service manager in the U.S., possibly the world" by *BusinessWeek*[1]—believes it is time to change how we provide customer service fundamentally. However, Eliason writes in a LinkedIn post, "companies cannot improve the way they deliver customer service without listening to the client." Eliason gained national attention when, in 2008, he and his team took on the challenge of addressing some of Comcast's then customer service issues. Eliason created the now famous '@ComcastCares' Twitter account and single-handedly interacted with more than 10,000 of Comcast's clients. In his book, *At Your Service: How to Attract New Customers, Increase Sales, and Grow Your Business Using Simple Customer Service Techniques*, Eliason suggests that we should refocus our business on those who matter most—customers and employees.

Stakeholders are assets. Customers (as well as managers and users) fall well within that definition. Their needs, partnership, commitment, and support along with our talents are the only assets we have. It behooves us to listen efficiently and address the concerns stated as much as those who are not. If our stakeholders are made to feel as if they are outsiders, they will eventually become outsiders. Let us stop assuming that our stakeholders will work with us and trust that they *want* to work with us; this procedure just needs our help. Do not assume that all of your stakeholders' needs will be solution related. Our focus for this chapter will be on the social aspects of acquiring stakeholder needs.

Thinking back to Gen-Y; I am not conducting a focus group with our millennial customers—at least not yet. Eventually, a focus group will identify attitudes and opinions about our goals and objectives. Before we engage our stakeholders, we first need to gather some research. Let us start with the hypothesis that a different style of training is necessary for the millennial generation.

With our external focus on macro-culture and our investigation of a particular perspective on the millennial's human-activity subset—specifically, their social structures, emotional intelligence, and micro-culture—our analysis will follow two learning/communication premises: the *politeness* and computer-mediated communication theories.

POLITENESS AS A GUIDE FOR NEEDS IDENTIFICATION

Searching the term *polite* gives us the following synonyms: well mannered, civil, courteous, mannerly, respectful, deferential, well behaved, well-bred, gentlemanly, ladylike, genteel, gracious, urbane, tactful, and diplomatic. Do these words define what it means to communicate politely? The politeness theory was developed in the 1970s and 1980s by two researchers from Stanford University: Penelope Brown, an American anthropological linguist, and Stephen Levinson, a British social scientist and linguistic anthropologist.

Brown and Levinson expanded an existing idea known as the face theory, which was developed by Canadian-American sociologist Erving Goffman. Goffman argued that we present a *face* to others in conjunction with how people interact in their daily lives. Claiming that everyone is concerned, to some extent, with how others perceive them, Goffman suggested that our behaviors maintain the identity we create for others to see—our public self-image. The expressions *saving face* and *losing face*, for example, were derived from this theory. To lose face is to suffer a diminished self-image publicly; while saving face takes a *line* while socializing. A line is a specific interaction such as an action or communication block combined with the receiver's evaluation of the person with whom they are interacting. Social interaction, according to Goffman, is a process that combines line and face, or *face-work*. Brown and Levinson use face-work to explain their theories of politeness (Goffman 1959).

Remember, our primitive brains have no capacity for language or rational thought. A tiger, a hunter with a spear, or a coworker who is irritated about something you did or if you are angry about something they did—it's all the same to your survival systems. Now, where do you think this all starts? That's right—your face, your posture, or in other words, your body! We already know that chronically elevated stress hormones link to many illnesses; but what's interesting is that stress also affects a decreased production of brain-derived neurotrophic factors, which are proteins that stimulate new brain cell formation. It follows, therefore, that we research what millennials consider polite behavior concerning online learning systems.

COMPUTER-MEDIATED COMMUNICATION THEORY

A Guide for Needs Identification

Any communication between two or more people that uses an electronic device as a medium, exclusively or in part, is computer-mediated communication. Seems simple enough; why then call it a theory? For that I recall a famed Canadian whom we Canadians all had to learn about in grammar school, philosopher Marshall McLuhan, and his ubiquitous phrase, "The medium is the message."

All messages transmit through a medium. The medium itself embeds into the message, forming a symbiotic relationship that ultimately influences our perception of the message. To understand this influence, we must understand the person receiving the message and how different mediums are likely to alter different messages. Among many theories, the three theories we cover are Social Presence Theory (SPT), SIDE, and SIP.

SPT

Derived from work initially described in Isaac Asimov's novel, *The Naked Sun* (1956), SPT was developed as a published theory in 1976 by communications theorist John Short, and academics Ederyn Williams and Bruce Christie, to explain the salience in relationships as they relate to the social psychology of communications through a medium. In this context, think of salience as the quality or state of *being there*. Salience may also refer to the quality of being particularly noticeable or significant. Project salience, in particular a stakeholder analysis, relates to power, urgency, influence, impact, and required participation.

In short, Williams and Christie's original thesis defined SPT as "the degree of salience of the other person in the interaction and the consequent salience of the interpersonal relationships" (Gunawardena 1995). This was later refined independently by Gunawardena and Zittle in 1995–1997 and again in the early half of this century by Boise State University Associate Professor Patrick Lowenthal. Respectively, each theorize social presence as "the degree to which a person is perceived as a *real person* in mediated communication" and "definitions of social presence tend to lie on a continuum where a focus on interpersonal emotional connection between communicators is on one end and a focus on if someone is perceived as being *present*, *there*, or *real* at the other end." In summary, social presence theory:

- Relates to the degree to which individuals perceive each other as a *real person* and the subsequent quality of interaction between the communication partners
- States that different media convey varying levels of perceived substance
- States that alternative media such as the internet, texting, Facebook, or other social specializations are not a quality substitution for a face-to-face connection
- Reveals that we are pattern-seeking, story-telling, social animals that thrive in a colocated face-to-face environment

SIDE

SIDE (Social Identity Model of Deindividuation Effects) was developed by Lea and Spears in 1991–1992 as a critique of the deindividuation theory. Deindividuation, which is similar to crowd psychology, suggests that in a crowd we lean toward behavior that we might not otherwise endorse. Also called *mob mentality*, the crowd provides us with cover and anonymity. Our behavior becomes less rational, allowing us to *get away* with things we know are socially impermissible (Thurlow, Lengel, and Tomic 2004).

This identifiability is common in groups that cannot directly interact with each other. Have you ever found yourself making faces or somehow demonstrating your disdain to the person on the other end of the conference line? You may not do this with your peers because there is still some richness in the communication event but left to your own devices, you are free to act as you desire, safe in the knowledge that your fellow stakeholders will never know. Even worse, the group may gang up on the unsuspecting voice on the other end of the telephone (Wood and Smith 2004).

Cognitively, anonymity changes the salience of personal identity and social identity, which profoundly affects behavior. This depersonalizes our social perceptions, which leads to stereotypes. Strategically, as it relates to organizational culture, our ability to express our personal and social identities also diminishes. Think about some of the in-groups and out-groups within your organization (Gaertner and Dovidio 2000).

SIP

Developed as an interpersonal communication theory and media studies theory by Joseph Walther in 1992, SIP (social information processing) theory attempts to explain how we express online interpersonal communication without nonverbal cues and how we develop and manage relationships in a computer-mediated environment. We are a very social species. Our need for bonding is the same regardless of how we communicate. Consider that for almost all of human history we have been in reasonable proximity to each other. Our society may have evolved beyond small tribes and villages, but our brains have not. We call it our communication imperative. We can compensate for nonverbal cues with our imagination and knowledge of our communication partner, but this is not very reliable. Using the Requirements, Elicitation, Planning, Analysis, and Collaboration Framework™ (REPAC®) collaboration superset and the analysis in this chapter, we can conclude the following needs for our millennials with respect to the design and support of an information management reference solution:

- Brief, visual, well-produced, scenario-based, computer-mediated training
- Learning that is designed to enhance their professional service portfolio without communicating in a style that is too casual, yet conveys a high degree of social presence
- Adapt and support the casual and informal use of Web 2.0 technologies by millennials
- Bridge the linguistic gap between younger and older generations for whom instant messaging is very formal

Millennials are digital natives; having grown up with sophisticated technology, their expectations for training and usage in the workplace differ vastly from those of older generations. Millennials have become pragmatic, which lends itself well to an agile mindset. They are adept at sorting through large volumes of data quickly and feel comfortable spending all of their time with and around technology (Prensky 2010; Prensky 2012). Any training solution created by The New Business Analyst, Inc. must keep these facts in mind. It will not be long before this group will be the largest consumer of educational material. We now have enough information to build an encapsulated construct of what is required to fulfill our stakeholders' needs.

REFERENCES AND ADDITIONAL SUGGESTED READINGS

Brown, Penelope and Stephen C. Levinson. 1987. *Politeness: Some Universals in Language Usage (Studies in Interactional Sociolinguistics 4)*. Cambridge University Press.

Eliason, Frank. 2012. *At Your Service: How to Attract New Customers, Increase Sales, and Grow Your Business Using Simple Customer Service Techniques*. Wiley.

Gaertner, Samuel L. and John F. Dovidio. 2000. *Reducing Intergroup Bias: The Common Ingroup Identity Model (Essays in Social Psychology)*. Psychology Press.

Goffman, Erving. 1959. *The Presentation of Self in Everyday Life*. Anchor.

Gunawardena, Charlotte N. 1995. "Social Presence Theory and Implications for Interaction and Collaborative Learning in Computer Conferences." *International Journal of Educational Telecommunications* 1, no. 2/3. 147–66.

Lowenthal, Patrick R. 2009. "Social Presence." *Social Computing: Concepts, Methodologies, Tools, and Applications* 1, pp. 129–36.

Metcalf, Eric. 2011. *The Impact of Media Selection on Organizational Communication: Testing Information Richness Theory With Agent-Based Models*. LAP Lambert Academic Publishing.

Prensky, Marc R. 2010. *Teaching Digital Natives: Partnering for Real Learning*. Corwin.

Prensky, Marc R. 2012. *From Digital Natives to Digital Wisdom: Hopeful Essays for 21st Century Learning*. Corwin.

Reisner, Rebecca. January 13, 2009. "Comcast's Twitter Man." *BusinessWeek*.

Sproull, Lee, Sara Kiesler, and Sara B. Kiesler. 1992. *Connections: New Ways of Working in the Networked Organization*. MIT press.

Thurlow, Crispin, Lara M. (Martin) Lengel, and Alice Tomic. 2004. *Computer Mediated Communication*. SAGE Publications Ltd.

Wood, Andrew F. and Matthew J. Smith. 2004. "Online Communication: Linking Technology, Identity, & Culture (Routledge Communication Series)," p. 264.

ENDNOTE

1. Rebecca Reisner. January 13, 2009. "Comcast's Twitter Man," *Business Week*.

21

ASSEMBLING THE IMPERATIVE

"Most of the world will make decisions by either guessing or using their gut. They will be either lucky or wrong."
—Suhail Doshi, CEO, Mixpanel

I recognize that some, perhaps most of you, may not capture all of the elements contained within a quantized imperative—nor should you; it is a collaborative effort! You, business analyst (BA), however, are solely responsible for managing the initial cause, following proposals, identifying needs, eliciting interrogatives, and designing logical (nonphysical) elements, all the way to delivering quantified customer value and organizational purpose.

We are assembling a quantized imperative. An abstract that contains all we require to satisfy a particular need. Consider the quantized imperative (or requirement if that word is more comfortable) as the physical wrapper for a user story, scenario, use case, process, or declarative statement. It contains everything we need to release and realize whatever you have elicited—data, value, purpose, functions, rules, tasks, everything!

Value propositions belong to customers (the paying kind), while organizational stakeholders and business partners (either external or internal) own the purpose. For instances where an internal stakeholder creates a need—a client services representative (CSR), for example—our instincts might consider the CSR as our customer, so we would naturally construct the requirement from their point of view. We would be wrong to do so, however. Who is the CSR's customer? Our internal representative asked for their need so she can serve her customer better. Thus, in almost any case where we must build something to satisfy a need, it will ultimately be an external stakeholder—the paying customer. Business analysis and all of its various activities is a social experience; this includes *writing imperatives (requirements).*

The following statement may surprise you: I stopped writing requirements long ago. I still refuse to sit and write a business requirements document (BRD). I am happy to write, model, and diagram encapsulated imperatives, but I will not capture requirements using such an old artifact. Granted, I must still capture the data, but there are far better ways to accomplish those goals. Getting the stakeholder's demands right is all about communication, teamwork, and effective stakeholder management.

Based on my experience with hundreds of students, most BAs still use a BRD, solutions requirements specifications document, or some such artifact to collect and document what they perceive as requirements—business, stakeholder, functional, nonfunctional, transition, and the like. In preparation for this book, I spent months researching and analyzing hundreds of requirements documents kindly passed to me by former students and colleagues. Of the many issues, one stood out among the rest.

A requirement—for example, "The system shall allow a user to enter a new employee's address as part of the new employee on-boarding change request for ABC System"—would be written on, say, page 143 within the *Functional Requirements* section and then either repeated in another section, drafted in a higher form, or not connected to the dozens of other provisions that a designer, developer, or tester would need to know about so they can realize and accept the specification.

A quantized imperative does away with requirements spread across many pages and documents by boxing all of the content into a single provision—a wrapped need, encapsulated with all of its required descriptors and imperatives. The ah-ha moment here uses the term *requirement* as a verb, not a noun. I do not expect a BA to document the imperative and all of its elements by him or herself—this is a team effort, as dictated by the team's project approach. I do, however, expect the BA to manage the imperative throughout the project and product life cycle. In an adaptive culture, for example, the wrapper for each imperative is a user story. Each of the member elements within the imperative is an element necessary to realize a need. The requirement is neither functional nor nonfunctional; it is not a reporting requirement nor a data requirement—it is all of those—it is an imperative with required elements encased within a logical wrapper.

REPAC QUANTIZED IMPERATIVE SUPERSET

Solutions have thousands of elements with hundreds of complex associations and interdependencies. Quantized imperatives inform and influence analysis, proofs of concept, design, development, testing, implementation, and future and unknown uses. Their effective communication is crucial for realizing organizational purpose and customer value. Regardless of the project management method or style (predictive, incremental, adaptive) applied, documentation is significant when considering communication, a shared understanding, delivery, continuous improvement, integration, interoperability, prioritization, life-cycle management, traceability, complexity, regulations, laws, organizational standards, reporting, accessibility, retention, quality, security, and approvals. Nevertheless, never document for documentation's sake and always challenge the necessity of each artifact, within reason—JEJIT (just enough, just-in-time).

It is now time to assemble a quantized package of what we require to meet our stakeholders' expectations. Figure 21.1 models everything we need to deliver on our team's promise. The REPAC quantized imperative superset extends a descriptor set and groups a data member and a properties member set, which carries an intent to transform a stakeholder need—which has a corporate purpose—into customer value. For a proposed solution or any of its components, an imperative member classifies as one or more of the following:

1. An ability to meet environmental conditions and accommodate existing or planned infrastructure, including infrastructure as a service (IaaS)
2. An ability to maintain the permanence, integrity, and accuracy of all data, objects, or entities
3. An ability to offer a chain of custody to data and physical or non-physical objects and entities
4. An ability to connect, create, change, transition, scale, extend[1], expand[1], retain, perform, and express specified states, policies, rules, standards, conditions, behaviors, characteristics, specifications,

features, functions, capabilities, events, actions, processes, tasks or operations with and without human or machine intervention

5. An ability to secure, store, retrieve, track, print/display, and query qualitative or quantitative data and physical or non-physical objects and entities
6. An ability to identify patterns, create algorithms, use statistical models, make inferences, derive, decide, calculate, inform, measure, predict, forecast, or anticipate with or without specific instructions or human intervention

SEGMENT SUBSET

The segment subset contains two members—data and properties. Each member drives and constrains, supports and sustains each other, thereby forming a closed loop within an open system. Of the two members, the data subset contains the most elements, concepts, and classifications. Much of what we deduce from stakeholders relates to data, or rather the information they wish to learn. Let's take a look at the data segment subset, which we see in the upper left portion of Figure 21.1.

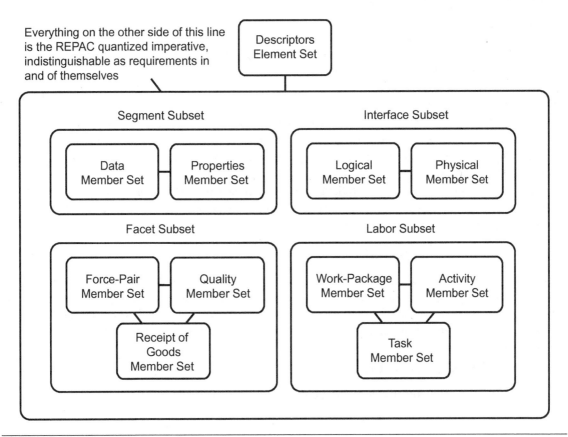

Figure 21.1 REPAC quantized imperative (© The New BA, Ltd.)

DATA MEMBER SET

The members and elements in this subset refer to the data that we require to satisfy a particular need. Although these members may resemble database arrangements such as tables, records, fields, entities, and rows, we do not assume that designers and developers use a traditional relational database in their solution.

When it comes to the acquisition, storage, and retrieval of data, we are not always information seekers. Sometimes organizations do not want to know particular things about themselves. Active information avoidance is a human phenomenon observed when we deliberately avoid costly information that we know exists. Organizations are like people (which makes sense since people run them) and they too can victimize themselves through active information avoidance regardless of the potential threats—ignorance is not bliss.

People and organizations like to live within an optimism bubble—going out of their way to avoid data that may bring their beliefs into question. Figure 21.2 expands the data member set to help us build a rich set of elements at this depth of analysis.

Data Concepts Element Set

Data Derivation Concept Element

Derivation refers to how we obtain the values—either through some action from a user, a calculation from a unit of code, or some machine state change.

Data Tuple Concept Element

Tuples are finite ordered lists of values—for example, *CourseID, CourseType, CourseName,* and *Course-Cost.* Tuples group *n* values into a single aggregate. Syntactically, a tuple is a comma-separated sequence—a data structure consisting of multiple parts. We consider a tuple to be an ordered set of data constituting a record. A record is an indivisible unique set.

Tuples require values such as keys and field names, which identify vertical columns. There must always be at least one value that can create a link with one or more other values. We call this the key value. Foreign key values are not native and are used to link one set of values to another.

Data Persistence Concept Element

Persistence denotes values that are infrequently accessed. These values are not likely to be modified over time. Conversely, dynamic or transactional values asynchronously change as updates become available. Developers and architects need to know the level of data persistence for optimal design and performance. Persistence also refers to the characteristic of a *state* that outlives the process that created the state.

Data Relation Concept Element Set

Data relates to other data (sometimes called multiplicity) in the following manner.

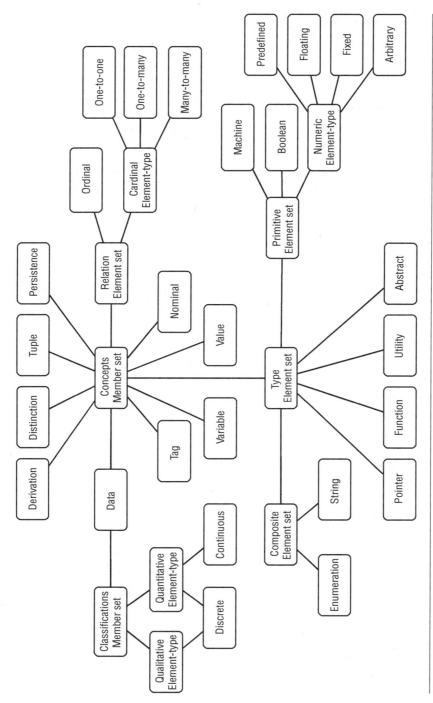

Figure 21.2 REPAC data member set (© The New BA, Ltd.)

Ordinal Data Relation Element

An ordinal is a value's position within a set. To give an example, imagine yourself shopping online. You will always have a one-to-one relationship to your default shipping address. You may have other addresses you want to use, but you will only ever have one and only one primary address.

Cardinal Data Relation Element

A cardinal is the number of elements in a set or other grouping as a property of that grouping. In data management, we use cardinals to manage the following relationships:

- *One-to-one data cardinal*: each side of a relationship may have, at most, only one value. A student's course would only have one identity value assigned. Your organization, for example, permits you to have only one swipe card.
- *One-to-many data cardinal*: a value on one side of a relationship may have several values related on the other side. The New Business Analyst, Inc. (TNBA) sells leadership courses, for example. Each course is part of the same type—leadership.
- *Many-to-many data cardinal*: there are cases where both sides of a relationship may have many values. TNBA may choose to organize its courses with courses listed in more than one type and a type may have multiple values. In another example, you may have many friends; in turn, each of them may have many other friends. This relationship or any other many-to-many relationship requires a junction to resolve.

Nominal Data Relation Element

Nominals are values that are used only as a name or identification. It is not a value, cardinal, or ordinal in and of itself. Consider your street address; the nominal value in your address string might be *7* or *9*—as in *9 Pleasant Drive*. The unit or house number's nominal reference in this example is nine. We would never use your address in an equation; except perhaps counting the number of houses on your block, in which case each complete address tuple represents a count of one. There are Σn addresses in your neighborhood resulting in X cardinal for your block set.

Data Variable Concept Element

Designers and developers must know the intent of each unit of datum. We use data variables if a value changes from one derivation, observation, instance, or transaction to another. We cannot know a variable until the machine derives it or a user enters it. Where possible we establish patterns. If the variables are not consistent from one transaction to the next, development becomes more complicated.

Data Tag Concept Element

Data tags or metadata are nonhierarchical values that we assign to other values. Tagging helps describe an item and allows it to be easily categorized, referenced, or indexed. Website search engine optimization designers often connote values that convey importance, drawing search engines to their site.

Data Value Concept Element

Values are the retained item; the data stored. Cardinals refer to how many values belong to a set. A cardinal value cannot be a fraction or decimal.

Data Type Concept Element Set

A datum of basic data types such as whole numbers or integers is considered complete in itself. Data classifies into the following.

Primitive Data Type Element

A *type of anything* is a just syntactic label associated with a variable of some kind. The primitive data that designers and developers have available depend on which programming language they are using.

Some languages have one-to-one relationships with the programming objects of that language. Standard programming objects include functions—an object with a single method, immutable. Regardless of a programming language's semantic nuances, each will make use of at least these primitive data types:

- *Primitive machine data type*: this type is the smallest unit of data, usually expressed as a group of bits called a byte or an octet, which is eight bits. The unit processed by machine is known as a *word*. These *words* usually read as binary numbers in 32- or 64-bit groups.
- *Primitive Boolean data type*: George Boole (1815–1864) developed a system of algebraic notations that represent logical propositions. As a binary variable, a Boolean has one of two possible states, *true* or *false*. The basic operators of Boolean algebra are *AND*, *OR*, and *NOT* combined with the proposition letters *P* and *Q*. In logic, the semantic concept *P* and *Q* states equivalency if they have the same truth value. This technique is a very compelling tool for designers and developers. If you can master it, you are many steps closer to speaking *their language*.

    We use truth tables to express how a data type, system, function, or rule is realized. Starting with a premise, usually denoted as *P*, we assume the proposition as either true or false—it can never hold a value in between. We call this the *law of the excluded middle*, and it is an axiom in logic. Next, we string additional true or false statements together using the basic operators *AND*, *OR*, and *NOT* (there are other gates such as *XOR*, but I will stick to the basics) until we have a fully expressed argument. Boolean logic is easy to understand but can be a bit confusing to follow.

    If proposition *Q* is true, then the negation of *P* or Not(*P*) would make *Q* false. For example, if today is TNBA's *Millennials Appreciation Day* (which I'll call MAD, for short) and we want to offer the 18–35 age bracket a discount off of online learning packages, then the system logic might *flag* in this manner (we use the setflag handler—pardons if my syntax is not perfect):

    - P = MAD SetFlag = *TRUE*
    - ¬P = Not(MAD) ¬SetFlag = *FALSE*

    We assign the variables *P* and *Q* or *SetFlag* in this example to data types that handle switching the promotion on and off. The system looks for MAD = false, and when it is, the SetFlag handler will not allow the promotion. If MAD is *not* false, then the system offers the promotion. Perhaps MAD represents a property of a calendar object, such as *HasDate*. *HasDate* looks for a value that a stakeholder specified as the promotion date. Someone in the marketing department, for example, might enter this data on an administration screen using one of those fancy *ChooseDate* objects you see on most websites.

- *Primitive numeric data type*: the last primitive data type we will examine is a numeric value or integer. An integer is a whole number, either positive or negative. Numeric data types come in a wide variety, such as predefined subtypes, which may be short or long; small, medium, or large; floating; fixed; or in rare cases, arbitrary precision (also known as bignum, multiple precision, or infinite precision).

Predefined Numeric Data Element

Predefined numeric data elements refer to functions that are already expounded by a programming language's interpreter. Users cannot redefine predefined data types. Short integers occupy two bits of computer space, while long integers double that at four bytes.

Floating Numeric Data Element

Values are usually rational numbers. Thinking back to grade school, a rational number is any value that expresses as the quotient or fraction of two integers; as in the numerator P and the denominator Q (P/Q). We often store floating data types with upper and lower limits and print them as decimals, in which case the output becomes fixed.

Fixed Numeric Data Element

We use the fixed point numeric primitive data type for values that have integers on both sides of a radix point. In mathematics, a radix is used to separate numbers, such as a period or a comma.

Arbitrary Precision Numeric Data Element

Arbitrary precision numeric types lack predefined limits, and for this reason, are used sparingly. Because there is no defined limit, we limit the machine's calculations by its available memory. Again, in contrast, the types listed previously are set with limits, thus allowing for faster calculations. We observe an example of irrationality with numbers that cannot express as a ratio of two integers.

Irrational numbers such as pi (π or 3.14159265359 . . .) which, as you know, calculates forever without ever repeating, and the square root of two (1.4142135623730950 . . .) are classic examples. We could express π as 22/7, but this is not accurate and would not be helpful to those who relied on it for statistical calculations and other mathematics. Can you imagine if we forgot to limit the machine's resolution of pi? As the string continues to grow, so does your memory allocation and within minutes, dozens of users are calling the helpdesk because of one tiny little data type error. This comment may seem overstated, but I assure you, I have seen hundreds of change requests over the years where the fix was some little thing that we might easily miss; this is another reason to use quantum level imperatives in place of traditional requirements writing.

Composite and Pointer Data Type Element

As the name suggests, composite types derive from more than one primitive. This composition creates a new data type. Arrays, lists, and enumerations are common examples of composite data. We often see composite data represented as strings, texts, blanks, or any alphanumeric sequence of characters. Pointers are simply data types whose value points to another value.

Function Data Type Element

Functions are computer operations, procedures, or routines with associated variables or parameters. Functions may or may not return a value, depending on which programming language our developer is using. We must be careful with our words. Procedures, in some languages, run operations but do not return a value, whereas functions do.

Abstract and Utility Data Type Element

Abstracts are mathematical models for data types. Mathematical models are composed of governing equations, defining equations, constitutive equations, and the model's constraints. Linear, nonlinear, static, dynamic, explicit, implicit, deterministic, and stochastic or probabilistic are examples of some of the forms these models might take. I like to call utility data types *save-me-some-time* data types. Most languages these days include a host of library options such as timers, date data types, memory management, and built-in types for handling most of the world's currency.

Data Classifications Element Set

Quantitative and Qualitative Elements

Quantitative data are values stored or derived as integers. Qualitative values are non-numeric and may be selected from a finite list or entered by a user as free text. We always try to limit the use of free text, as it creates a potential for too many variants.

Discrete and Continuous Element Sets

Discrete data can only be certain values. Discrete data may take the form of an integer or we may consider the value categorical such as the color of your eyes or a list of learning difficulty levels—beginner, intermediate, and advanced. If we capture how many courses a client has taken with TNBA, we will use a discrete quantitative integer. In this example, we would recognize the discrete business rule for the number of courses taken (which must resolve to a whole number) as a condition within the property segment subset.

As you can see, data is an essential aspect of any solution. When we think about the importance of data and the information derived (remember, information is data in context), it becomes clear that without it, there is no action. You cannot do anything in life without first knowing something about what you are doing. Data allows us to make informed decisions, build strategies, set goals, create objectives, find causes, determine needs, fulfill imperatives, build elegant solutions, and deliver value and purpose.

PROPERTY MEMBER SET

The property subset contains element members whose conditions and characteristics, which are either event or component based, describe distinctive qualities and states possessed by the behavior and other elements within the imperative. We observe the members of the property member set within the top right portion of Figure 21.1 of the imperative super set.

Characteristic Element Set

Characteristics drive and constrain conditions, actions, and responses. These items, in turn, support and sustain specific elements identified within the imperative. Either event- or component-based characteristics and conditions affect the solution in different ways.

Event-Based Characteristics Element

These characteristics are qualities attached to the relevant elements and provide occurrence-based needs for the realization of the imperative. Event-based characteristics manifest as part of some condition.

Component-Based Characteristics Element

These characteristics are similar to event and component characteristics in that they provide structural needs for the realization of the imperative.

Condition Element Set

Conditions are unique elements that the imperative must follow as a matter of structure or process. As expected, we see both event-based and component-based conditions.

Event-Based Element

Conditions are rules that specify any action or response within the imperative. Actions and responses are members of a forced pair subset contained within the quality superset.

Component-Based Element

Conditions are also rulings specific to any structural element within the imperative. Within the condition element, observed in Figure 21.3, we see a substructure. All business rules root within a policy. A person or official body must endorse policies. Endorsements drive and constrain policies, while the policies must support and sustain the endorsement. Policies are either internal or external to the organization. Regardless of their source, they drive and constrain business rules. Business rules group or organize into rule statements that relate to each other. Rules, of course, support and sustain policies and are sub-organized as procedural or structural. Finally, all business rules and the policies from which they derive must construct by following the Business Rules Manifesto.[2]

FACET SUBSET

Keep your stakeholders focused on their needs by ferreting out behaviors. Repeat the six interrogatives over and over—always starting with *why*. "[Stakeholder], *why* do you *need* this? [Stakeholder], what *must* it *do* for you?" The quality of the imperative depends on our understanding of its required behaviors. In repeating the words *why, be, what, do,* and *you,* we eventually come to rest on a particular need. Typical business analysis techniques are out of the scope for this book; however, the five whys approach is a great example in this instance. Figure 21.4 zooms in on the facet subset's member sets.

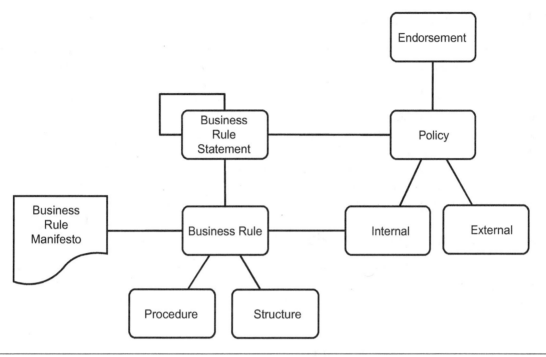

Figure 21.3   REPAC condition member set (© The New BA, Ltd.)

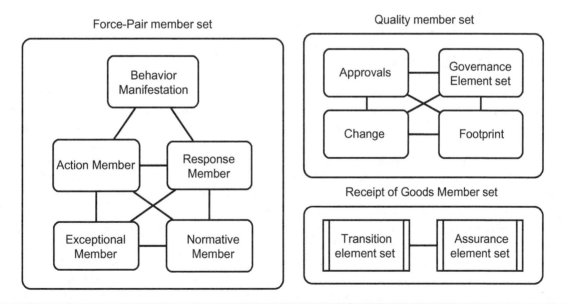

Figure 21.4   REPAC facet subset (© The New BA, Ltd.)

FORCE-PAIR MEMBER SET

When someone acts upon a machine, process, or person—when they *work purposefully* at their job—they exert energy, creating some value. This *purposeful-work-for-value* is their force-pair relationship. The same applies to our projects and solutions. The work that goes into the project or solution must equal the value. Too much work creates waste, while too little affects entropy. Recall, the entropy of something is a measure of the amount of energy unavailable to do purposeful work—purposeful work creates customer value. We use entropy as a measure of the number of possible states a project, solution, system, service, service result, or some item can have. The higher its entropy, the more arrangements the things we measure have. Consequently, the more uncertain we are about its purpose and value, the higher the entropy and the greater the disorder. Either way, we experience an imbalance—a loss of equilibrium. Recall that earned value or a burn-up chart is an effective means to measure these phenomena.

Action/Response Normative Element

Regarding a use case, the normative or standard actions and responses are those that we intend and deliberately design. Process and activity diagrams are typically used to document actions and responses. Other diagrams such as UML interactive overviews or sequence diagrams are also great ways to illustrate action response pairs.

Action/Response Exceptional Element

Again, using the use case as a reference, exception actions and responses are behavioral steps that must account for when elements of the imperative or behavior encounter something outside the boundaries of normal operations.

QUALITY MEMBER SET

Engineering governance is always a challenge. That is, creating artifacts which allow organizations to conduct the policy, actions, and affairs of itself and its resources. The hard question is, how much control and influence should the organization have over its staff, their actions, or the resulting course of events. There are many theories; some require more governing than others. It is out of the scope of this book to suggest a new model. We will, however, outline basic principles. The business must define and manage this framework. It is no longer acceptable for information technology (IT) departments to establish and own a governance model. Figure 21.5 provides visual clarity for the quality member set.

The approval and change (project or solution change requests) elements do not need much explanation. Footprint refers to the physical space that a solution takes up regarding the people, process, and technology; the amount of memory or disk space required by the applications; and the logical *area* that the solution requires. For example: how far does the solution extend into the organization? What does it *touch*? Who and what does it affect? Who and what is changed? Any spider diagram will help display this kind of information. Each line extending from the solution would document which of the six interrogatives we must capture. Figures 21.6 to 21.8 decompose the quality member set.

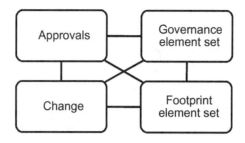

Figure 21.5 REPAC quantized imperative superset, facet subset, quality member set (© The New BA, Ltd.)

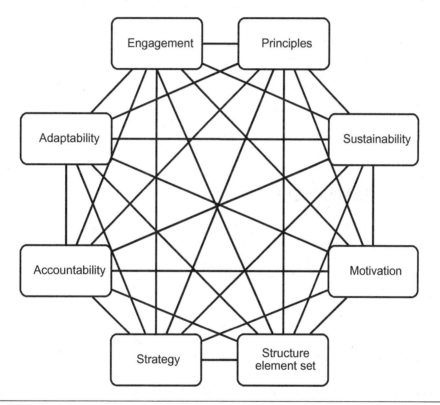

Figure 21.6 REPAC governance element set (© The New BA, Ltd.)

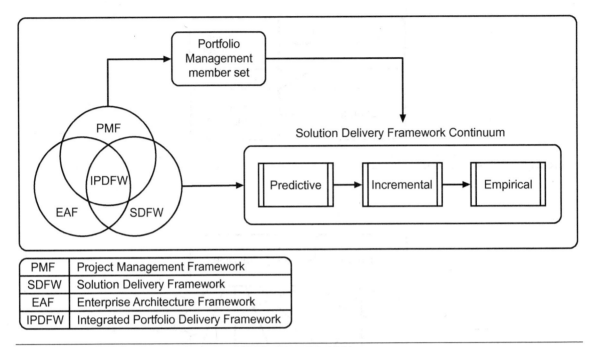

Figure 21.7   REPAC structure element set (© The New BA, Ltd.)

GOVERNANCE ELEMENT SET

Imperative or requirement governance is a very underrated element within projects. Not all items require governing consideration. The ones that do, however, if overlooked, can completely derail a project. Something as simple as a single data element, if required to behave a particular way, may be the *crux* of an entire solution. In these cases, it is the BA's responsibility to understand the substructure of organizational governance.

Engagement

There are many ways to engage employees—the objective of employee/organizational relationship management—many of which we have already discussed. In this context, I refer to engaging project staff about governance itself. Regardless of context, an engaged employee is someone who is fully absorbed, emotionally charged, and genuinely empathic to the organization's mission, values, goals, and objectives. Engaged people actively seek out ways to further an organization's footprint. In the context of governance, engaged employees actively follow and shape the rules, norms, and actions that structure, sustain, regulate, and account for actions within the people, process, technology, policy, and culture model.

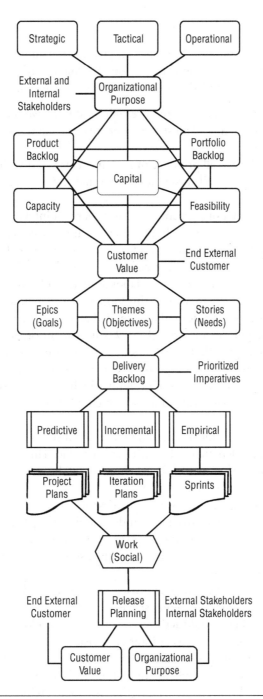

Figure 21.8 REPAC portfolio element member set (© The New BA, Ltd.)

Principles

The *Anglo-American model* of corporate governance emphasizes the interests of shareholders. Whether or not we believe this is fair is not relevant here. I focus on IT-related principles with a few honorable mentions to common themes. I have provided an outline for categorizing principles:

- *Rule of Law*: foremost, all governance requires fair legal frameworks enforced by an impartial regulatory body for the protection of all stakeholders (external and internal), regardless of organizational salience.
- *Integrity and ethical behavior*: all principle models must also start with the fair, equitable, inclusive, and participative treatment of all stakeholders (external and internal), regardless of organizational salience.
- *Transparency*: we know that organizations cannot share all information with all of its employees all of the time. Transparency is more about hidden agendas or not creating an environment that is conducive to collaboration, cooperation, and collective decision making.
- *Consensus oriented*: as with transparency, governance must also allow for equity and inclusiveness in its efforts to reach consensus through collaboration and collective decision making.
- *Effectiveness and efficiency*: you may think this too obvious to mention; however, it is common that efficacy, the ability to produce a desired or intended result, is often overlooked for overblown, redundant departmental policies and procedures. I believe many organizations come by it innocently enough through organic growth; nevertheless, it remains a problem. Consider evolution through natural selection as a model for comparison. Our genes contain redundant *protocols* (a unit of heredity that instructs the production of proteins which determine some characteristic of an offspring, determining some part of its function which, over time, could lead to mutations, illness, disorders, and disease).
- *Accountability*: organizations remain accountable to themselves and, for the most part, their employees. It is the stakeholders themselves who concern me. This idea is where I observe a breakdown in the accountability between each stakeholder and the groups they belong to. End the blame game and stop playing the role of the victim.
- *Ownership of solutions*: business units own business systems (i.e., business applications and data) and are accountable for their effectiveness. Guides should be created and followed to determine the best options on reusing, buying, or building organizational solutions.
- *Access location*: work location should not restrict the users from having access to the processes and data required to perform their roles.
- *Product market mix*: a company's architecture team should allow for the development of innovative goods and services and support customer service excellence.
- *Joint development*: a business should actively consider joint development of programs, services, and tools with other similar organizations or internal divisions.
- *Security and privacy*: security and confidentiality policies should always be a key driver when designing systems for accessing, storing, manipulating, and sharing data.
- *Architecture vitality*: the business model and the enterprise architecture (EA) that supports it are *living* virtual organisms that are subject to the same Darwinian laws as any other life form or ecosystem.

- *Working environment*: companies should enable a modern and progressive IT work environment that provides the right resources (e.g., technology tools) at the right time to meet legitimate business needs.
- *Architecture compliance*: where companies undertake the goals of EA, those principles, processes, and standards should be mandated (unless the exception is endorsed and documented by an EA review process).
- *Partnership*: a partnership should cultivate collaboration between the various business areas (e.g., HR, strategic planning, IT, operations, etc.) from the start of any strategic, operational, or project-related plan.

There are other principle concepts to consider, such as the principle of the social structure of a useful governance model. Consider:

- *Governance structure*: as in the substructure's strategic purpose, its accountability, and its ability to adapt to changing markets and stakeholders' needs. This principle includes a capacity to reflect a single source for policies, rules, risks, and a systematic plan of action; and control statements that direct operations, sustainability, adaptability, and responsiveness.
- *Single source accessibility*: for that which we require to satisfy a stakeholder's needs is of particular importance. When encapsulating the fundamental imperatives into a single superset, it becomes critical to ensure cross-references from one encapsulated element to another. Data elements come to mind. Parts of data often spread across different needs. It is imperative to know which data point is in use—and where. We must also catalog other *business terms*—the nouns and verb-noun phrases of the organization. I cannot stress the importance of this concept enough. It is still possible to use the REPAC Framework with tables and spreadsheets; however, cross-referencing between elements would be a full-time job, in and of itself.
- *Accountability*: here I refer to the history and repository of things that the business has done, links from what the company wanted to do, and what the business did—an organizational memory.
- *Delivery*: in practical terms, the organization must lead key enabling processes and tools to maximize communication between the project management office (PMO), the software delivery cycle, and the compliance to architecture before we achieve any structure or responsiveness to business needs.

Looking back at this model you can see that I have included a waterfall or predictive style along with incremental and empirical. Although we want an agile approach as much as possible, a good governance model structure must recognize the need for predictive plan-based management where appropriate.

RECEIPT OF GOODS MEMBER SET

The transition process expressed in Figures 21.9, 21.10, and 21.11 is fairly typical except for its use of the goal-oriented change management model—the awareness, desire, knowledge, ability, and reinforcement (ADKAR®) method. Concerning change, organizations tend to be capability or process-centric.

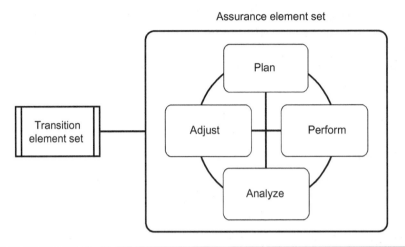

Figure 21.9   REPAC receipt of goods member set (© The New BA, Ltd.)

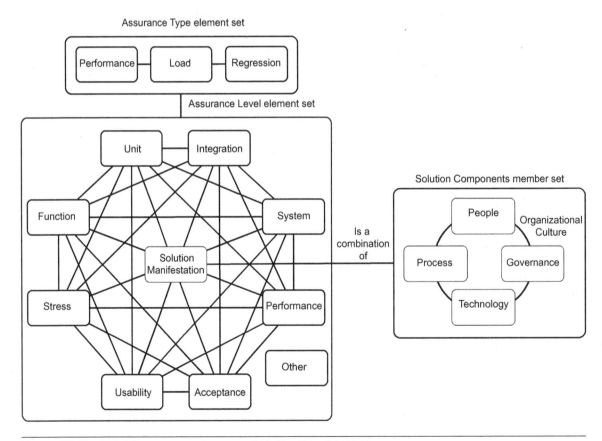

Figure 21.10   REPAC assurance element set (© The New BA, Ltd.)

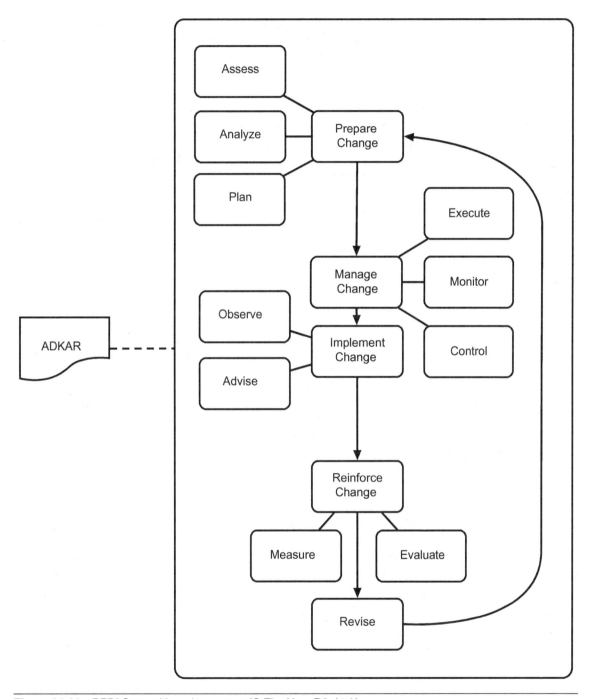

Figure 21.11   REPAC transition element set (© The New BA, Ltd.)

Focusing capabilities allows for innovation and the production of new outcomes by capitalizing on what the organization already does well. When organizing capabilities into relationship-driven functional sets or hierarchical decompositions, gaps become simpler to identify.

If our goal is to enhance performance, we choose a process-centric point of view. Workflows and procedures tend to organize using linear logic. This end-to-end perspective creates value chains. A value chain is the sum of activities contained within a process or workflow.

The value should increase through the workflow, along with the processes predictably and measurably—this is an example of emergence. Through purposeful work, the total value delivered by a business to its paying customers is the sum of each incremental value-add created by each person, team, department, division, and line of business throughout the entire organization. Michael Porter first developed this concept in 1980; it has since become an essential part of international business development and sustainability (Porter 1998).

ASSURANCE ELEMENT SET

The terms within this substructure should be familiar because they all refer to different types of testing. According to the International Institute of Business Analysis (IIBA), the BA does not test; however, at the very least, the BA ensures that the tests are completed, managed, and communicated. Where defects occur, business analysis must continue until resolution. Assurance concerning an imperative and its elements safeguards conformance to the need. The assurance subset is:

- The degree to which an imperative and its quantized components fulfill what we require to satisfy a need, produce customer value, and realize the external or internal organizational purpose
- The degree to which an imperative and its quantized components are fit for use by their intended primary, secondary, tertiary, and extended audiences
- The degree to which an imperative and its quantized components follow their established quality standards

Assuring quality uses the following elements:

- *Quality planning*: determines the standards we must meet and the work we must perform to achieve those standards
- *Quality control*: monitors and measures compliance to the agreed standards through the identification of defective imperatives or their individual ingredients

Focusing on quality in this manner helps ensure a reduction in rework—consequently decreasing costs and raising productivity and team morale while improving the team and customer satisfaction. Although BAs are not responsible for conducting tests, they often need to communicate the results and efficiently manage the workflow itself. Regardless of the project approach (planned or adaptive), a well-conceived test strategy considers the following:

- Strategy and coverage align with solution objectives
- Effective tracking of defects and resolutions
- Established traceability and dependencies between elements within and outside of an encapsulated imperative

- Scheme for managing imperatives and their elements for reuse
- The collection and reporting of relevant metrics

Solutions are comprised of many elements, processes, policies, rules, training, regulations, and activities, to name a few. We must separate ourselves from the notion that systems and solutions are machine oriented. The mechanical aspects of a solution are a means to an end.

Today's solutions require one or more elements from each of these concepts. People and their culture are the glue that holds an organization together. Ironically, however, transformation projects tend to focus on process and technology, leaving people to fend for themselves. Subsequently, these change initiatives do not achieve their desired results. According to the Project Management Institute and other sources, as many as three-quarters of North American organizations do not meet or maintain their desired long-term results.

The most cited reason is the inability to establish and maintain healthy relationships with internal (and sometimes external) stakeholders. Lack of focus on the organization's people and culture engenders resentment and a belief that the company only cares about revenue.

Much of a BA professional's actions must relate to an efficient transformation method that focuses on developing critical organizational competencies around organizational culture transformation and process improvement, resulting in a more effective and sustainable change effort.

INTERFACE SUBSET

The IIBA refers to interface analysis as a means "to understand the interaction, and characteristics of that interaction, between two entities, such as two systems, two organizations, or two people or roles" (IIBA 2015).

An interface is merely a shared boundary across two separate sometimes disparate things. Application program interfaces are often used to specify how boundaries interact. Interfaces may be physical objects such as people, computer hardware, or peripheral devices. An interface may also be logical as in a software entity consisting of an IP address. Regardless, an interface is either internal (within the walls of the organization) or external. Interfaces represent boundaries of scope.

Traditional interfaces had no intelligence, they were just physical connections. For example, a simple binary circuit designed to change the flow of electrons creating a communication of balanced and unbalanced signals could only send simple messages. Developers coded the communication protocols into the application's modules rather than the interface. Modern interfaces, however, are far more intelligent than their distant cousins. They can make decisions for themselves based on the input they receive and restrict access supported by the standards encoded. Today's interfaces typically store communication protocols within. Consequently, most of the communication channel's control is determined by the interface itself, which requires users to follow the rules of whatever standards the interface employs.

LOGICAL INTERFACE MEMBER SET

A logical interface (LIF) does not have a physical presence. A virtual interface is a type of LIF. Logical and virtual interfaces are system configurations that allow other parts of the system to function. An IP address is a simple example. Again, I would not expect business analysis professionals to document these ingredients; however, it is important to be aware of their indented use. Remember, this is a team effort. Each member identifies what aspects of the quantized imperative they need to realize as part of the tasks they have assigned to themselves.

As data increases in importance within our organizations, interface analysis—that is, using the six interrogatives (who, what, when, where, why, how) to determine what information must exchange between people, process, and solution components across solution boundaries—becomes crucial.

PHYSICAL INTERFACE MEMBER SET

A physical interface is an interconnection between two material things such as people and computers, hardware, or machinery. Most solutions require several interfaces to exchange information with other solution components, organizational units, or business processes.

Human Machine Interface Element

People interact with computers and machines in many ways. The most common metaphoric interface, known as the graphical user interface (GUI), has changed the way humans interact with technology immeasurably. The first commercially available GUI operating system came from Xerox, circa 1981. Known as the Star Workstation, it was the first commercially available computer to use a mouse-driven GUI. Although not a commercial success, the work that came out of the Palo Alto Research Center went on to change the world.

Common traits of a GUI interface include checkboxes and radio buttons, menus, and forms. GUIs have become the standard way in which we interact with our computers. However, as computational power becomes increasingly prevalent, we find ourselves reaching the useful limits of the GUI—enter learning machines.

Not all interfaces rely on a GUI. Natural language user interfaces (LUI or NLUI) are becoming increasingly reliable and necessary for situations where focusing on a traditional user interface may be too complicated, distracting, or dangerous. Natural language-based systems use voice commands as their input. These systems become problematic if the tongue or accent spoken is not native to those who designed the solution. Perhaps the cost of developing a voice-activated system that will support multiple languages outweighs its investment. As so-called *smart homes* or *wearable technology* continues to evolve, the need for NLUI becomes fundamental.

Communication Interface Element

In computer science, a communication interface is an electronic circuit that allows machines to communicate with each other. We broadly define a communication interface as any point of interaction between any number of work groups or systems. Communication interfaces manifest as schedules, human interactions, computer systems, printers, copiers, or any other material medium of interaction.

DESCRIPTORS SUBSET

Figure 21.12 details the metadata we capture for an imperative and each of its components. A consequence of encapsulating required elements in this manner demands we pay particular attention to the elements we use across more than one imperative superset. Most configuration management solutions accomplish this traceability.

VALUE AND PURPOSE SUBSET

Most professionals use the term *value* or *value proposition* to describe why we undertake a particular initiative. I prefer to separate value and purpose, reserving value exclusively for the end customer's measure of desire for the solution. Value is the regard that a person or thing holds as worth or importance. Value is either intrinsic or extrinsic and has no measurable utility. Purpose, on the other hand, represents a person's sense of resolution or the reason something exists—its quantifiable utility. As members of a project team, our goal is to maximize our service or purpose to others—this is servant leadership. Figure 21.13 specifies the value and purpose subset.

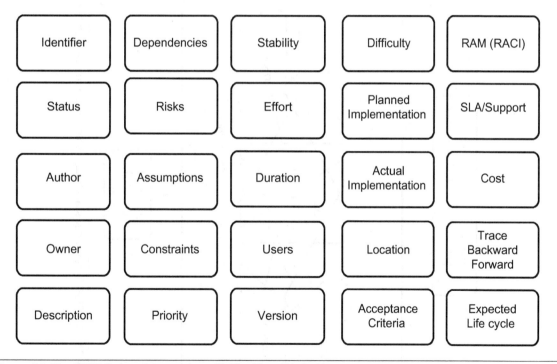

Figure 21.12 REPAC descriptors subset (© The New BA, Ltd.)

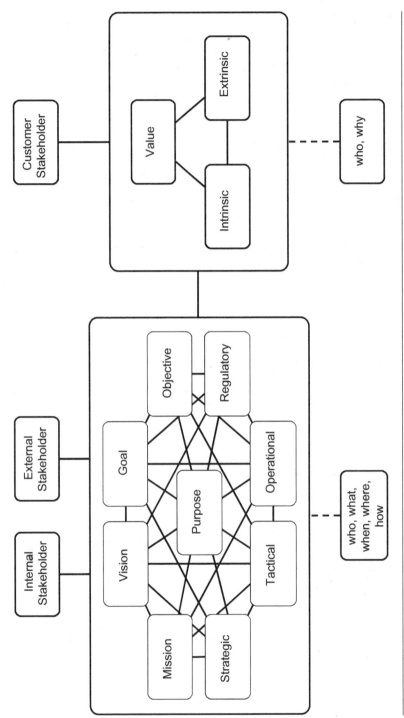

Figure 21.13   REPAC customer stakeholder value and purpose members (© The New BA, Ltd.)

REPAC PURPOSE ELEMENT SET

Separating value from purpose allows us to distinguish between *what* value customers require and *why* we purposefully fulfill those needs. The REPAC purpose member refers to both external and internal organizational stakeholders. Purpose expresses as missions, visions, goals, and objectives whether they are strategic, tactical, operational, or regulatory.

Mission Level Element

An organization's mission or mission statement is, in essence, the reason why the organization exists. If we want our customers to accept why we do what we do, then we must have a compelling and straightforward declarative statement. Among others, an active mission element drives everything the organization does, its ethics and values, its culture, and its motivations for decision making. Some of the most inspiring, clearly articulated mission statements are:

- "To build the Web's most convenient, secure, cost-effective payment solution."—PayPal
- "To give everyone the power to create and share ideas and information instantly, without barriers."—Twitter
- "To become the number one fashion destination for 20-somethings, globally."—ASOS
- "Man is the creator of change in this world. As such, he should be above systems and structures, and not subordinate to them."—Steve Jobs, Apple's unofficial mission statement, circa 1980s

Picking on Apple for a moment; the statement by Steve Jobs reads more like a manifesto rather than a clear statement of organizational purpose. I have read many sources on the life and times of Jobs and his relationship with Apple Inc. and I suspect that he deliberately intended his statement to read as a philosophy rather than an achievable fiduciary statement of purpose. The official mission statement on Apple's corporate website reads more as a list of products and past accomplishments.

"Apple designs Macs, the best personal computers in the world, along with OS X, iLife, iWork and professional software. Apple leads the digital music revolution with its iPods and iTunes online store. Apple has reinvented the mobile phone with its revolutionary iPhone and App Store, and has recently introduced iPad 2 which is defining the future of mobile media and computing devices." This is not a good example of a mission statement. However, Apple ends all of its press releases with: *"Apple is committed to bringing the best personal computing experience to students, educators, creative professionals and consumers around the world through its innovative hardware, software and Internet offerings."*

In this example, as well as ASOS, we know exactly who the customer is. Understanding who is most likely to be the end customer is critical for any elicitation or analysis event. Except for legal and regulatory constraints, we consider *all* other stakeholders *after* the client stakeholder, regardless of the change requested. Change your mission—and you fundamentally change who you are.

Vision Level Element

The organization's mission statement clarifies why we do things and for whom. The mission statement should be relatively immutable. Because of changes to an organization's ecosystem, a vision statement changes every five years or so. The organization's vision identifies what and how the organization does what it does. As organizations grow, their goals and objectives change. The vision is a *sum* reflection of the company's goals.

Goal Level Element

Visions (which reflect missions) become separate value-added discrete qualitative goal statements. Goals are places we want to be without regard to how we will get there. A goal serves as the object of an organization's particular ambition or direction, such as making it easier for a student to register for an online class. What does *easier* mean in this context? Our objectives will tell us.

Objective Level Element

If a goal serves as the object of an organization's particular ambition or direction, then an objective level element or an objective is an expression of something abstract in concrete form. Usually, we consider it rude to objectify people and things. In the case of goals, however, objectification is key to understanding stakeholders' needs. Effectively, we make the goal specific, measurable, agreed to, realistic (completable within anticipated resources, risks, constraints, and assumptions), and time-bound.

TYPE ELEMENT SET

Strategic Type Purpose Element

Strategic purpose provides a future-oriented, larger overall plan for the organization as a whole. The plans, created to realize strategic value, typically contain several smaller tactical plans. Strategic plans achieve results over an extended plane and, as such, are subject to project or product entropy. An example of a vision-level, strategic type purpose element might read: "*We will be very customer focused this year, creating a better experience regardless of how they connect.*"

Tactical Type Purpose Element

Tactical purpose represents the plans and projects that organizations carry out in response to strategic directives. Strategic purpose drives and constrains tactical purpose. Conversely, tactics support and sustain strategy—the perspective of tactical type purpose is far narrower than strategic purpose. Imagine funneling toward tactical and operational objectives that lead to projects.

Co-opted from the military, tactical purpose in a business context relates to the planned actions that will reach the project's objectives. The strategy is our end game, while tactics refer to the individual plays that will get us there. Tactics are directions to follow. Most of the projects in which we participate are tactical. A project should never have to make choices regarding how to solve a problem or which direction to take. Others should have already made a choice. The project's job is to implement agreed-to tactical decisions. Following the previous example, a goal-level, tactical-type purpose element would read: "*This year the care center will increase the results of the customer satisfaction survey to align with the customer focus initiative strategy launched at last month's annual retreat.*"If we continue to objectify this line of reasoning, we would see the following results:

- *Objective level, tactical purpose*: "Begin a business case to explore solution options that meet the goal of increasing the score of our post engagement customer satisfaction survey from 76% to 95% by the end of the third quarter of this calendar year."
- *Objective level, tactical research project*: "In response to the business case, charter a short-term tactical project to understand the current state of the client care center customer complaint ticketing process. Its scope must recommend areas for improvement, which should be tactically sound and align with the customer's experience vision statement that was released earlier this year."
- *Objective level, tactical implementation project*: "Charter a second project to design, build, and implement the options chosen by the organization and its stakeholders. These choices align strategically with our customer's experience and align tactically with our customer satisfaction survey."

Operational and Regulatory Purpose Elements

Operational purpose elements respond to and support strategic and tactical visions, goals, and objectives. Thus, the operative purpose maintains targets set by the project. Regulatory purpose elements are self-evident. Many organizations are driven and constrained by external and internal laws and regulations. Compliance *trumps* any visions, strategies, goals, and objectives.

VALUE PROPOSITION MEMBER

Separating value and purpose in this manner elevates the customer's need and delineates its purpose. This approach allows for a comparison of the two concepts, closing the loop on missing solution components. We perceive value as either extrinsic or intrinsic. Extrinsic value is the benefits of a thing associated with an external agent; which is an action or intervention, producing a particular effect. Intrinsic value belongs to a thing by its very nature. Figure 21.14 offers a revolutionary model of customer value. Developed by the management consulting company, Bain & Company, through the lens of Maslow's hierarchy of needs, this value pyramid, as it is known, identifies the 30 elements of value that customers want. Every customer identifies with one or more of these elements. Observe that the value elements that are most likely to be realized are at the very bottom of the pyramid. The pyramid's first level maps to Maslow's physiological and safety concepts—the fundamental components required to keep a company alive. Further observe that the higher an element is, the more intrinsic the value seems.

Extrinsic Value

Think of external value as a means to an end or a chain of derivation. The outer value of 'A' traces to the extrinsic value of 'D' through 'B' and 'C.' Money has extrinsic value because you can buy garments to cover your body; those clothes, in turn, have extrinsic value because they protect you from the elements; while protecting you, the garments offer social acceptance intrinsically through attributes such as fit, color, and design.

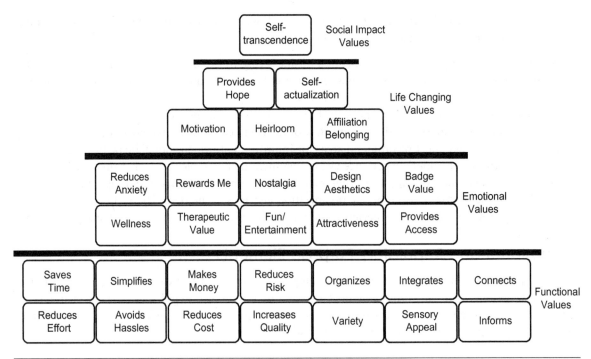

Figure 21.14　Quantized imperative superset, customer stakeholder value proposition, element set (© Bain & Company)

Intrinsic Value

As a philosophical property, the belief that a thing can have value in and of itself is considered intrinsic. We observe intrinsic value as either intangible or tangible. Intangibly, my clothes offer membership to a social group. As a belief system, intangible value is the underlying perception of real value based on the sum of all other value-add considerations. As an economic principle, once we produce something or solve a problem, the cost of its production is intrinsically embedded within the object or solution and cannot be removed (remember, the resolution includes all of its components within the people, process, things triad).

Value and purpose are conceived, conceptualized, and realized through a value chain. Because I am separating purpose from value, I will call it a value-purpose chain. Figure 21.15 illustrates the panoramic perspective required of a PMO wishing to engage in both organizational stakeholder and customer-centric purpose and value.

We prefer to structure our imperatives within a configuration management system, allowing for complex relationships, traces, dependencies, and reports; however, many organizations still believe the Microsoft (MS) suite of tools is adequate. Although difficult, it is possible to extend the REPAC assembly framework to a word processor. A spreadsheet can work well, provided the dependencies and tracing are kept up to date.

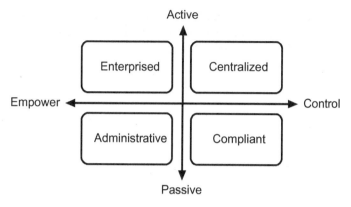

Panoramic Perspective, Empirical Culture, Event Driven

Myopic Perspective, Predictive Culture, Report Driven

Figure 21.15   Organizational panoramic to myopic perspectives (© The New BA, Ltd.)

Do you find this structure unintelligible? More than a dozen diagrams to explain how to assemble what is required to satisfy a need does seem a bit much. Remember you may not need to *build* all of these elements, but you must consider them individually and assess their usefulness. Using a fastidious, finicky, and methodical approach to constructing a requirement, as you would your home, ensures a much higher stakeholder satisfaction probability. It has been more than a decade since the term *business analysis professional* came to our attention by the IIBA, and in all that time little has been done to lock down how a requirement should appear. Remember, this is not a model framework to *follow* as such; it is an ontology you reference so that you can have the right conversations with the right people at the time.

All BAs do not need to know how to code, but they should take the time to learn how different languages and designs work. Understanding requirements in this way helps with identifying differences between programming paradigms such as imperatives, procedural, declarative, object-oriented, and the like. Understanding how the assembler interprets these languages helps a BA write requirements and specifications which closely align to the work that the designers and developers need to perform to realize the solution and all of its components.

REFERENCES

IIBA. 2015. *A Guide to the Business Analysis Body of Knowledge (BABOK® Guide) v3*. International Institute of Business Analysis.

Michael Porter. 1998. *Competitive Strategy: Techniques for Analyzing Industries and Competitors 60th edition*. The Free Press.

ENDNOTES

1. Although we often use extend and expand interchangeably, extend applies to things that stretch out, while expand applies to things which spread out. One implies length; the other, area.
2. Business Rules Group, Version 2.0, 2003, Ronald G. Ross, et al., businessrulesgroup.org.

22

SOME FINAL THOUGHTS

"The capacity to learn is a gift; the ability to learn is a skill; the willingness to learn is a choice."
—Brian Herbert

A quantum requirement is a deliberate grouping of all the elements typically spread throughout several requirements documents and all of their sundry diagrams, tables, equations, and the like. Requirements necessitate the joining of components such as their purpose and value, characteristics, and the effects they have on their environment. The most visual example I can give is one I often show to my students: No Mess Playfoam® distributed by Educational Insights®—it is "squishy, squashy, shaping fun."

> *"Preschoolers are free to express their creativity—plus no mess to clean up afterward! Just squish the Playfoam, shape it however you like, squash it back down, and start all over again. Playfoam never dries out so the creativity never ends—and the secret no-stick formula means you can take it anywhere for creative fun on the go."*

Figure 22.1 illustrates an analogy in the form of a cute fish. This is how we should handle all of our required needs. Each *Playfoam* element is a small sphere that can stick to any other *Playfoam* sphere. Imagine each bit as a part of an imperative (requirement). In and of themselves, they do not offer much, but when we stick a bunch of them together, we have an encapsulated imperative of what we require to

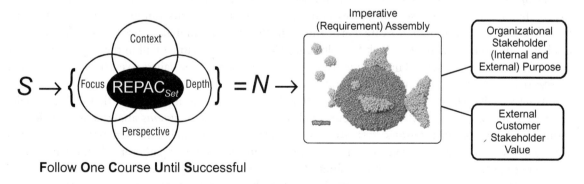

Figure 22.1 *Playfoam* fish as an analogy to a quantized imperative

satisfy a need. Figure 22.1 demonstrates how each *Playfoam* element comes together to create the fish. If we take away a few of the balls, we might not notice a difference, but the fish does! Our business solutions work the same way.

Playfoam's electrons loosely bond together—that's what makes it *work*. The only way for our requirements to *work* is to quantize and bond them together in an encapsulated shell or imperative. I have had my share of unfriendly discussions on this point of view. Regardless of how heated the debate becomes, the disagreement is never the idea itself. Everyone seems to agree that this is the approach to take. The differences come from how to adapt these ideas—how to help management understand the need for encapsulated imperatives managed holistically.

I often compare a business analyst (BA) to that of a medical doctor who is a general practitioner (GP). A business architect who is a specialist, for example, might relate to a rheumatologist who specializes in rheumatic diseases of the bones, joints, and muscles. Let us explore this comparison through an examination of the term *system*.

Would you agree that an organization is a system? The International Institute of Business Analysis speaks of a *system* as: "A set of interdependent components that interact in various ways to produce a set of desired outcomes." I read that statement as the function of a system, not a definition. A *system* is any portion of the organization we choose to analyze. From our atoms to our clothes, we are dozens of systems all encapsulated, one upon another, until something greater than the sum of its parts emerges. Our cells are nothing more than inert chemical bonds which, over billions of years of mutation and random chance, arranged into something we call life. Let's give our businesses solutions the same intellectual respect, but please don't take billions of years to organize your stakeholder's imperatives into purpose and value.

An organizational system attempts to adapt and change by interacting with itself and its external environment by taking inputs from itself and its environment, transforming them, and then sending the results of the transformation back to itself as (internal or external) organizational-stakeholder purpose, and the environment as customer-stakeholder value.

If the transformation executed well, the organization minimizes entropy and, as an extension, waste. This redefinition requires us to accept that a business system contains all aspects of a solution, which by extension includes people, process, culture, the technology, and everything in between—the solution and all of its components.

Let's reexamine the correlation between a doctor and a BA. A business analysis professional must have a working knowledge of the business system as a whole, not unlike a GP. The BA will invite other experts to give their opinions, diagnoses, prognoses, and recommended treatments, but in the end, the GP is primarily responsible for the patient's care. He or she keeps the records and makes sure the stakeholder finds a suitable solution. Similarly, BAs look for solutions. They will not document all of the requirements but will make sure the encapsulated imperative is passed along to the right specialists so each can capture what is essential to satisfy the need from their point of view.

Business analysis professionals should conduct systems analysis, but not in a way that is traditionally conceived by organizations. BAs are systems analysts, rather, *business-systems* analysts. My worldview promotes the profession as *business-systems analysis professionals*; utilizing a hyphen between the words creates a new model for our profession. BAs are more than requirements gatherers, document writers, and sometime-testers. We have a unique ability to focus on the many perspectives of business systems and the multiple components within. Our depth of analysis may be qualitative, quantitative, logical, physical, behavioral, or structural. Our perspective of focus may be on interactions between the people and the processes, the policies and the culture, or the customer's perceived value and the organization's intended purpose.

We must abandon the current ideas of what a business system is and account for all of the combinations and permutations therein. Organizations have shortsightedly defined *systems* in the *machine sense*, limiting a BA's exposure and wholly underestimating the value they bring to the physical issues as well as the behavioral. This is more than a simple transformation of our profession; it is a coming-of-age movement.

Make every moment in your project productive. Call out and challenge waste, but in a way that offers suggestions for improvement—perhaps some from this very book. Teams are social groups. Projects and work, in general, are a social experience. Our social nature builds from a foundation of communication. Sure, trust and respect, among other traits are important too, but communication (and reciprocal collaboration, among others) is the foundation upon which we built our society. Thus, every project must begin with a robust collaborative, communication framework. When it comes to requirements, you cannot do much better than the Requirement, Elicitation, Planning, Analysis, and Collaboration Framework™ (REPAC®). Just about every question or piece of information you need to elicit, document, and manage lays within the pages of this book. The apparent fine tuning of what we require to satisfy needs in a manner presented here will elevate you and your stakeholders to center stage. Remember, rather than asking our stakeholders, "what are your requirements?" focus on their needs and ask ourselves and other subject matter experts, "What do we, as a team, require to satisfy a need in a way that provides purpose to the organization and its stakeholders, and value to its customers."[1]

This book is a detailed examination of project management and business analysis as seen through the lenses of information theory and linguistics, organizational and behavioral psychology, and propositional logic—with a touch of mesh theory applied to human systems. Business analysis is not an information technology-based profession. Business analysis primarily belongs within the social sciences because of our social systems interactions—the interplay between people, the processes they use, and the tools and technology that help them work purposefully to bring value to their customers. This entire book is an attempt to recognize this perception and provide tools and techniques that will make business analysis professionals more efficient.

This book started with a simple premise; what would happen if we change the word *requirement* from a noun to a verb? In response, it quickly became apparent that I needed to invent a framework to help BAs and project teams understand all the elements relevant to their organizational needs. Enter REPAC—a requirement, planning, analysis, and collaboration framework; an idea that uses set theory and an extended mesh network of interrelated, interdependent elements which help identify on what we should focus, the perspective of that focus, and how deep the analysis of that focus and perspective should descend. I created an interlaced connection of super sets and subsets with a set builder to identify permutations of related elements that are useful for conversation, problem solving, planning, needs identification, and constructing the imperatives required to satisfy stakeholders' needs. REPAC depends on effective communication. If we have not taken the time to establish lasting and productive relationships with our stakeholders, no amount of analysis will bring them value. Within the context of building relationships, let's take a last look at how the REPAC framework keeps our course true.

FOCUS

As far as we know, atoms make up the observable universe. Quantum mechanics teaches that the universe consists of twelve *matter* particles, which are just waves of energy bound together by other waves of energy—you, me, a banana, whatever. It stands to reason, therefore, that a BA should be able to do the same with a *requirement*. For BAs, removing themselves from the classic view requires them to imagine *requirements* as force-carriers of work, rather than discrete things in and of themselves. To identify the imperatives or what is necessary to satisfy the needs of stakeholders, a BA must focus his or her thoughts and conversations using the discrete elements found in the REPAC focus superset—such as governance, suppliers, investors, or operational principles. Examining the organization and the business ecosystem to which it belongs helps identify the essential elements of a requirement, which upon closer examination, link to each other to the point where they are inseparable.

PERSPECTIVE

The REPAC perspective subset assists the BA's efforts with sets such as contextual, material, human, and procedural points of view. These groupings contain elements like organizational culture, circumstantial, performance, succession, computations, ordinals, conditions, and events and extents. Using this standard typology removes much of the discord and subjectiveness. There may still be disagreements regarding a solution approach, but with everyone using the same terms in the same way the conversations begin from a common point of reference.

DEPTH

A contextual analysis gives rise to meaning. Remember, without context, there is no meaning. The following are some examples of words that help describe contextual thinking: fixed, archetype, established, or immutable. A contextual analysis illustrates pattern-based reasoning and helps identify the elements that we use to inform scope.

Conceptual thinking, on the other hand, is an instance of the context. Words related to conceptual thinking are relative, informed, appropriate, tangible, or specific. Theoretical reasoning illustrates thinking that is specific to scope. "How will we use these patterns to solve our issues in this instance?" The elements identified at this order inform our solution options.

Finally, we complete our analysis of depth, transforming our identified needs into quantized imperatives using the REPAC assembly superset, which we document just enough, just in time. Of course, this is a highly iterative process with no clear beginning or end. You must enter REPAC wherever it makes sense and leave for reentry once you are ready to take on another problem or opportunity.

The REPAC Framework™ helps project teams center their efforts around what matters most to stakeholders—their needs. REPAC:

- Provides a means for developing plans and structuring conversations for maximum benefit to elicit needs, from which we construct and manage requirements

- Builds thousands of communication sets with specific instances of focus and perspective, allowing business analysts and project teams to analyze and collaborate, and drive workshops, interviews, and focus groups
- Helps BAs, project teams, and stakeholders facilitate repeatable, measurable, traceable, and reportable requirements

Thank you, reader, for giving me some of your precious time. I hope this book becomes a central reference guide for you as you elicit your stakeholder's needs and plan your interviews, workshops, and story building sessions. Use this framework to analyze the focus, depth, and perspective of particular needs, and collaborate with customers, stakeholders, and team members about what you require to solve problems and create solutions that create organizational purpose and provide customer-centric value. Oh, and one more thing:

"Take chances, make mistakes, and get messy!"[2]

The end.

ENDNOTES

1. Once we understand the need, we, along with designers, developers, and the like, determine what we require to satisfy the need.
2. Miss Frizzle, Magic School Bus, PBS Kids, Scholastic Entertainment.

INDEX

Note: Page numbers followed by "f" indicate figures; and those followed by "t" indicate tables.